How to Start a Virtual Bankruptcy Assistant Service

FIRST EDITION

Everything you need to know to start, operate and market a virtual bankruptcy service working for bankruptcy attorneys nationwide.

by

Victoria Ring
Certified Paralegal, Speaker and CEO, 713Training.Com

First printing, May 2006

ISBN: 0-9761591-7-1
LCCN: 2006922641

ATTENTION CORPORATIONS, UNIVERSITIES, COLLEGES, AND PROFESSIONAL ORGANIZATIONS. Quantity discounts are available on bulk purchases of this book for educational, gift purposes or as premiums for increasing magazine subscriptions or renewals. Special books or book excerpts can also be produced to fit specific needs.

For information, please contact Graphico Publishing, 1601 West Fifth Avenue, Suite 123, Columbus, Ohio 43212-2303 or www.graphicopublishing.com.

Graphico Publishing
a subsidiary of 50 State Notary
1601 West Fifth Avenue, Suite 123
Columbus, Ohio 43212-2303
Website: http://www.graphicopublishing.com

Special Notice about the Bankruptcy Abuse Prevention and Consumer Protection Act of 2005

(signed into law on October 17, 2005)

Even though the new bankruptcy law was enacted on October 17, 2005 there were still minor changes in the law being made at the time this book was written. As we are informed of updates we will announce them to the Bankruptcy Club Members at the **713Training.Com** website. If the updates are substantial I may need to revise this book in the future; however, at the time of this writing, this book has been proofed by bankruptcy professionals to ensure the information is as accurate and current as possible.

Note: Do not be alarmed if minor changes in the bankruptcy law occur over the next several years. This is common practice when federal laws are changed. You can keep up-to-date with these changes by checking the **713Training.Com** website at **http://www.713training.com**

Special Recognition to Gloria Joyce

I chose to have Gloria Joyce appear on the front cover of this book with me because she has been an important part of my business and personal life for the past 20 years. From 1986 thru 1988, Gloria was the supervisor of the Proposal Center when I worked at *Battelle Memorial Institute.* After *Battelle* downsized and I lost my job, Gloria and I continued our friendship. Her faith in my abilities and daily encouragement have greatly contributed to my decision to write and publish this book.

Today, Gloria Joyce works fulltime as an immigration paralegal and part-time for *50 State Notary* as the Manager of the Shipping Department. Her dedicated friendship is very rare to find and often occurs once in a person's lifetime. I feel very blessed that Gloria and her family are a part of my daily business and personal life.

-- *Victoria Ring*

Dedication

This book, *How to Start a Virtual Bankruptcy Assistant Service,* is dedicated to the following bankruptcy attorneys who were the first to believe in my ideas and utilize the services of my online business, *The Lawyer Assistant:*

- Brandon Barnett, Esq.
- Lloyd Cohen, Esq.
- Matthew Fisher, Esq.
- Bradley Goldbloom, Esq.
- Charley Hess, Esq.
- Scott Jay, Esq.
- Brandon Keltner, Esq.
- Keith Knochel, Esq.
- Robert Miller, Esq.
- Justin Perryman, Esq.
- Raoul Revord, Esq.
- Greg Revord, Esq.
- Terry Thomas, Esq.
- Roy True, Esq.
- Roger Weaver, Esq.
- Jerry Weinstein, Esq.
- Scott Sidner, Esq.

Legal Disclaimer

The author, Victoria Ring is NOT an attorney.

The information contained in *How to Start a Virtual Bankruptcy Assistant Service* is for training purposes only and should not be considered legal advice. The sole purpose of this material is to provide the reader with the information they need to better perform their job duties as a virtual bankruptcy assistant, grow their business and become a greater asset to the attorneys they are working for.

Additionally, the information in this book is NOT intended to be used for preparing bankruptcy petitions for the general public without the aide of an attorney. Doing so could result in violation of unauthorized practice of law regulations in your state.

All the material in this book is written from the perspective of Victoria Ring, an experienced bankruptcy paralegal who has never attended law school and is not authorized to practice law in any state.

The author and publisher do not warrant or guarantee any of the website references or products described herein. By following the instructions contained herein, the reader willingly assumes all risks in connection with any transactions.

The author and publisher make no representations or warranties of any kind; nor are any such representations implied with respect to the material set forth herein, and the author and publisher takes no responsibility with respect to such material The author and publisher shall not be liable for any special, consequential, or exemplary damages resulting in whole or in part from the reader's use of, or reliance upon this material.

Table of Contents

Chapter 3
Performing Your Job as a Virtual Bankruptcy Assistant

Chapter 4
The Client Intake Interview

Chapter 5
Drafting the Bankruptcy Petition

Chapter 6
The Means Test Training Course

Chapter 7
Advanced Tips and Techniques for Virtual Bankruptcy Assistants

Chapter 8
Marketing and Growing Your Virtual Bankruptcy Assistant Service

Chapter 9
Resource Links for Virtual Bankruptcy Assistants

Chapter 10
Legal Dictionary for Virtual Bankruptcy Assistants

Introduction

The author, Victoria Ring, was the first paralegal to develop an online virtual bankruptcy service dedicated to providing debtor bankruptcy attorneys nationwide with electronic online services. The inspiration for this idea actually began when a bankruptcy attorney Victoria was working for set her up in a home business processing his bankruptcy petitions.

Through the encouragement of other attorneys, Victoria developed an online company she named *Bankruptcy Paralegal Services* in 2001. This company provided document preparation services directly to consumers. Its purpose was to target the group of people who were unable to afford an attorney and wanted to represent themselves in court which is the right of every American citizen.

However, after a few months of operation the local bankruptcy court required the word *paralegal* to be removed from the company name because they said it contained the word *legal.* This was a violation of the unauthorized practice of law regulations. But even after the company was renamed *Bankruptcy 2 Go* to comply with the rules of the bankruptcy court, the court continued to scrutinize the success of the business and eventually forced Victoria to transfer the company to a new owner or close it down entirely.

However, the court's decision turned out to be a blessing in disguise. When Victoria could no longer prepare petitions directly for consumers she developed a company named *The Lawyer Assistant* and marketed her services nationwide to bankruptcy attorneys.

However, this new idea was not as well accepted as Victoria originally thought it would be to attorneys in the Columbus Ohio area. When she began marketing this new idea of electronic forms processing services to the attorneys, she received quite a bit of resistance. It took awhile before she discovered the problem was not the actual business idea, but the fact that most bankruptcy attorneys in the Columbus, Ohio area were just barely learning how to use email at the time. The concept of hiring a an independent virtual bankruptcy assistant to prepare a bankruptcy petition in PDF format that is emailed to the attorney and electronically filed with the court was technologically impossible for them to comprehend.

But this realization again turned out to be another blessing in disguise. Victoria then decided to market *The Lawyer Assistant* to other states outside Ohio that already had electronic court filing procedures in place. She also attempted to find bankruptcy attorneys who were more up-to-date on the latest technology. This decision paid off! Within less than one year, *The Lawyer Assistant* grew to a point that Victoria was faced with a major decision: Sell the company or rent office space and hire employees. Victoria chose to sell the company to David Gonzalez, Esq., an attorney in Bronxville, New York. This enabled her to take her knowledge to the masses through the development of books and video training products. The book you are reading now is a brand new edition that was published after the new bankruptcy law went into effect. The first book Victoria Ring wrote after selling *The Lawyer Assistant* was How to Start a Bankruptcy Forms Processing Service, ISBN: 0976159112 It was taken out of print in March 2006 and copies are no longer available for sale.

However, a large majority of the original books' content has been preserved throughout the book you are reading now. Victoria used the original book as a base. She then removed all the material that was no longer compliant under the new bankruptcy law as it related to virtual bankruptcy assistants. Victoria then edited the book entirely and wrote over 175 pages of new material.

Also included is a large section of the book that is dedicated to providing you with training in drafting the actual Forms and Schedules of the bankruptcy petition. This way, you will be able to do a better job for the attorneys you are working for.

Finally, the marketing section teaches you how to sell your services to attorneys. Armed with this information, you will be able to duplicate Victoria's marketing efforts and build a successful virtual bankruptcy service of your own like many others are now doing.

> **Note:** If you learn best by visual methods, you should consider ordering the 2-Hour Training Video: How to Market Your Virtual Bankruptcy Assistant Business. Please visit **https://www.713training.com/cart**

Chapter 1

Is The Virtual Bankruptcy Assistant Service Business Right for You?

Is The Virtual Bankruptcy Assistant Business Right for You?

What is a Virtual Bankruptcy Assistant?

A virtual bankruptcy assistant is a person (like you and me) that works for bankruptcy attorneys as an independent contractor. You own your own business. You bill the attorney for work that you perform and the attorney pays you. You are not an employee of the attorney. Instead, the attorney is your customer. Additionally, you are responsible for paying your own income, state and other applicable taxes and keeping good accounting records as any business owner should.

The words *virtual assistant* simply means that a person works off-site and communicates with their customer through the internet.

The words *bankruptcy assistant* is a term used for people (like you and me) who gathers information from clients and drafts the bankruptcy petition. You then submit this information to the attorney (via the internet in PDF format.) The attorney reviews your work, submits revisions and you provide the final completed bankruptcy petition to the attorney, ready for filing in the court.

At the time this book is written, people are still finding it difficult to change their way of thinking to adapt to the new technology. Some attorneys who have been filing bankruptcy petitions the same way for the past 25 years find it difficult to adapt to the mindset that most of their work can be done outside the office. Therefore, if you decide to start this type of business (which I assume you do since you purchased this book) you may need to educate some of the attorneys you come into contact with about the advantages of utilizing the new electronic technology. Once you get them to understand the advantages your services will be to their law firm, and how much money you are going to save them, you will have more business than you can handle and an excellent career to boot!

How can I make this strong statement? Because I have already done it. I didn't just research the subject and decide to write this book like some authors do. In fact, I started the first online company dedicated to providing services to bankruptcy attorneys nationwide so I have already paved the way for you. I know all too well that the virtual bankruptcy assistant service business is a booming business. Within nine months after I started *The Lawyer Assistant,* I had a customer base of 56 attorneys; and in this book, I will teach you how to do the same thing.

But before we jump into training, please take a moment and answer the quiz questions on Page 3 to find out if this business is right for you.

Is This Business Right for You?

Be truthful and answer the questions below by placing a checkmark next to the box that most closely matches your response to the question.

1 If you had 4 hours of time to do anything you wanted, what activity from the list below would you find the most enjoyable?

- ☐ Reading and enjoying quiet times
- ☐ Planning an event and entertaining friends
- ☐ Fast-paced physical activities
- ☐ Listening and helping others

2 From the list below, choose the work-related activity that you would most enjoy:

- ☐ Researching topics for a quarterly report
- ☐ Interaction with a variety of different people with different personality types
- ☐ Managing a group of people and implementing work procedures based on company goals
- ☐ Typing, data entry or other clerical duties
- ☐ None of the above

3 What procedure do you use to check for mistakes after you have completed a job?

- ☐ I am so detail-oriented that I rarely make mistakes and therefore do not check my work after completion.
- ☐ I consistently check my work for mistakes and then recheck everything again after the completion of the job.
- ☐ I give my work to someone else to check for me.
- ☐ I complete the job and then wait to see if there are any problems later. Then, when problems arise, I quickly fix them.
- ☐ I double-check everything I do and intentionally look for errors so that my completed project is as near perfect as possible.

Quiz continued on next page

4 **What type of office-related experience have you had?**

- ☐ I have worked in an office most of my adult life.
- ☐ I have worked as a manager or supervisor in an office.
- ☐ I used to work in an office but have not worked outside my home for 2 years or more
- ☐ I have never worked in an office environment.

5 **What level of computer experience do you have?**

- ☐ I purchased my first computer less than 1 year ago.
- ☐ I surf the internet often and am familiar with my computer.
- ☐ I have purchased at least 3 computers within the past 10 years.
- ☐ My children know more about computers than I do.

Now, to complete your assessment, compare your answers to the Quiz Analysis that begins on the next page.

Quiz Analysis

1 **If you had 4 hours of time to do anything you wanted, what activity from the list below would you find the most enjoyable?**

☐ Reading and enjoying quiet times

If you chose this activity you will probably love working as an independent virtual bankruptcy assistant but you may need someone else to handle the telephone calls from attorneys and clients. People who enjoy a quiet, peaceful existence find it hard to work creatively when their concentration is repeatedly interrupted by phone calls.

☐ Planning an event and entertaining friends

If you chose this activity you are undoubtedly a people-person. You would do well working with clients, such as following up on required documentation and communicating with them during the initial client intake.

☐ Fast-paced physical activities

If you chose this activity you would probably enjoy working in the office with the bankruptcy attorney. Bankruptcy offices are normally very busy and you may need the fast pace to keep you focused.

☐ Listening and helping others

If you chose this activity, you will probably love working as an independent virtual bankruptcy assistant. It takes a level of patience, understanding and flexibility to work with clients and attorneys outside the law office. You also cannot be someone who is judgmental of others and you must be able to respect the privacy of all parties you come into contact with to maintain confidentiality. Above all, you should be a good listener.

2 From the list below, choose the work-related activity that you would most enjoy:

☐ Researching topics for a quarterly report

If you are the type of person that has the perseverance to research topics and obtain non-biased information to arrive at a decision based on facts, you will be an excellent virtual bankruptcy assistant.

☐ Interaction with a variety of different people with different personality types

If you enjoy interacting with other people and have the ability to deal with a wide variety of different personality types, you will be an excellent virtual bankruptcy assistant. Every client will have a different life story to tell. Some stories will be heartbreaking. Others will have lived lifestyles you do not personally agree with. If you have self-confidence in yourself you will be less likely to judge others and will be open-minded to helping them regardless if you agree with their lifestyle or not.

☐ Managing a group of people and implementing work procedures based on company goals

If you enjoy managing rather than actually doing the labor involved in getting a job done, you may enjoy putting together a network of virtual bankruptcy assistants. This way, you can work directly with attorneys and have the processors perform the actual work. However, you must first learn how to draft bankruptcy petitions yourself before you can properly manage the people doing the work for you.

☐ Typing, data entry or other clerical duties

If you enjoy sitting at the computer and doing repetitive work without a lot of thought, you are probably not suited for the field of bankruptcy forms processing. Drafting bankruptcy petitions is a very detailed job that requires a logical mind and attention to detail. If you do not enjoy using your mind and thinking *outside the box* you may want to seek starting a business in another area of law - such as legal transcription.

☐ None of the above

If you selected this answer, you may not be suited for the virtual bankruptcy assistant field. It would be to your benefit to interview a paralegal currently working in the field of bankruptcy to determine if this field is something you truly want to pursue.

3 What procedure do you use to check for mistakes after you have completed a job?

☐ I am so detail-oriented that I rarely make mistakes and therefore do not check my work after completion.

If you chose this answer you will need to alter your habits in order to work as a virtual bankruptcy assistant. It is imperative that you know how to check and recheck your work because all human beings make mistakes regardless of their level of experience. In the virtual bankruptcy assistant field, if you make a mistake and it is overlooked by the attorney, that mistake could substantially effect the lives of people who are depending on you.

☐ I consistently check my work for mistakes and then recheck everything again after the completion of the job.

Excellent answer! You have the skills needed to work as a virtual bankruptcy assistant.

☐ I give my work to someone else to check for me.

If you depend on others to tell you if your work is acceptable or not you will never improve your own skills. Even if the other person finds a mistake you made and you correct it, you will never know when or why you made that mistake in the first place so that it doesn't happen again. No one is going to provide you with the high level of detail you need for checking your work except you.

☐ I complete the job and then wait to see if there are any problems later. Then, when problems arise, I quickly fix them.

This is not the correct mindset for working as a virtual bankruptcy assistant. The Federal Government now requires that all bankruptcy petitions be well-detailed and the information backed up with documentation. If you wait for problems to happen after the bankruptcy petition is filed, you could wreck havoc on the attorney as well as the lives of the clients who are already very emotional over the fact they are filing bankruptcy.

☐ I double-check everything I do and intentionally look for errors so that my completed project is as near perfect as possible.

Excellent answer! You definitely have the skills needed to work as a virtual bankruptcy assistant.

4 What type of office-related experience have you had?

☐ I have worked in an office most of my adult life.

Excellent answer! You probably have the skills needed to work as a virtual bankruptcy assistant and to succeed in your own business.

☐ I have worked as a manager or supervisor in an office.

You may do very well working as a virtual bankruptcy assistant, but you must also be flexible enough to enjoy doing the actual day-to-day work. Managing your home office is an excellent skill to have for running your business but you must also be a hard worker or you will need to hire others to do the day-to-day work for you. This could get expensive if you are just getting your business started and every penny counts.

☐ I used to work in an office but have not worked outside my home for 2 years or more

If you chose this answer, you may experience a large learning curve working at home and running your own business. Perhaps you should consider working for temporary employment agencies either as a part-time or fulltime employee in an office atmosphere to gain some recent office experience before starting your own company.

☐ I have never worked in an office environment.

You could have a great deal of start-up problems if you have no skills working in an office outside your home. Unless you have a great deal of computer experience, you may consider enrolling in an introductory business course or studying business magazines to gain some beginning business skills before starting your company.

5 What level of computer experience do you have?

☐ I purchased my first computer less than 1 year ago.

If you worked most of your adult life in a job that required no exposure to a computer, and you recently purchased your first one - you definitely should consider some type of basic computer training before you open a business and work as a virtual bankruptcy assistant. This field requires you to have a good working knowledge of computer software and the ability to electronically file documents for the attorneys that employ you (if requested.) If you don't know what a PDF document is, you definitely need to learn basic computer and software skills.

☐ I surf the internet often and am familiar with my computer.

Excellent answer. You have the skills needed to use the internet to research and communicate with the attorneys you are working for and the ability to electronically file documents if requested.

☐ I have purchased at least 3 computers within the past 10 years.

Excellent answer. You probably know how to install a wide variety of software and solve common computer problems as they occur. These skills will help you when conducting online research, working with software programs and electronic documents.

☐ My children know more about computers than I do.

Suggestion: Get your children to teach you everything they know, then take an advanced computer class in your area before starting your virtual bankruptcy assistant service business.

Important Questions and Answers About The Job

What Are the Job Duties of a Virtual Bankruptcy Assistant?

You are already familiar with the process involved in preparing and filing your tax returns each year. Normally you gather up your W2s, 1099s or other income records and transfer this information to the correct lines on the IRS Tax Form. Most people purchase software programs to do the job for them while others go to tax preparers and pay them to do the job. However, if you are like most people and are familiar with the process of entering your income and expense information into a software program (that does most of the work for you) - the process of drafting bankruptcy petitions is a similar process. Essentially, you take information from the Client Intake Forms that the clients fill out and place this information on the proper Forms and Schedules of the Federal bankruptcy petition forms.

On the surface this process may sound easy, but it is not as simple as it sounds. There is a skill involved in learning the level of detail you need to provide to the attorney you are working for and the ability to gather the right information needed to document all the statements within the petition. This skill is the same utilized by tax preparers who have been trained to know where to place tax figures into the proper areas of the Federal Tax Forms in order to provide their clients with the largest return. As a virtual bankruptcy assistant you must work through an initial *learning curve* in order to acquire the skill to know where to place information into the proper areas of the Federal Bankruptcy Forms. This skill can be easily learned if you have the willingness and determination to learn it. However, if you are just looking to make some fast money - the virtual bankruptcy assistant field is not for you. Instead, the virtual bankruptcy assistant field should be thought of as a chosen career that you grow and learn with over time.

How Much Money Can I Earn Working as a Virtual Bankruptcy Assistant?

This is an impossible question to answer. It's the same thing as asking me what your next employer will pay you in wages. I am not the person to ask this question. The only person who can answer it is YOU. That's because your income is determined by how hard you work and how much money you spend to make your business grow. Although you can start a business working as a virtual bankruptcy assistant for less than $1,000 (including the software), only YOU can pick up the tools and use them properly. That is a decision only you can make.

But to provide you with some type of idea as to how much money people are actually making in this field at the time of this writing, most virtual bankruptcy assistants are charging on the average of $250 to $400 per bankruptcy petition they draft. In most areas of the United States, bankruptcy attorneys charge upwards of $1,500 to represent their clients in a Chapter 7 and $2,000 for a Chapter 13. Since a virtual bankruptcy assistant will be doing most of the actual labor drafting the bankruptcy petition and gathering the information for a well-documented bankruptcy petition, attorneys are more than willing to pay $250 to $400 for each one you process if you do a detailed, professional job and save them money.

To give you a better idea of the type of money you can earn as a virtual bankruptcy assistant; if you only had 3 attorneys that you independently worked for, and each one of those attorneys assigned you 5 petitions per week, you would be processing 15 petitions. 15 x $250 = $3,750 per week or $15,000 per month. Imagine what would happen if you had more than 3 attorneys? You would need to hire outside help just to keep up with the workload like I did!

REALITY CHECK: Don't allow the income potential of this business to overwhelm you. In order to make that kind of money you must provide an acceptable level of professional service to the attorneys you are working for. Attorneys will normally not *babysit you* if you make mistakes. Instead, you will be out of business very fast. Therefore, in order to succeed at this type of business you must obtain good training and practice drafting several bankruptcy petitions before you can begin to contact attorneys and start earning any level of income.

Do I Need to be a Paralegal to be a Virtual Bankruptcy Assistant?

No. You do NOT need to obtain a paralegal certificate to become a virtual bankruptcy assistant. In fact, the information in the training products sold by 713Training.Com is NOT taught in any law school or paralegal program. It is only taught at expensive paralegal seminars and through personal on-the-job training from an attorney or paralegal.

Also, drafting bankruptcy petitions is normally not a job that falls under the category of *paralegal duties.* Paralegals are often involved in drafting motions and pleadings, conducting legal research and assisting the attorney in appeals cases. This is why the services of a virtual bankruptcy assistant are welcome at law firms. You are not taking anyone's job away from them and you are instrumental in relieving a heavy workload from the office staff.

Can I Only Work for Attorneys in My Area?

No. You can live anywhere and draft petitions for bankruptcy attorneys in any state. It doesn't matter if you live in Cheyenne Wells, Colorado – you can still draft bankruptcy petitions for attorneys in California, Texas or any other state. There are no jurisdictional limits because bankruptcy is governed by federal law not state law.

Is this Legal to Do in Any State?

You may have already heard horror stories concerning unauthorized practice of law (UPL) charges brought against non-attorney petition preparers who prepare bankruptcy petitions for the general public. **The difference between a bankruptcy petition preparer and a virtual bankruptcy assistant is that virtual bankruptcy assistants work solely for attorneys -- not the general public.** Your name does not appear on the bankruptcy petition as a non-attorney preparer. Therefore, you are immune from any possibility of committing UPL unless you take it upon yourself to answer legal questions from the client instead of referring the legal question to the attorney. Your job as a virtual bankruptcy assistant is to obtain factual information and place it into the proper areas on the bankruptcy petition, not advise clients on legal matters.

Is This Type of Business Considered to Be Sharing Fees?

No! Virtual bankruptcy assistants never share fees with the attorney. The debtors pay the attorney directly for his or her representation. The virtual bankruptcy assistant is simply processing the paperwork for the attorney and gathering general information about the client. This is the same a law firm employee would perform their duties if they worked in the law firm drafting the bankruptcy petition.

How Can I Get Started in This Business?

You have taken the first step in purchasing this book. However, below is a list to help you take the second step and beyond:

1. Read this entire book and work through the training on Pages __ to __.

2. Join the Bankruptcy Teleconference Club at https://www.713training.com/administrator/signup.php and learn how others in this field built their virtual bankruptcy service.

3. Download the FREE Getting-Started Training Ebook at http://www.713training.com/freetraining/

4. Purchase additional training videos and books at: http://www.713training.com

5. Get listed in the Nationwide Bankruptcy Directory so bankruptcy attorneys can locate you for jobs: http://www.713training.com/directory/whyorder.html

6. Download a free set of Client Intake Forms https://www.713training.com/intake_forms/

7. Research more about this field at the bankruptcy links at: http://www.713training.com/links/

Chapter 2

The First Steps in Starting a Virtual Bankruptcy Assistant Service

The First Steps to Starting a Virtual Bankruptcy Assistant Service

The information in this chapter is designed to help lay the initial foundation for building your virtual bankruptcy service. First we will cover whether obtaining advanced legal education is necessary. Next, I will provide you with a recommended method of structuring your business and client base. Finally, this chapter ends with tips and techniques for setting up your office, establishing efficient office procedures and purchasing software and hardware for your bankruptcy business.

Should You Obtain Advanced Education Before Starting This Type of Business?

This is another one of those questions I cannot answer for you. Every person is different. Some people can pick up a job and instantly know what to do, or who to contact to get answers so they know what to do. Other people need hands-on guidance and intense training before they have the self-confidence to do a job correctly. Only you can make the determination whether you need to enroll in a few courses or sign up for a paralegal program before you open your virtual bankruptcy service.

As stated previously, there are no requirements that you have any legal experience to draft bankruptcy petitions for attorneys. There are no paralegal programs that teach this skill. While some paralegal programs do cover an overview of the bankruptcy law, no education exists at this time to teach you step-by-step how to draft bankruptcy petitions. The only available knowledge of this kind outside of law firms and seminars is within the training materials provided by *713Training.Com.*

But if you should decide that you want to obtain legal training before you start this type of business, a few places on the internet where you can enroll in paralegal training courses are located at:

- Constitutional Educational Research Foundation
  http://calparalegal.com/
- Ashworth College (Associates Degree in Paralegal Studies)
  http://www.ashworthcollege.com/
- The Washington Online Learning Institute
  http://www.theparalegalschool.com/
- American Association for Paralegal Education
  http://www.aafpe.org/

By enrolling in an online paralegal class, you can complete the training at your own pace, study on your own time schedule and earn your Paralegal Certificate often within less than one year.

Another Method of Obtaining Your Paralegal Education

I personally believe that the best education you can receive is on-the-job training provided by an experienced attorney. This is where I obtained my initial training in bankruptcy. Paralegal training courses are excellent but they do not give you real-life experience. My suggestion would be for a person interested in a career as a paralegal to work for an attorney before enrolling in a paralegal training course. If you start a training course with absolutely no legal experience you may become overwhelmed. If you are working for an attorney while you are enrolled in the training course you will be able to benefit from the formal education as well as the real-life education at the same time and increase your knowledge much more rapidly. But of course, this applies to those of you who enjoy the legal field so much that you want to expand to include additional services to attorneys. As a virtual bankruptcy assistant, the information in this book and my other video training products may be everything you need to work in this field without investing in other paralegal training courses. Learning how to train and educate yourself is a very good skill to have.

Structuring Your Client Base

As a virtual bankruptcy assistant you may be thinking about the possibility of not only working for several attorneys but also preparing documents for consumers who are unable to afford an attorney. I cannot stress the fact enough that you should NEVER prepare bankruptcy petitions directly for consumers who are filing on a *pro se* basis without an attorney. The paralegal regulations in every state (except California) make it impossible for paralegals and virtual bankruptcy assistants to work independently for the general public, especially with the changes in the bankruptcy law enacted on October 17, 2005.

To avoid these problems, I strongly suggest you use the knowledge in this book to work under the direct supervision of attorneys. Besides, as I will explain later in this book, you will make more money working directly for attorneys and create a smoother income flow that cannot be achieved working for consumers.

Starting at Ground Zero

Okay, so you have decided to start a virtual bankruptcy service. I am sure you put a lot of thought and planning into this venture and I am happy that you have chosen this field of bankruptcy law to work in. However, I must warn you; working with debtor(s) and creditors is not a *piece of cake*. But you will find this fact is true with any business that deals directly with the general public. Ask any grocery cashier to tell you what it is like dealing with the general public every day. You will hear some pretty interesting stories about how *unrealistic* some customers can be. Their behavior is often shocking!

It is no different in bankruptcy since you are also dealing with the general public – only the general public you will be dealing with are people under a lot more stress than they would be if they were standing in a grocery checkout line.

This highly stressful, emotional state only adds fuel to the fire. So be prepared to accept the fact there will be many days when you will be mentally drained working in the area of debtor bankruptcy law. However, you will find that the rewards will always outweigh the drawbacks.

One reward of being a part of the debtor bankruptcy process is that you are helping to change people's lives!! Filing bankruptcy is a life-changing event that normally occurs only once in the average person's lifetime. Bankruptcy law is a very powerful law because bankruptcy is federal law. It even has the power to stop collection procedures from the IRS. Now, that's powerful!

For me, the greatest reward of working in bankruptcy was when a debtor called and said: *I just wanted you to know how very much I appreciated your help. It's rare these days to find people willing and eager to help someone. I just wanted to say thank you and hope you know you have made me and my husband's life just a little easier because you were there.*

Just knowing that my work is very important and has such an impact on thousands of people's lives was enough to keep me working in the field of bankruptcy for several years. In fact, bankruptcy was the most rewarding area of law I have ever encountered in the 24 years I have worked in the legal field. In many areas of law, a legal assistant is involved with the preparation of paperwork. After awhile, people tend to appear nothing more than a name on a piece of paper. But with bankruptcy you have human interaction and can experience the important role you play in people's lives. This had a lot of meaning to me personally.

I believe you feel the same way or you would have not decided to purchase this book and start a virtual bankruptcy service. If your goal was only to make money, I am sure you would have chosen another field.

Setting Up Shop

It really does not take much money to start an online or offline virtual bankruptcy service. Even a bankruptcy attorney can start his or her law practice from a spare room in their home. The virtual bankruptcy assistant can network their home office computer with the attorney's computer if both parties decide to work together on an ongoing basis. In this type of setting, the only time a virtual bankruptcy assistant would need to leave their home office is if the attorney wanted them to physically conduct client intake interviews or go to court with him or her. But even face-to-face client intake interviews can often be eliminated under this scenario also. For instance, I found that clients preferred me to interview them over the telephone in the evenings and on weekends when they were away from their jobsite. Who wants to take time off work to come into an attorney's office or discuss their private debts at work during business hours where co-workers could overhear the conversation?

Additionally, if you communicate with clients by email, the email will serve the same purpose as any written correspondence. Get in the habit of printing every email for the client file (or saving the file to an electronic folder) for each attorney you are working for. This habit has saved me from many catastrophes in the past.

In addition, people who are filing bankruptcy are not normally concerned about whether your business looks like a corporate giant or not. Most average people who file bankruptcy are in a desperate state of mind. Their main concern will be whether a creditor is going to take their home or their car and what effect filing bankruptcy will have on their life. Although I am not suggesting that you conduct business in a basement with cob webs dangling from the ceiling – I am also not suggesting that you go out and spend $1,000 on an original painting to hang on your office wall to impress your clients. Unless you are working in the field of Chapter 11 bankruptcy, you will rarely encounter high-profile clients. In the majority of cases, Chapter 7 and Chapter 13 bankruptcy normally consists of working-class people, or the average *John Q Public.*

Saving Money on Office Start-Up Supplies

Even if your rich uncle just left you $5 million dollars last week, this is still no excuse to waste money. The following are some money-saving tips for purchasing start-up supplies for your virtual bankruptcy service:

Office Furniture

You will need a computer desk and good office chair because you will be spending a great deal of time at the computer. Do not skimp on price when it comes to office chairs. Also, make sure you visit the store and sit in a few chairs before making a purchase. If you purchase a chair that is not designed for long hours of use or does not fit your body properly, you could end up with major back and muscle problems resulting in permanent physical damage.

Almost every large city has an office warehouse store. Here in Columbus, Ohio we have a store located downtown named *The Office Furniture Warehouse.* I have outfitted many new start-up offices from this fantastic store. Office chairs start out at a price of $15 and nothing is wrong with them except the fabric may not be a popular color. They also have hundreds of office desks, executive chairs and other furniture to outfit your office at a savings of 50% to 75%. I have never once found a piece of junk at *The Office Furniture Warehouse.* The furniture they sell is always strong, sturdy and designed for years of use in an office.

To find an office furniture warehouse in your area you could start by looking in your local yellow pages. If you live in New York, you can contact the *Salvation Army* who has a large selection of good, lightly used office furniture. Or, you can do a search on the internet by going to any search engine like www.google.com and type in the search words: *discount office furniture, used office furniture* or just try the search words: *office furniture* and begin your shopping experience.

Office Supplies

Office supplies will be something you will use for as long as you remain in business. It is extremely important to select the right office supply company to do business with at the beginning of start-up because as your business grows you will have less and less time to spend on comparing prices to save the most money.

Three office supply companies that have been in business for many years that I use on a consistent basis are:

- Quill Corporation, http://www.quillcorp.com
- Viking Office Supplies, http://www.vikingop.com
- Reliable Office Supplies, http://www.reliable.com

These companies offer excellent prices. Although the brand name companies like Staples (http://www.staples.com) and Office Max (http://www.officemax.com) give Quill, Viking and Reliable some stiff competition – I still prefer the fantastic customer service and savings perks that Quill, Viking and Reliable offer. My suggestion is to establish accounts with all five companies so you can take advantage of the tremendous discounts and choose the one that best fits your needs.

I have had a few attorneys and paralegals ask me to visit their office and give them some ideas about saving money on their overhead expenses. The first question I always ask is: *Where do you order your office supplies from?* Normally, the answer I receive from the attorney will be: *I don't know. I believe my secretary orders through some catalog.* You know something is definitely wrong when the owner of a company does not know where their office supplies come from. That is because they overlook the importance of how the purchase of office supplies can hurt or help their business and you can take steps now to make sure you do not make the same mistakes by establishing good business procedures for your company.

For example – every bankruptcy office will use a lot of paper. At current prices, paper can range in price from $2.50 per ream (500 sheets) to $11.00 per ream. In the beginning of your business it probably won't have any effect on your profits if you save a few dollars on each ream of paper you purchase. That is because you will probably only be using three or four reams of paper per month (if that.) However, as your business grows, the savings of a few dollars per ream could make a large dent in your profits. This is only one example to demonstrate the importance the cost that office supplies play in your growing business.

Another suggestion is that when your business grows and you hire people to work for you, one person should be designated to be in charge of ordering office supplies. This prevents double ordering as well as employee abuse. If everyone working in the office has the ability to order their own office supplies, your business will soon be wasting money on expensive designer pens and other nonessential items. After researching the operations of one law firm that allowed the employees to order their own office supplies, I found the following to be true:

1. Office supplies were being delivered almost on a daily basis because no one knew when someone else was going to place an order. Gloria might order paper clips today and Angie at the front desk may order a case of them tomorrow. Because both orders were placed on different days, they will be delivered on different days and there will be two delivery charges. If only Gloria and Angie would have known this, they could have combined their order and saved the additional delivery charge.

2. Over-ordering and double-ordering was a major problem. Gloria goes to the supply cabinet to get a box of binder clips and finds she is taking the last box. She immediately goes to her office and places an order for two cases of binder clips because she knows this is a necessary item that is used on a daily basis in the office. However, Angie already noticed the supply was getting low a couple of days ago and he ordered three cases of binder clips that arrived the same day

Gloria placed her order. Now the office has enough binder clips to do them for six months or more. This was unnecessary inventory that not only took up space, but was an unnecessary expense that could have been easily spread out over six months.

Selecting one person to be in charge of ordering office supplies would completely eliminate these types of problems. In addition, when one person places the office supply order, he or she begins to form a business relationship with the office supply company and will be able to spot special savings, discounts and other perks that will save your business additional money. In the beginning, it would be best to have the person obtain your approval before ordering any office supplies so that you can monitor their process. Once this person is properly trained and you feel confident they know what they are doing – make sure you inform the staff to submit any request for office supplies to the person you have chosen. One way to maintain consistency in implementing this process is to have a standard Office Supply Request Form like this:

OFFICE SUPPLY REQUEST FORM			
Catalog Order No.	**Description**	**Quantity**	**Price**
8674-B	Yellow File Folders	100	$5.18

You may be wondering why I included a place to write in the *price* on the above form. The logic is very simple. Most employees do not look for ways to save your business money. But, being forced to look at a price and write it down, they will be more apt not to order expensive items. Employees don't always order expensive items just for the sheer joy of costing your business money. The main thing on an employees mind is getting the supplies they need to do their job. But I have seen it proven time and time again. If an employee places an order and is forced to look at the price and write it on the request form – they often will stop and rethink about ordering the item or find a lower-cost alternative if the item is excessively priced. This normally happens because they do not want to appear extravagant to their co-workers.

I tried this experiment in one bankruptcy office and I listened to employees as they made comments about the products they ordered from the office supply store. A paralegal by the name of David was going to order a stapler for his desk but when he looked at the price he saw it was $57.00. He knew the employer would never approve this price so he searched and found a similar stapler for only $12.00. If David had never been forced to look at the price, he would have probably ordered the $57.00 stapler which would cost your company money.

Note: Although as a virtual bankruptcy assistant you may not be interested in how to manage the office supply ordering process at this time; you can use this knowledge if an attorney hires you to help set up their bankruptcy office. Believe it or not, an attorney may decided to start a bankruptcy practice when he or she finds out how much money they can make utilizing your virtual bankruptcy assistant services.

Computer Equipment

The lack of proper computer equipment to run a business is one of the main causes for a substantial loss in company profits. For example, I have worked in many law firms that had several different computer systems all networked together under different operating systems. One computer may be running Windows 98, another Windows 2000 and another Windows XP. This problem is caused by purchasing a computer whenever the need arises instead of purchasing several computers at one time so the operating systems will all be the same.

One time I worked in an office where the attorney was using a computer that was over five years old and still running the old Windows 3.1 operating system. When his business grew and he hired a paralegal, he bought her a new computer. This new computer was operating under the Windows XP operating system and the attorney could not figure out why the two computers (networked together) crashed all the time. He estimated he had a production loss of at least five hours per week (including added stress and frustration) resolving computer problems.

When I installed Windows XP on the attorney's computer a large majority of the computer problems ended. But because of the age of his computer, Windows XP operated very slow. It was easy for me to find a more updated computer that was only two years old (instead of five) for less than $300 – which is a small price to pay compared to losing five hours per week in production time as well as the added stress and frustration.

I believe what bothers people the most about upgrading their computer (or the operating system software) is the possible loss of production time. In this case, you may want to hire a computer technician to transfer all your software programs and files and set up your new computer for you. The computer technician arrives after the office has closed and the next day when you return to work, your new upgraded system will be ready. With this method, you should have a minimal loss in production time.

Note: Where can you find a computer technician in your area to help you? The resource I use for my company is Monkey Productions, owned by Geoff Gratz. You can contact him by phone at 614-668-5037 or by email at ggratz@columbus.rr.com.

The type of computers I personally purchase are Dell Computers. I have owned 9 of them and never had a problem. However, I shop at the Dell Outlet store at http://www.dell.com/outlet/ and save money on pre-built systems.

> Also, you can go online to http://www.guru.com/ and search through thousands of programmers in your immediate area. Post a job request and you will receive bids from actual programmers. Review their resume and select the right person for the job. If you find one that really knows what they are doing – make sure you keep them around. Computer problems are a part of life and having an experienced computer guru who is familiar with your set-up and who will work for you on an *as needed* basis is a resource every business should have.

Laser Printer

A laser printer is the most economical type of printer you can buy. I highly recommend Hewlett Packard LaserJet printers because they are compatible with the widest range of software programs. You can pick up a laser printer today for under $300 and I am sure the price will be even lower as time passes by. The reasons you need to invest into a laser printer (versus an ink jet printer) are:

1. Court documents are required to be printed on a laser printer. Documents printed on an ink jet printer can easily be altered and the ink may also smear.

2. The cost for ink jet cartridges range from $15 to $40 or more and you can print about 1,000 copies. The average cost for toner cartridges for a laser printer is approximately $80-$90 and it will yield about 5,000 printed pages.

3. Black and white laser printers print faster and the copies remain crisp, clear and professional. Since ink jet printers print using a wet ink, the quality is not the same. Ink jet printers are best used for printing photos, brochures and other materials that require color. Only unless you plan to do a great deal of color printing, you should buy a black and white laser printer, not a color one.

Fax Machine

A fax machine is essential to any business whether it be a virtual bankruptcy service or a pet store business. At the time this book is written, you can purchase a fax machine for less than $200. I prefer the Brother IntelliFax 2800 but there are many other models to choose from. A fax machine will need to be hooked up to a telephone line, so make sure have the telephone company install a separate telephone line in your house for your fax machine. It is important to have a dedicated fax machine that is not connected to your office or home phone. This is because you will be on the telephone talking to clients and attorneys for long periods of time and being interrupted by incoming faxes will drive you crazy. Also three-way conference calling will prevent the transfer of any fax during the conversation.

You may also want to sign up for an efax service like Maxemail at www.maxemail.com. This service is very efficient because you not only have a dedicated fax line (separate from your telephone line) but you will save paper because the fax will be accessed on the internet. You will print the pages on your laser printer or you can decide to delete or save the fax without printing it.

But regardless of which fax method you choose, always test out your fax machine before your attorneys have a chance to. Go to another fax machine and fax several pages to yourself. Find out how many times the fax machine rings before it picks up. You want to make it convenient for your attorney so the fax machine should answer on the first ring. Also, analyze the same process your attorney will go through when sending a fax to you. Then fix any problems before you ask attorneys to start using it to send Client Intake Forms for processing.

Bankruptcy Software

If you are just getting started in this business, I do not recommend that you make an investment into purchasing bankruptcy software. Instead, you should download a free demo from Best Case software at http://www.bestcase.com and use the demo version to practice inputting a bankruptcy petition. You can do this easily by installing Best Case, starting a new file and inputting bogus information. Continue filling in the blank boxes with information just to get a basic feel of the type of work you will be doing as a virtual bankruptcy assistant. Once you see exactly how this business operates and the type of work involved you will be in a better position to determine the software program you need to purchase for your particular needs.

However, when the time comes to purchase bankruptcy software to run your virtual bankruptcy service, the software program you choose for the day-to-day operations of your business is one of the most important decisions you will make. That is why it is important to work with the demo version of Best Case software first. Then you will be in a better position to locate the right software program to meet your particular needs. The following is a list of the software programs you may want to try before purchasing:

- A1 Law Firm Software
  http://www.lawfirmsoftware.com/
- Bankruptcy 2005
  http://www.bankruptcysoftware.com/
- Bankruptcy Case
  http://nationallawforms.com/bankruptcy/software-bankruptcy.htm
- Bankruptcy Disk
  http://www.lawdisks.com/bcydisk.htm
- Bankruptcy Plus
  http://www.syscommedia.net/bankruptcy_plus_software.asp
- Bankruptcy Pro
  http://www.legal-pro.com/

- Best Case
  http://www.bestcase.com/
- EZ Filing
  http://www.ezfiling.com/

Prices for the bankruptcy software will range from $250 to $800 so take your time and choose the one you like the best. Also, each software program will have different prices for a Single User, Multi-User and Network Version. Sometimes, two or more people will go together and buy a Multi-User license and save money. So check the website of the bankruptcy software manufacturer and consider the different pricing options available for each one.

However, under NO CIRCUMSTANCES should you ever ask your customers to purchase the bankruptcy software for you. Below is an article I wrote for The Teleconference News that specifically addresses this topic:

Article that appeared in:
Issue 122 of The Teleconference News
published by 50 State Notary and 713Training.Com

DON'T MAKE THIS MARKETING MISTAKE

One day last week I stopped by to visit with my friend who is a bankruptcy attorney. During our conversation I was shocked to find out that a few people who had purchased my bankruptcy book had actually found his name in the book and decided to market their bankruptcy forms processing service to him.

Although it is not unethical to contact my friends and business associates for work, the first mistake these people made was in pursuing my market. Why? Because the bankruptcy attorneys that I know and work for are

article continued on next page

dedicated customers. The chances of someone getting work from an attorney that I have spent years building up a solid working relationship with are non-existent; so it was a waste of their time.

Secondly, one of those persons who purchased my book actually had the nerve to ask my attorney to purchase Best Case software for them. My attorney was just as embarrassed as I was about this. Who in their right mind would make this type of offer to a customer? Can you imagine someone knocking on your door and asking: *Would you like for me to mow your grass this summer?* You tell them that you would like to hire them. Then, they reply: *I will be happy to do it if you will buy me a lawn mower.* How would you feel? Would you slam the door in their face?

The only explanation I can come up as to why someone would take this approach to marketing is that the people who approached my attorney must have never spent one minute of research to understand what owning a business is all about. People who work for employers their entire life are accustomed to employers suppling the tools they need to work for them. But when you own your own business – you buy your own tools because you are the employer.

The customer that pays you for your services is paying only for your services – not your software, computer, printer, pens, paper and other supplies. Those are expenses you must invest to start your own business and run your own company. It is the same thing as Wal Mart asking you to buy the shelves the merchandise is sitting on before they will sell you a box of cereal. I am sure you would be offended if Wal Mart asked you to do this – and this is exactly how the attorney felt when the people who had purchased my book asked him to buy their Best Case software.

NEVER, NEVER, NEVER ask an attorney or any other customer you plan to work for to purchase your office supplies and overhead expenses. This will put you out of business very fast and you will have to return to working for an employer. Unfortunately, the people who contacted my

article continued on next page

attorney will never know why no attorney in Columbus, Ohio will probably ever hire them. Why? Because my attorney has already told his other attorney friends about this incident and passed along the names of these parties.

So, be careful what you do. The legal industry has a small-town attitude. Everyone knows someone, who knows someone. If you demonstrate poor business and marketing techniques to one attorney, hundreds more will find out through the close contacts and networking that people have within the legal community.

This does not mean that you cannot make mistakes. Everyone makes mistakes and as long as you correct them the attorney will forgive you. But expecting an attorney to spend his or her own money so you can have a business of your own is going past the acceptable point.

My suggestion is to attend the teleconferences offered by *713Training.Com* and join the Bankruptcy or Notary Club. At each meeting we have interesting special guests who reveal the marketing techniques they used to build their own companies. You can learn everything you need to know from these successful people so you can duplicate their efforts. And if you decide to try a marketing technique you are not sure about – feel free to join in on the teleconference and ask the experts before you go out and make mistakes that could be detrimental to your future as a business owner.

The Teleconference News is free and you can subscribe at: http://www.50statenotary.com/subscribe.html

Establishing Good Office Procedures

There is one more important step to take before you start your business. You will need to establish office procedures for processing orders as well as the accounting system you plan to use. To help you get started, here is a list of the procedures I used in my virtual bankruptcy service when I processed a bankruptcy petitions for attorneys:

1. The attorney faxed me the Client Intake Forms once the client had properly filled them out.

2. I immediately placed all the pages into a letter-size file folder (I preferred the yellow-colored ones because they were easier to identify in a stack of papers.) I labeled the file folder like the sample at right:

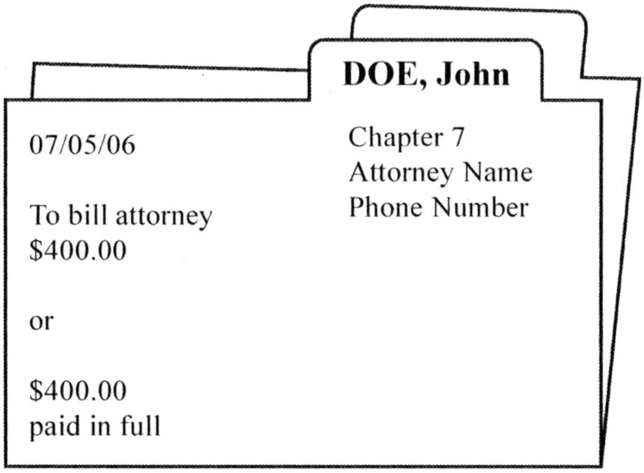

Labeling the folders in this manner helped me to easily find client files as well as keep track of which attorney was to be billed or had paid in full. Some of the attorneys who were using my services on a steady basis were provided with a free company account. This way, the attorney did not have to pay for each petition individually and was conveniently invoiced once a month.

By noting the method of payment on the front of the client's file folder when a petition was completed, I could quickly look at the information and either add the charge to the attorney's account or record the amount paid in my accounting records.

3. Next, I began preparation of the bankruptcy petition. As I input information obtained from the Client Intake Forms if I found missing information or information that needed explanation, I would make a list of questions in a standard MS Word document. I kept the MS Word document open on my desktop as I was preparing the petition. That way, I could make notes as I went along. If you wait until after you have drafted the petition to make your list of questions and notes, you will overlook something – believe me!

On Page 38 is a sample of a sample Attorney Cover Page I prepared along with the questions I might have on my list.

If the Client Intake Forms were filled out completely, you should not have more than five or six questions on your Attorney Cover Page. If your list of questions grows to more than two pages in length, you need to seriously talk to your attorney about reviewing the Client Intake Forms before giving them to you. It is the attorney's job to make sure the forms are filled out completely but most attorneys that I worked for were sloppy in this area and faxed me incomplete forms. This only delayed the processing of the bankruptcy petition by several days and even weeks because the client needed to be contacted and a telephone interview conducted to obtain the missing information before starting the bankruptcy petition.

Because this is such a common problem, I use this situation to my advantage in marketing. I explain to the attorney that I will contact the client to obtain any missing information on the Client Intake Forms, then I factor this service into my final price. I personally would not recommend that you charge an extra fee for contacting the client to obtain missing information. Instead, it should be factored into your price. Besides, you will pick up so much more information by talking directly to the client, which adds to the quality and detail of the bankruptcy petition. When you get the *whole story* about the client's current financial situation directly from the client, you will be able to record more detail within the bankruptcy petition which makes the job of the attorney and trustee much easier.

Then, if you do work for an attorney that makes sure all the information is properly filled out on the Client Intake Forms, you still charge the same price but send them a *Thank You* gift because they helped to make your job much easier.

SAMPLE ATTORNEY COVER PAGE

Client Name: **John and Betty Doe**
Attorney Name: **Angie Lawyer**
Date Client Intake Forms Received: 05.16.06
Date this Attorney Cover Sheet Faxed to Attorney: 05.22.06
Fax answers to Virtual Bankruptcy Assistant: 614.555.5555

1. Betty did not provide her middle name on the General Information form. Please find out if she has a middle name or not and what it is. I put NMN (NMN = no middle name) on the petition.

2. Debtors state that have a dependent granddaughter. We need to know:
   a. Where is the mother of the child living?
   b. Does the mother pay John and Betty any money to care for the child?
   c. Since the child is an infant, are there additional expenses that John and Betty pay for such as diapers, formula, medications, etc. that were not included in their monthly living expenses?
   d. Does the dad pay child support?
   e. If so, who does he pay it to?
   f. Do John and Betty pay any support to their daughter? (food, rent, etc.)

3. Notice that John and Betty's home has not been appraised since 2002. A recent appraisal needs to be done to reflect the current market value on Schedule A for their property at 123 Main Street, Cheyenne Wells CO.

4. The software reports $4,308.00 of unexempt equity in property located at 123 Main Street. If the recent appraisal shows the home valued at more than the 2002 figure of $137,000 there may be even more unexempt equity.

continued on next page

5. Notice that John and Betty's rental property at 642 Anytown Street, Espanola NM has not been appraised since 1999. A recent appraisal needs to be done which could result in unexempt equity for this debt.

6. What type of Government Bonds do John and Betty have valued at $500?

7. What is the name and city and state location of the bank where John and Betty have a $2,000 Certificate of Deposit?

> **Note:** Do not be concerned if this sample Attorney Cover Page is confusing. It is not important for you understand the reasoning behind these 7 questions at this point in your training. It is only necessary that you understand how the Attorney Cover Page is structured and the type of information it contains.

4. After the Attorney Cover Page was compiled in MS Word, I saved the document under the client folder on my computer. (I made a separate file folder for each attorney and within that attorney's folder I created subfolders for each of their clients.) For some attorneys, I emailed the list of questions so they could make contact with the client and obtain the information. For other attorneys that requested it, I called the client and obtained the missing information myself.

I structured my company so that my service was personalized to the needs of each attorney. By personalizing my services to fit his or her office procedures, my reputation grew for providing good reliable customer service as well as helping to maintain a smoother workflow for the attorney and his or her office staff.

5. After the client answered the list of questions on the Attorney Cover Page I updated the bankruptcy petition and saved it in PDF format. (My bankruptcy software, Best Case, could automatically do this for me.) I then emailed the PDF file to the attorney and he or she reviewed it. If there were any changes that needed made, the attorney either called me on the phone or sent me an email.

6. Upon final approval by the attorney I electronically filed the bankruptcy petition and emailed a final PDF copy to the attorney. But you will only provide this service after you have established a good business relationship with the attorney you are working for. When you do a petition for an attorney the first time, they will normally electronically file their own petition using their private username and password.

7. After my job was completed, I made the entry into my accounting records and placed the file folder in a banker's box. Once the banker's box was filled, I stored it in my office closet to be used as an off-site backup for all my attorneys. I also archived the client files for each attorney on a CD-Rom and mailed it to them once a year or as they requested.

Establishing Procedures for First Time Attorney Clients

Before you can begin drafting a bankruptcy petition, you will need to know the following information about the attorney handling the bankruptcy case. The initial information you need is:

- Full name of attorney
- Name of law firm (for the attorney who is a sole-proprietor, the law firm name may be the same as the attorney's name.)
- Address, city, state and zip code of law firm
- Telephone and fax number

- Email address (used when documents are electronically filed so the attorney receives a copy containing the case number.)
- Attorney bar number (this is the number issued by the Federal Bankruptcy Court so that this attorney may practice law in front of a federal judge.)
- Total amount this attorney charged for the bankruptcy petition including the filing fee. (This information is recorded on the Attorney Compensation Statement within the bankruptcy petition.)

Should You Provide an Agreement to the Attorney for Your Services?

When I worked for attorneys I did not provide them with any type of legal agreement to perform virtual bankruptcy assistant services. The attorney simply called me up, discussed the case with me; I provided the services and was paid by the attorney within 30 days. However, some people feel more comfortable in providing the attorneys they work for with an agreement for their services.

The document on the next page can be used as a guideline to write your own that is customized for your particular business. Keep in mind that I am NOT an attorney and I do not make any statements that this sample agreement is legal in any state. Therefore, I highly recommend that you write your own agreement and only use the sample as a template so that you can edit it to fit your situation.

Next, I suggest you take your agreement to a licensed contract attorney in your state and for a consultation fee of approximately $50, the attorney will review the agreement and provide you with suggestions to comply with your individual state laws. Or, you can have the attorney you are working for review it for free and let them know you are willing to make any changes to the agreement they deem necessary before working for them.

SAMPLE AGREEMENT

This Agreement is made between **Your Name**, residing at _________________________________ (hereinafter referred to as "Independent Contractor") and **Attorney Name**, with offices at _________________________________ (hereinafter referred to as "Attorney") on **Date Here.**

Employment Status

Your Name will be employed as an independent contractor by **Attorney Name**. **Your Name** will be responsible for the reporting of his/her own income taxes, expenses, social security and other requirements stipulated by the laws of the jurisdiction where **Your Name** is residing and performing his/her duties.

Payment Agreement

Attorney Name will pay **Your Name** a flat-rate payment of $___________ per bankruptcy petition that is drafted under the direction of **Attorney Name** and upon complete satisfaction of services.

Attorney Name agrees to pay **Your Name** within ___ days after the finalized bankruptcy petition has been filed with the court.

Services to Be Performed

Your Name agress to provide the following services to **Attorney Name:**

1. Input of client intake information into bankruptcy software.
2. Compile additional questions client did not provide the answer to (or needs to provide clarification for) and provide to attorney for review and direction.
3. Lien search on internet for additional debts.

continued on next page

Sample Agreement (continued from previous page)

4. Judgment search on internet for additional fines and debts
5. Print-out from Black Book to substantiate motor vehicle values recorded within the bankruptcy petition.
6. Revision to draft of bankruptcy petition.
7. Final bankruptcy petition ready to electronically file.
8. Printed copy mailed to debtor(s.)
9. Back-up copy provided to attorney on CD along with all customer files and correspondence.
10. Print-out for customer file of all correspondence including correspondence by mail or in written form.

Confidentiality Agreement

Your Name agrees to maintain in confidence and not to disclose any confidential client information received from **Attorney Name** other than to employees or agents who have a need to know the confidential information and approved by **Attorney Name** for release. **Your Name** further agrees not to make any copies in whole or in part of confidential information or analyze samples of tangible materials included therein, which are not available on the open market or from other sources, for any purposes and will, upon request by the attorney, return all tangible materials furnished hereunder and any notes or memoranda of conversations relating thereto, including any copies thereof.

AGREED: (2 Pages)

______________________	______________________
Your Name	**Attorney Name**
Your Company Name	Attorney Law Firm Name
Date: ________________	Date: ________________

Naming Your Business

The name you give to your bankruptcy business should match the domain name you select for your online bankruptcy business. Here is a way to start getting ideas for business names:

1. Go to http://www.dnwiz.com/ and type in some keywords, select the criteria for your search and you will get a list of 100s of different domain names to choose from.

2. Also, go to http://www.google.com and type in the search words: *What should I name my company?* and you will come up with several websites that provide you with a wide variety of ideas.

3. Once you have located the domain name you want for your business, select a web host like Bummer Hosting at www.bummerhosting.com and secure the name so you don't risk losing it. Even if you are not going to establish a web site at this time, you can still *park the domain* so it is registered to you and you alone.

Should You Incorporate or Get a Business License?

Since I do not know your situation, I cannot advise you whether to incorporate your business or not. My experience has been that many people start a business, find out how much work is involved and they decide to close the company. If it were me, I would suggest that you work the business for awhile until you reach a point where you are making money and you enjoy the work. At that time you can look into incorporating your business in order to protect your personal assets.

But keep in mind; as a virtual bankruptcy assistant service you are working under the direction of attorneys. It is doubtful they would ever try and sue you for making a mistake on a bankruptcy petition. Ultimately, it is the attorney's responsibility to catch mistakes before signing their name on the bankruptcy petition and filing it in court anyway. In the many years I have worked independently for law firms, not one has tried to sue me so therefore I never incorporated my business.

As far as whether or not you should apply for a business license, you will need to check with the requirements under your particular state law. For example, in Ohio there is no business license for a homebased internet service business. The closest type of license available in Ohio is a vendors license. Since service businesses normally do not buy products from a wholesaler and resell them to the public, my type of service business does not qualify. However, when I lived in Tennessee, it was required for any business to get a business license. At that time, the business license for a homebased service business was only $11.00.

The Next Step ...

Now that you have set up your business and are ready to begin, we will cover some of the knowledge you will need about bankruptcy in order to do your job properly as a virtual bankruptcy assistant. Please understand that the information that follows is not intended to take the place of any competent advice from a licensed attorney in your state. Further, the information that follows has been reviewed by a wide variety of bankruptcy attorneys in different U.S. states and revised before publishing. I even include some of the information I taught at bankruptcy seminars. This seminar materials was approved for CLE credits by The National Federation of Paralegal Associations (NFPA.) That's right! Many people have paid up to $275 to attend seminars to obtain the information in this book. So, you have already saved yourself a great deal of money just by purchasing *How to Start a Virtual Bankruptcy Assistant Service!*

So, let's get started and learn more about the field of bankruptcy as it relates to the virtual bankruptcy assistant in the next chapter.

Chapter 3

Performing Your Job as a Virtual Bankruptcy Assistant

Performing Your Job as a Virtual Bankruptcy Assistant

Bankruptcy law is a fascinating field because it involves a wide range of different areas of law. For instance, if a couple are divorced one spouse may be paying child or spousal support, thereby affecting the income of the debtor filing bankruptcy. Therefore, a basic knowledge of divorce law may be needed to help with the preparation of the bankruptcy petition. A bit of knowledge about tax law also is necessary when dealing with debtor(s), because many of them may owe federal, state or local taxes which must be listed as an unsecured *priority* debt. Corporate law comes into play when preparing Chapter 11 bankruptcy filings and a basic knowledge in criminal law comes into play when the debtor has been arrested and owes money for unpaid fines and other misdemeanors.

Also, bankruptcy law has two unique and different sides to it: *debtor* and *creditor*. Personally, I prefer working in debtor law because I have the opportunity to actually work with real consumers and know I am helping them to change their lives. On the other side of the coin, a virtual bankruptcy assistant normally working in creditor bankruptcy essentially fills out routine forms like a Motion for Relief From Stay or Proof of Claim. Therefore, there is very little direct contact with consumers.

Working on the debtor side of bankruptcy, my life somehow takes on new meaning. When I draft a wage garnishment notice to prevent a creditor from garnishing a debtor(s) wages this week, it is a good feeling to know a single mother may be able to afford the groceries she needs. With my attorney's approval, I am thrilled to call the electric company in order to get a debtor's service turned back on so her son can do his homework tonight. It's also a joy to have a debtor come into to the office, give me a hug and tell me how thankful they are that creditors are no longer harassing them and their neighbors. Dealing with debtor(s) also provides me with the ability to actually use my mind and I in turn learn a great deal about people in the process.

Susan Burns, a bankruptcy paralegal in Fair Oaks, California had the following to say about working on the debtor side of bankruptcy:

> *Prior to working in bankruptcy, I worked for several years in family law (divorce.) I also was a word processor for a corporate lawyer many years ago and worked six months as a personal injury secretary but I recently found myself exposed to the debtor bankruptcy field. At first I thought bankruptcy would be "snooze-ville" but there is no such thing as a boring case file. Each case file contains someone's life. And everyone has a vastly different life. I really 'feel' for these bankruptcy people. It's like many of them are on the edge and it's our job to let them know things will probably be okay and even better if we do our job right. It's a rewarding feeling to know that you helped to change someone's life.*

Can you see what I mean by the bankruptcy field of law being fascinating? Why then do some people make a sad face when I mention the word *bankruptcy?* I believe it is because filing for bankruptcy is still considered to be admitting the debtor was a failure. He or she did not properly plan their finances and because of their poor judgment they are now in a financial position where they have no choice but to file bankruptcy. And because of this general negative opinion, people who know nothing about bankruptcy law will continue thinking this way until they are educated about the positive side.

The Bankruptcy Abuse Prevention and Consumer Protection Act of 2005 (BAPCPA)

After almost five years of litigation, President George Bush signed the new Bankruptcy Abuse Prevention and Consumer Protection Act of 2005 into law on

October 17, 2005. Prior to the changes in the law there were many rumors going around that the new law would make it harder for people to file bankruptcy. In fact, the rumors grew so great in number that they caused a panic within the general population. Record numbers rushed to file bankruptcy before the law changed just because of these rumors. In fact, there was such a rush of new bankruptcy filings that many bankruptcy courts opened on Sunday just to accommodate the long lines of people on October 16, 2005.

But after the dust settled and the new law went into effect, petition preparers found there were very few changes in the actual Forms and Schedules of the bankruptcy petition. Also, attorneys discovered that if a person qualified for a Chapter 7 under the old law they would probably qualify under the new law. In fact, the changes made in the new bankruptcy law (in my opinion) are very fair. While some people will disagree with me - I have witnessed abuse under the old bankruptcy law and I am glad to see a stop has been put to it under the guidelines of the new bankruptcy law.

If you are interested in obtaining more information about the changes from the old bankruptcy law to the new one, please visit http://www.713training.com/links/ on my website. I keep these links up to date with the latest information.

The Need for Virtual Bankruptcy Assistant Services is Increasing

With bankruptcy filings increasing by record-breaking proportions (and it does not appear there will be an end to this rise any time soon) many attorneys are adding bankruptcy services to their current practice. These attorneys in turn need virtual bankruptcy assistants skilled in this field to assist them. Unfortunately, since bankruptcy has not been a popular topic in the past, paralegals are not normally trained specifically in this area of law.

Because of the lack of education offered to paralegals in the area of debtor bankruptcy law, many attorneys have had no choice but to take the *inside* approach to personally training their paralegals in bankruptcy. But simply being trained by an attorney about bankruptcy law is not the education a bankruptcy paralegal needs for their day-to-day duties. Additionally, many attorneys may have not practiced in this area before so it would be impossible for them to properly train their paralegals (or assistants) in the day-to-day skills they need.

The result for the paralegal (or virtual assistant) often becomes a frustrating experience because they are forced to learn from their mistakes while on the job. This causes additional work for the bankruptcy court that must find these mistakes and send out a notice that delays the processing of the petition. In addition, the paralegal (or virtual assistant) and attorney need to spend time fixing the mistakes. However, if the paralegal (or virtual assistant) had been properly trained in the first place to prepare a well-detailed and accurate bankruptcy petition, the lost time and delay could have been avoided. So lets get started and learn some basic information about bankruptcy they normally never teach you in paralegal school.

Bankruptcy Basics

A person just doesn't wake up one morning and say, *Hey, I think I will file bankruptcy today.* Instead, it is normally a long process of worry, struggle and guilt before people reach this point. However, the decision to file bankruptcy is the legal right of every citizen in the United States.

To give you a quick history lesson, the bankruptcy law is derived from the laws established by the Jewish people in the Old Testament period of our history. Every seven years a person's debts would be forgiven and they could start a new debt-free life. (It was called the *Year of Jubilee.*) These laws were not enacted solely because the society loved their neighbor. The reason goes much deeper than that. It was done because they knew that keeping people under debt forever was not good for their society as a whole. By *forgiving* debts every seven years, those experiencing the heavy burden of debt could now afford to put money back into the economy and hopefully stay out of debt so the problem did not occur again, thereby causing the society as a whole to grow and prosper.

Our United States government also knows that if there was no way to forgive heavy, burdensome debts, many people would eventually end up on welfare just to survive, thereby raising taxes, causing high unemployment, affecting prices and causing other companies to go out of business because the majority of people couldn't afford to buy their products. This situation would eventually collapse the economy of our society, so the bankruptcy law was established to keep our economy balanced.

Note: As of October 17, 2005 when the new bankruptcy law went into effect, the six (6) year requirement was extended to eight (8) years for the first time in bankruptcy history.

Some Bankruptcy Terms You Need to Know

If you have worked in another area of law, you are already familiar with the terms *Plaintiff* and *Defendant.* However, in bankruptcy those words change to *Debtor* and *Creditor.* In addition, in litigation there are two parties (Plaintiff and Defendant) that are parties to a lawsuit. However, in bankruptcy there is only one party (debtor and/or debtor's spouse.) When a husband and wife file a bankruptcy petition together, the husband becomes the *debtor* and the wife is the *co-debtor.*

Unmarried couples (including domestic partners) cannot file a bankruptcy petition together; regardless of how many years they have lived together. Unmarried couples must each file separate bankruptcy petitions although they can live in the same or separate residences.

Common Bankruptcy Words in Layman's Terms

Creditor — This is the person or company the debtor(s) owe money to regardless if the debt is secure or unsecure.

Debtor or Co-Debtor — This is the person(s) filing bankruptcy.

Secured Debt — This is a debt owed for an item that could be repossessed from the debtor(s) if they don't pay the bill. For instance, if the debtor(s) do not make a house payment, the creditor (or bank) can repossess their house. However, if the house is no longer in the debtor(s) possession, the item becomes *unsecured* regardless of the fact that the original loan was secure.

Unsecured Debt — This is a debt owed for something that *cannot* be repossessed from the debtor(s) if they do not pay the bill. For instance, unsecure credit cards, medical bills, repossessed vehicles no longer in the debtor's possession and other similar debts are *unsecured debts.*

Asset — This is something the debtor(s) own that has a monetary value. An asset can be something as small as a set of carpenter's tools, a $10 watch, a security deposit with a landlord or utility company, a 401K plan, all the way to more expensive items the debtor(s) own such as a house or a car. In other words, anything the debtor(s) own or have in their possession is an asset.

Real Property — Real property is considered anything that is attached to *God's green earth.* A mobile home is normally not attached to the earth because it sits on wheels. Therefore, a mobile home is considered personal property unless the wheels have been removed and it is physically attached to the earth.

Personal Property — Personal property is everything else the debtor(s) own that is not real property or the item does not have a deed or title.

Bankruptcy Discharge — This is a notice the debtor(s) receive from the bankruptcy court letting them know their case has ended. A bankruptcy can end because the trustee files a Motion to either dismiss the case, convert it to another Chapter, or the judge discharges the debts in a Chapter 7 and/or approves the Chapter 13 plan of repayment.

Reaffirmation Agreement — This is an agreement filed with the bankruptcy court when the debtor(s) want to continue paying a debt and the creditor agrees to the payment terms. This agreement will contain the names of both parties, the total amount owed to the creditor, the interest rate and payment terms, etc. In Chapter 7 and Chapter 13 bankruptcy cases, Reaffirmation Agreements are normally used for mortgages and motor vehicles so the debtor(s) can keep the collateral and make payments. The creditor will normally initiate the Reaffirmation Agreement when they receive a notice from the court that the debtor(s) wish to reaffirm the debt. Other creditors will bring the Reaffirmation Agreement with them to the 341 Meeting for the debtor(s) to sign.

Normally, if the debtor(s) are up-to-date on their payments, most creditors will agree to a Reaffirmation Agreement. Where you may run into problems is if the debtor(s) are behind in their payments and are financially unable to pay them in full before their 341 Meeting of Creditors. Of course, this all depends on the creditor, the type of debt, value of the property and the debtor(s) prior payment history with the creditor. The attorney will need to advise the debtor(s) in matters like these.

Conversion — A conversion occurs when the debtor(s) file one Chapter of bankruptcy and converts over to another Chapter after they have filed. For example: debtor(s) file a Chapter 7 but their income increases in order to qualify them for a Chapter 13. The attorney will file a document in court to convert the case to a Chapter 13 so they don't lose any assets, or for any other number of reasons.

Exemption — Many people are fearful when they file bankruptcy because someone told them they will lose everything they own. This is not true! There are a variety of exemption allowances allowed by the bankruptcy court to protect the assets the debtor(s) own. Each state has its own set of exemption allowances. These exemptions are necessary to help the debtor(s) to continue living a normal life and not be stripped of everything they own. For instance, people need a house to live in, a car to drive, clothes to wear and furniture in their home to continue living a normal life. The law allows debtor(s) to keep all or most of these types of items by allowing exemptions for them. When anything the debtor(s) own is totally exempt from the bankruptcy, no one can take the item away from them.

However, exemptions do not cover everything. For instance, if the debtor(s) own a home with an appraised value of $100,000, but they only owe $50,000 to the mortgage company, this means the debtor(s) will have $50,000 in equity. If your state exemption allowance is only $25,000 on real property the debtor will have $25,000 left in *unexempt* equity that may be requested by the bankruptcy court to divide between their creditors. Of course, this is only a general example, but it is provided to help you understand what exemptions are and how they work.

Automatic Stay — Filing a petition *automatically stays* (the word *stay* means *stops*) most collection actions against the debtor or the debtor's property. But filing the bankruptcy petition does not *stay* certain types of actions listed under the new Bankruptcy Code. In fact, the *stay* may be effective only for a short period of time in some situations. The *stay* requires no judicial action. As long as the *stay* is in effect, creditors generally may not start or continue lawsuits, wage garnishments or even telephone calls demanding payments. The bankruptcy clerk gives notice of the bankruptcy case to all creditors whose names and addresses appear on the Creditor's Matrix of the bankruptcy petition. After the creditors receive this notice, all collection procedures for the debtor(s) should stop and any further communication will be made by the creditor to the attorney or bankruptcy court.

Motion for Relief From Stay — This is a court order requested by a creditor, who asks the court to lift the *Automatic Stay* that was immediately put in place when the bankruptcy petition was filed. If a creditor is granted a *Relief from Stay,* the debtor(s) will receive notice from the court of its existence and the bankruptcy attorney will prepare a Motion on the debtor(s) behalf to request the court remove the *Relief from Stay.*

Trustee — This is an attorney appointed by the bankruptcy court. When your attorney and the debtor(s) attend the 341 Meeting of Creditors, they will meet the trustee assigned to their case. He or she will review the bankruptcy petition, ask questions, verify information, allow any questions of creditors who may be present and request any additional documents before recommending the case for confirmation to the judge. The trustee is *supposed* to be an impartial person who works for the benefit of the creditor as well as for the debtor(s.) His or her job is to find unexempt assets to distribute to creditors or to declare the bankruptcy filing as a *no asset case* among other things.

Dismissal — A bankruptcy case can be dismissed at any time if the attorney or debtor(s) fail to comply with any rules of the court. Also, a bankruptcy case is *discharged* if the debtor(s) completely pays off their Chapter 13 or when their Chapter 7 is completely dismissed with prejudice.

Chapter 7 Basics

Under the old bankruptcy law, the bankruptcy judge had the power to dismiss a Chapter 7 case if he or she thought the debtor had enough disposable income to be in a Chapter 13 repayment plan. There were no hard and fast rules that dictated when a judge should dismiss a case on these grounds — it depended on the facts of the case and the attitude of the judge. Now that the new bankruptcy law has gone into effect, clear criteria now exists that dictates who will be allowed to stay in a Chapter 7 and who will be forced to file a Chapter 13. Disabled veterans whose debts were made during active duty and people whose debts come primarily from the operation of a business get a *fast pass* to Chapter 7. All others must meet the following requirements:

- Debtor(s) must have resided in the bankruptcy jurisdiction they are filing a petition in for a minimum of 180 days (6 months) or in their state for two (2) years.

- Debtor(s) must not have received a Chapter 7 bankruptcy discharge within the last eight (8) years or filed a Chapter 13 case within the last six (6) years from the date of filing. (Example: a debtor who files a Chapter 7 on July 5, 2005 is not eligible to file another Chapter 7 until *after* July 5, 2013.)

- Debtor(s) must be able to pass the Means Test for income requirements. You can find median income tables, by state and family size, at the website of the United States Trustee at http://www.usdoj.gov/ust (click "Means Testing Information") or the link from the *713Training.Com* website.

- Debtor(s) must meet the Debt Counseling Certification as required under Section 109(h) of the bankruptcy code.

- Debtor(s) cannot file a Chapter 7 bankruptcy if a previous Chapter 7 or Chapter 13 case was dismissed within the past 180 days because: (1) the debtor(s) violated a court order; (2) the court ruled that the debtor(s) filing was fraudulent or constituted an abuse of the bankruptcy system, or (3) the debtor(s) requested the dismissal after a creditor asked for relief from the automatic stay.

Chapter 13 Basics

In order to be eligible to file a Chapter 13 bankruptcy, debtor(s) must be able to meet the following basic guidelines:

- Debtor(s) must reside or have a domicile, a place of business or property in the United States; and

- Debtor(s) must be an individual or married couple. This means that the debtor(s) cannot be a corporation, partnership or some other company entity; and

- Debtor(s) must have income that exceeds their monthly expenses. The reason for this is to ensure creditors and other interested parties of the debtor's have the financial ability to afford to be in the plan; and

- Debtor(s) must have noncontingent, liquidated, unsecured debts of less than $307,675 and non contingent, liquidated, secured debts of less than $922,975 on the date of filing. These two figures will change from time to time based on inflation standards. But presently these figures act as a ceiling for secured and unsecured debt; and

- Debtor(s) must be able to pass the Means Test for income requirements. You can find median income tables, by state and family size, at the website of the United States Trustee at http://www.usdoj.gov/ust (click *Means Testing Information)* or the link from the *713Training.Com* website; and

- Debtor(s) must meet the Debt Counseling Certification as required under Section 109(h) of the bankruptcy code.

Chapter 13 allows debtor(s) to reorganize their finances and pay a certain percentage of their debts over a period of five years (or 100% if they have the income to afford it.) The unpaid balance of unsecured non-priority debts (if any) is discharged after the payment plan is completed. Payments are usually made by the debtor(s) through a payroll deduction and paid directly to the Chapter 13 Trustee.

But do not be confused. A Chapter 13 is *not* a bill consolidation loan, although some debtor(s) think of it that way. While it may appear to be a similar concept, a bill consolidation loan is money actually loaned to a person to repay other creditors and the person in turn pays back the lender. In a Chapter 13, no money is loaned to debtor(s) because they make monthly payments to the bankruptcy trustee who disburses the money to the creditors.

Priority claims are paid first in a Chapter 13. Priority claims include debts for items such as a mortgage, taxes, child support, etc. Priority claims are listed in the bankruptcy petition on Schedules A, B, D, E and sometimes Schedule G. Debts listed on Schedule F are not considered to be priority claims. Instead, they are unsecured, non-priority debts.

In a Chapter 13, debtor(s) are normally permitted to keep everything they own as long as regular payments are made to the Chapter 13 Trustee and payment of arrearages under the Plan is provided for. If the debtor(s) get behind in their Chapter 13 payments the trustee may dismiss the case and the debtor(s) could be *back to square one* and will have to wait a certain period of time before they can refile.

A Chapter 13 plan is also prepared for submission to the court when a Chapter 13 petition is filed. From the perspective of a virtual bankruptcy assistant, this is the only difference between a Chapter 13 and a Chapter 7 because the Forms and Schedules are essentially the same in both Chapters.

Unfortunately, many legal professionals (including attorneys) have difficulty preparing a Chapter 13 plan and many of them choose only to accept Chapter 7 cases because of this. This is unfortunate because a Chapter 13 plan is not difficult to understand. It is essentially an overview of exactly how the debtor(s) propose to repay their debts. Once you understand the basics, you should have no problem drafting them for your attorney. Besides, most bankruptcy software programs (including Best Case) have built-in functions that do the calculations for a Chapter 13 plan automatically; ready for your attorney to review.

If the debtor(s) are eligible to file a Chapter 13 bankruptcy, one of the first questions they may ask is: *How much are my monthly payments going to be?"* Only an attorney can provide an answer to this question; so never make an attempt to answer it. Instead, you could say something like: *The attorney is the only one permitted to give you the exact figure for your proposed Chapter 13 Plan Payment. But be assured, your attorney will make sure you can afford the payment because it would not be worthwhile to put you into a payment plan that you cannot afford. I can contact the attorney and find out if he is willing to release this information and I get back to you as soon as possible.*

Changes During a Chapter 13 Bankruptcy

Nothing stays the same. During the five years that the debtor(s) are making their regular payments to the Chapter 13 Trustee anything could happen. One or both debtor(s) may lose their job, change employment, need to purchase a replacement vehicle, sell their home, file for divorce, inherit money, or any other number of life-changing events. Any one of these circumstances can cause the Chapter 13 plan payment to be decreased or increased, depending upon the situation.

Unfortunately, when a life-changing event occurs for debtor(s), they normally do not think about contacting their bankruptcy attorney. However, if they take it upon themselves to stop paying their Chapter 13 plan payment without notifying their attorney, it may result in their case being dismissed. At this point, the debtor(s) may not be eligible to refile their petition or the attorney may have the virtual bankruptcy assistant draft a Motion to Reinstate the Case. Either way, this will cause the virtual bankruptcy assistant to spend time preparing additional paperwork which results in delays for everyone concerned.

To prevent this from happening, make sure the attorney sends a letter informing the debtor(s) to contact the attorney if they require any changes to their Chapter 13 plan payment or if one of the debtor(s) should change employment or lose their job. I have noticed that in the majority of cases where debtor(s) stop making their Chapter 13 plan payment, one or both of the debtor(s) lost their job. They thought they would get another job soon but that didn't happen. Pretty soon, the debtor(s) are seriously delinquent in their Chapter 13 plan payments and this is usually when they notify the attorney. Let the clients know to contact the attorney immediately before the situation turns from bad to worse so the attorney can take steps to make sure their Chapter 13 bankruptcy is not discharged for nonpayment.

Filing the Bankruptcy Petition

Attorneys in all 50 U.S. states are required to file petitions electronically via the internet. Most bankruptcy software programs have this feature built in, or the attorney may need to login to their PACER account and upload the PDF file of the actual bankruptcy petition. Currently there is a filing fee of $299 for a Chapter 7 and $274 for a Chapter 13. Most courts provide their local rules on their website. Print them out and review them with your attorney so you will learn the state's filing requirements.

To find links to your local bankruptcy court's Local Rules visit http://www.uscourts.gov/rules/bk-localrules.html

Below is the list of the Forms and Schedules currently required to file a Chapter 7 and Chapter 13 bankruptcy petition. An actual sample of a fully complete bankruptcy petition is provided in the publication: The Virtual Bankruptcy Assistant Training Workbook, which is available at the *713Training.Com* website.

- Form 1: Voluntary or Involuntary Petition

- Form 6: Summary of Schedules
- Schedule A (real property)
- Schedule B (personal property)
- Schedule C (property claimed as exempt)
- Schedule D (secure creditors holding secure claims on property listed on Schedule A and Schedule B)
- Schedule E (unsecured PRIORITY claims; i.e., student loans, fines, child support, taxes and other debts not eligible for discharge)
- Schedule F (unsecured NON-PRIORITY claims; i.e., credit cards, medical bills, repossessed items no longer in the debtor(s) possession, etc.)
- Schedule G (executory contracts and unexpired leases; i.e., cell phone contracts, automobile leases, any and all other contracts and leases)
- Schedule H (co-debtors) Note: If a husband and wife are filing a bankruptcy petition together, they do not need to be listed on the co-debtor form. However, if a married debtor is filing without his/her spouse (but his/her spouse is a co-signer or co-debtor on any debt) their name, address and relationship to the debtor will need to be listed on this form.
- Schedule I (current income of debtor)
- Schedule J (current monthly expenses of debtor)
- Declaration Concerning Debtor's Schedules
- Form 7: Statement of Affairs
- Form 8: Chapter 7 Individual Debtor's Statement of Intention
- Compensation Statement of Attorney for the Debtor(s)
- Notice to Individual Consumer Debtor of Available Chapters
- Verification of Creditor's Matrix
- Creditor Address Matrix
- Form 21: Statement of Social Security Number
- Form 22A: Statement of Current Monthly Income/Means Test
- Any additional local forms required by your specific bankruptcy court

Additional Forms Required to File a Chapter 13:

- Omit: Form 8: Chapter 7 Individual Debtor's Statement of Intention
- Chapter 13 Plan
- Form 22C: Current Monthly Income/Disposable Income

The Skeleton Bankruptcy Petition

In some extreme circumstances, a *skeleton* petition may be filed by the attorney for his or her client. Skeleton petitions consist of the Voluntary Petition and Creditor's Matrix only. However, if a skeleton petition is filed you will only have a short period of time to file the remaining schedules and forms or the case will be dismissed. Skeleton petition filings are only necessary in an extreme emergency situation. For example, if the virtual bankruptcy assistant or attorney does not have the time to properly prepare the petition but the debtor(s) need to stop a foreclosure, a Sheriff's sale, a wage garnishment, a repossession or if utilities have been turned off, the attorney may decide to file a skeleton petition so a *bankruptcy stay* can be put into effect immediately.

The Umbrella Effect of the Bankruptcy Stay

Regardless of whether an entire petition or a skeleton petition is filed, the very moment the bankruptcy petition is filed with the bankruptcy court, a type of *umbrella* of protection for the debtor(s) is put into effect that we previously discussed on Page 56. The *bankruptcy stay* helps some common emergencies:

- **Utility disconnections.** If the debtor(s) are behind on a utility bill and the utility company is threatening to disconnect their water, electric, gas, or telephone service, the automatic stay will prevent the disconnection for at least 20 days. (Also, bankruptcy will probably discharge the past due debts for utility service.)

- **Foreclosure.** If the debtor(s) home mortgage is being foreclosed on, the automatic stay temporarily stops the foreclosure, but the creditor will often be able to proceed sooner or later. If the debtor(s) are facing foreclosure, Chapter 13 bankruptcy is usually a better remedy than Chapter 7 bankruptcy if the debtor(s) wish to keep their house, but it depends on the result of the Means Test.

- **Eviction.** If the debtor(s) are being evicted from their rented home, the automatic stay may provide some help — but the new bankruptcy law makes it easier for landlords to proceed with evictions. If the landlord already has a judgment of possession against the debtor(s) when they file bankruptcy, the automatic stay won't affect these eviction proceedings. The landlord can continue with the eviction just as if the debtor(s) had not filed bankruptcy. And if the landlord believes that the debtor(s) have been endangering the property or using controlled substances there, the automatic stay will not have much effect. In other cases, the automatic stay might buy the debtor(s) a few days or weeks, but the landlord will most likely ask the court to lift the automatic stay and allow the eviction — and the court will probably agree.

- **Collection of overpayments of public benefits.** If the debtor(s) receive public benefits and were overpaid, normally the agency is entitled to collect the overpayment out of their future checks. The automatic stay prevents this collection. However, if the debtor(s) become ineligible for benefits, the automatic stay doesn't prevent the agency from denying or terminating benefits for that reason.

- **Multiple wage garnishments.** Filing for bankruptcy will automatically stop wage garnishments. Not only will the debtor(s) be able to take home a full paycheck, but they also may be able to discharge the debt in bankruptcy. Although no more than 25% of a debtor(s) wages may be garnished to pay court judgments (up to 50% for child support and alimony), many people file for bankruptcy if more than one wage garnishment is threatened. For some people, who are living from paycheck-to-paycheck, any loss of income is devastating. Also, some employers become intolerant toward the employee because of the time and expense of initiating a wage garnishment. Although federal law prohibits an employee from being fired for one wage garnishment, an employer can fire an employee for multiple garnishments.

What the Automatic Stay Cannot Prevent

In a few instances, the automatic stay is unable to help debtor(s.) These reasons are:

- **Certain tax proceedings.** The IRS can still audit the debtor(s), issue a tax deficiency notice, demand a tax return (which often leads to an audit), issue a tax assessment, or demand the payment of such an assessment. However, the *automatic stay* does stop the IRS from issuing a tax lien or taking the debtor(s) property or income.

- **Support actions.** A lawsuit against debtor(s) who are seeking to establish paternity or to establish, modify, or collect child support or alimony is not stopped by the bankruptcy filing.

- **Criminal proceedings.** A criminal proceeding that can be broken down into criminal and debt components will be divided, and the criminal component is not affected by the automatic stay. For example, if a debtor were convicted of writing a bad check, sentenced to community service, and ordered to pay a fine, their obligation to do community service will not be stopped by filing for bankruptcy.

- **Loans from a pension.** Despite the automatic stay, money can be withheld from a debtor(s) income to repay a loan from certain types of pensions (including most job-related pensions and IRAs.)

- **Multiple filings.** If the debtor(s) had a bankruptcy case pending during the previous year, the bankruptcy stay will automatically terminate after 30 days unless the debtor(s), the trustee, the U.S. Trustee, or a creditor asks for the stay to continue and proves that the current case was filed in good faith. If a creditor filed a motion to lift the stay that is pending during the previous case, the court may assume the debtor(s) acted in bad faith, and they will need to disprove this assumption to get the protection of the automatic stay in their current case.

How Can Creditors Get Around the Automatic Stay?

Usually, a creditor can get around the automatic stay by asking the bankruptcy court to *lift* (also known as *remove*) the stay, if it is not serving its intended purpose. For example, say that John Smith files for bankruptcy the day before his house is sold in foreclosure. John has no equity in the house, he cannot pay the mortgage arrears (back payments), and there is no other way for John to keep the property. The creditor who is foreclosing on the property will probably go to the court soon after John files for bankruptcy and ask for permission to proceed with the foreclosure - and that permission is likely to be granted.

What Happens After the Bankruptcy Petition is Filed?

After a bankruptcy petition is filed, the bankruptcy court will send a notice to all the creditors listed on the debtor(s) Creditor's Matrix. This notice is normally mailed out within five days after the petition is filed but each bankruptcy court has its own time schedule. In most courts, a third party company receives the Creditor's Matrix from the bankruptcy court and mails out the notices. These notices let the creditors know the debtor(s) filed bankruptcy as well as providing them with the bankruptcy case number, a statement about the automatic stay, the name of the trustee assigned to the case, the date set for the 341 Meeting of Creditors, the deadline (if any) for filing objections to the discharge of the debtor(s) and/or specific debts, and whether to file and where to file claims. The exact information on the notice will differ depending on the chapter under which the bankruptcy case is filed.

In a Chapter 7 case involving an individual debtor, the creditors generally have sixty (60) days from the first date of the Meeting of Creditors to object to the discharge of the debtor(s) and/or a specific debt. If the creditor misses the deadline and does not file an objection, the court will issue a discharge order. If any objections are filed they will be heard by the court, but this will not delay the granting of a discharge for other debts.

An Objection to Discharge of the Dischargeability of Certain Debts is considered to be a separate lawsuit (an adversary proceeding) within the bankruptcy. This could result in a trial before the judge who has been assigned to the case. Corporate and partnership business Chapter 7 debtors do not receive discharges. Because there is no property from which any money can be paid, the trustee will prepare a report of no distribution and the case will be closed. If there is property that is not exempt, there is money left over for distribution to creditors. The court will set deadline dates for claims and will notify all the creditors to file their claims. The trustee will then proceed to collect the assets, sell them and distribute the proceeds to the creditors. When all the money has been distributed, and all assets administrated, the court will close the case.

In a Chapter 13 case, creditors are provided with the opportunity to object to the Chapter 13 plan. If no objection is filed by the creditors or the trustee, the plan may be confirmed and filed in court. Once the plan is confirmed, the trustee will being sending payments to the creditors as the debtor(s) send payments to the court. This cycle continues until the debtor(s) complete the Chapter 13 plan or the court dismisses or converts the case. After completion of the Chapter 13 plan, the court will issue a discharge order; the trustee will prepare a final report and the case will be closed.

The 341 Meeting (or Creditor's Meeting)

Debtor(s) do not normally understand what a 341 Meeting of Creditor's really is. All they know is that they are going to court with their attorney. In fact, most debtor(s) relate the 341 Meeting of Creditor's to a court hearing they might attend if they were involved in a civil action or committed a criminal act.

If the debtor(s) ask you about their court hearing, help them to relax by letting them know this is an informal meeting with a trustee and a judge will probably not be present. But like everything else, court procedures vary from state to state and city to city. However, the fact remains, a bankruptcy court appearance is not the same as a criminal action and the debtor(s) cannot be put in jail or fined (unless they have committed intentional fraud in the information they provided to the bankruptcy court that warrants a federal crime.)

Instead, at the 341 Meeting (which is normally scheduled twenty (20) to forty (40) days after the filing of the bankruptcy petition) the trustee will review the debtor(s) bankruptcy petition and ask specific questions about it. The debtor(s) and/or attorney may be asked to provide copies of tax returns, bank statements, paycheck stubs, titles to motor vehicles, an appraisal of a home along with a recorded mortgage and deed or the trustee may be satisfied with the information provided in a well-detailed bankruptcy petition and not request anything at all.

Most debtor(s) will get a little nervous when they find out that creditors may show up at their 341 Meeting. However, in most *no asset* cases, creditors rarely appear at these hearings simply because it is a waste of their time since there is normally no chance of receiving any payment. But even if a creditor does show up at the 341 Meeting of Creditor's, the debtor(s) do not need to be nervous because the creditors will normally talk with the trustee or attorney directly. Help the debtor(s) understand that no one is going to *rope and tie* them and put them in jail. The 341 Meeting of Creditor's is normally a sit-down informal meeting and some of the fees they paid their attorney are being used for his or her representation at this meeting. Therefore, the debtor(s) will probably not need to say anything.

Note: A *no asset* case means that the debtor(s) have no assets (everything they own was exempted) that can be used to satisfy any of the debts owed to their creditors. If there is nothing for an unsecure creditor to obtain in order to pay a portion or all of the debt, the creditor would normally rather *write off* the debt versus spending time appearing in court. Normally, the creditors I have witnessed that appeared at 341 Meeting of Creditor's were secure creditors who had a secured interest in the debtor(s) real or personal property. However, I did experience a dentist that showed up one time at a no asset 341 Meeting. He was there to confront the debtor(s) after the court hearing to ask them to pay him outside the bankruptcy.

If the bankruptcy petition is detailed and provides all the information the trustee requires, the 341 Meeting will normally only last a few minutes. Remember to stress to the debtor(s) that they are not going to court because they committed a crime and have to appear in front of a judge for sentencing. (Although this sounds bizarre, some people actually believe this.) Make them understand that filing for bankruptcy was a *voluntary* choice the debtor(s) made. One good tip is to encourage the debtor(s) to arrive at their 341 Meeting of Creditor's approximately 45 minutes before their scheduled meeting. If they watch some of the other cases before their case comes up, they will see how quickly the process is.

This may help them to become more relaxed and aide in making the attorney's job easier and less complicated.

Keep in mind that filing bankruptcy is a life-changing event for the debtor(s.) More than likely, the debtor(s) will never go through this event again. They paid good money for this bankruptcy filing and they have been waiting at home for several weeks or months for this important day. If an attorney arrives late, is unprepared or does not appear to care about the debtor(s) it will cause unnecessary stress on the debtor(s.) Most debtor(s) already feel bad enough for having to file bankruptcy. They don't need to feel they are just another *name on a piece of paper* at this stage of the process. Unfortunately, you may not have control over the attorney's attitude, but knowing the entire process may help you to keep the debtor(s) calm and prevent undue stress.

Other Basic Facts You Need to Know as a Virtual Bankruptcy Assistant

- Any debts made by the debtor(s) *after* they file their bankruptcy petition cannot be included in the bankruptcy. However, before the 341 Meeting of Creditors, debts can be added that were left out of the original bankruptcy petition as long as the debt was made *prior* to filing bankruptcy. To add debts, you would draft the proper Amendment along with an Amended Creditor's Matrix. Court filing fees for most Amendments are around $25.00 in all of the 50 states but check with your local bankruptcy court to be sure.

- After the bankruptcy is discharged and the creditors have been satisfied, any lien the debtor(s) have on their property is *not* automatically removed. The attorney will still need to file the proper paperwork to remove the lien once the debt is paid in full.

Debtor(s) are normally charged an additional fee by the attorney for this service and this is just one of many ways an attorney can add more income to his or her bankruptcy law practice.

- Debtor(s) should never make the mistake of running up debts on all their charge cards and then filing bankruptcy immediately thereafter. Debtor(s) could be held responsible for any purchases they made within ninety (90) days prior to filing if these expenses were not necessary for their day-to-day living needs. It is understandable for some people to use credit cards for food, rent and transportation prior to deciding to file bankruptcy; however debtor(s) cannot take exotic vacations or add unnecessary debts simply because they know they can file bankruptcy and get the debt erased. This is considered fraud and the debtor(s) may not receive a discharge.

However, if the debtor(s) have made purchases on their credit cards (other than basic living expenses) or obtained loans 90 days prior to filing bankruptcy, the virtual bankruptcy assistant should list these recent purchases on Schedule F of the bankruptcy petition to save the trustee and attorney time.

Debts That Cannot be Discharged in Bankruptcy

There are certain debts that cannot be discharged in bankruptcy. For example, bankruptcy will not allow people to keep property they have not paid for. Filing bankruptcy will also not stop the payment of child support or alimony, and it will offer only limited help if the person(s) are trying to get rid of a tax debt or student loan. Here are other ways a bankruptcy cannot help debtor(s):

- **Prevent a secured creditor from repossessing property.** As previously stated above, a bankruptcy discharge eliminates debts, but it does not eliminate liens which is why the bankruptcy attorney will need to be hired to follow-up and file the necessary paperwork to eliminate the lien after the bankruptcy discharge. Therefore, if the debtor(s) have a secured debt (a debt where the creditor has a lien on their property and can repossess it if they don't pay the debt), a bankruptcy can eliminate the debt, but it does not prevent the creditor from repossessing the property. However, after the repossession, bankruptcy does prevent the creditor from coming after the debtor(s) for additional money if the sale of the collateral did not generate enough cash to pay off the amount they were left owing.

- **Eliminate child support and alimony obligations.** Child support and alimony cannot be discharged and the debtor(s) will still owe these debts in full just as if they never filed for bankruptcy. If the debtor(s) file a Chapter 13, the Chapter 13 plan must include repayment of these debts in full. No partial payment is permitted and the Chapter 13 plan will not be dismissed until they are paid.

- **Wipe out student loans, except in very limited circumstances.** Student loans can be discharged in bankruptcy only if the debtor(s) can show *extreme hardship* - a standard that is very tough to meet. The debtor(s) must be able to show that they not only cannot afford to pay their student loans now, but also that they have very little likelihood of being able to pay the loan in the future. The court will also consider whether the debtor(s) made a good faith effort to repay at least some of what they owe, taking advantage of the partial-payment options offered under various laws.

- **Eliminate most tax debts.** Eliminating tax debt in bankruptcy is not easy but it is possible in some cases. There are many requirements to be met which the attorney will discuss with the debtor(s.)

- **Eliminate other nondischargeable debts.** The following debts are not dischargeable under either Chapter 7 or Chapter 13 bankruptcy. If the debtor(s) file for Chapter 7, these debts will remain when the case is over. If the debtor(s) file for Chapter 13, these debts will need to be paid in full during their repayment plan. If they are not repaid in full, the balance will remain at the end of the bankruptcy case.

❖ debts not listed in the bankruptcy petition unless the creditor learns of the bankruptcy case;

❖ debts for personal injury or death caused while driving intoxicated;

❖ fines and penalties imposed for violating the law, such as traffic tickets and criminal restitution, and

❖ recent income tax debts and all other tax debts.

In addition, some types of debts may not be discharged if the creditor convinces the judge that they should survive the bankruptcy. These include debts incurred through fraud, such as lying on a credit application or passing off borrowed property as the debtor(s) own to use as collateral for a loan.

Now that you understand the overall general procedure for debtor bankruptcy, we will advance into learning the actual day-to-day skills to help you do your job better as a virtual bankruptcy assistant. Keep in mind that some of the skills I cover may or may not be required of you. For instance, if you do not work onsite for the bankruptcy attorney, you will probably not be involved in the initial client intake interview or scheduling of appointments. But it is good for you to still understand these procedures so you will be able to work with the onsite office staff more effectively.

Chapter 4

The Client Intake Interview

The Client Intake Interview

If you decide to market your virtual bankruptcy assistant services on the internet the bulk of your attorney client base will probably be located out of state and you would be unable to conduct the client intake interview. However, there is still the opportunity to work as a freelance virtual bankruptcy assistant for bankruptcy attorneys in your local area. I had three attorneys that I worked for in Columbus, Ohio and they preferred that I come to their office to conduct client intake interviews.

The information in this chapter will help you to learn how to conduct onsite client intake interviews for attorneys you work for in your local area. But even if your attorney client base is located out of state and you do not plan to do any client intake interviews, the information in this chapter will help you to better understand the overall process. Additionally, you can use this information to train the office staff so that they do a better job gathering information for the Client Intake Forms, which in turn makes your job a lot easier.

FREE CLIENT INTAKE FORMS
https://www.713training.com/intake_forms/
Download the free version or order a personalized version. You also may link to this web page so that attorneys visiting your website can download a free set of their own. Or you can order a personalized set and upload to your website for your future attorney clients.

Scheduling the Appointment with the Debtor(s)

After the virtual bankruptcy assistant or attorney has spoken with the new client and the initial consultation interview is scheduled, you should ask the client(s) to bring the following items with them to the interview:

- Copies of all the most recent billing statements from every creditor the debtor(s) owe money to. If the debtor(s) do not have a recent statement from a creditor, ask them to write down the following information on a sheet of paper about each debt they have no statement for:

- Name and complete mailing address of who the debtor(s) owes;
- Account number;
- The name of the person who is responsible for the debt (husband, wife or both);
- The total balance owed to this creditor
- Amount of normal monthly payments for this creditor;
- The date or year the debtor(s) originally made this debt with the creditor. (If the debtor(s) cannot remember the exact date, an approximate year [i.e., 2004, 2005, 2006, etc.] within a two-year time frame will do.) The main purpose here is to determine if purchases were made within the past 90 days prior to filing bankruptcy because their recent purchase could be considered fraudulent;

- If the debtor(s) have made a purchase with a creditor within the last 90 days, ask them for documentation that verifies the reason for these purchases and the dollar amount of the debt. This information will be essential in recording on the bankruptcy petition or for documentation if a creditor objects to the bankruptcy discharge and/or files a fraud claim with the court;

- Copies of at least six months of the debtor(s) paycheck (or other income) stubs. If the debtor(s) have their checks automatically deposited in their checking or savings account, they should also bring six months of bank statements showing these deposits. (This information is needed to complete the Means Test and to determine if these debtor(s) will be eligible to file a Chapter 7 or Chapter 13 bankruptcy petition);

- If the debtor(s) are unemployed, ask them to bring in copies of documents showing any income they receive(d) from unemployment, worker's compensation, child support, SSI, social security, food stamps, retirement, estate, etc.;

- Copies of the mortgage and deed if the debtor(s) own or are purchasing a home or other real property (i.e., land, apartment complex, etc.); Deeds normally can be found online through the County Auditor's website.

- Copies of all titles to cars, boats, motorcycles, mobile homes or any of type of motor vehicle;

- Copies of the last two years of tax returns. If the debtor(s) have not filed a tax return, the attorney will normally refer them to a tax preparer so their taxes will be properly filed before filing bankruptcy;

- Copies of any court proceedings or collection letters; and

- Copy of the divorce decree if divorced within the past two (2) years.

Of course most debtor(s) will not remember everything on the list when you read it off to them over the telephone. You must follow-up with a letter in order to keep the process operating in a smooth manner. The best way to do this is to set up a standard letter template that is mailed to the new clients the same day the initial appointment is made.

The following is a sample of a letter your attorney may want to use; but remember to get his or her approval before using it. It is a violation of unauthorized practice of law to send out letters to clients under an attorneys name without his or her approval.

SAMPLE LETTER TEMPLATE
First Appointment Letter

Dear Mr. and Mrs. Doe:

Thank you for choosing our law firm to discuss the possible filing of your bankruptcy. Your appointment has been scheduled for July 5 at 2:00 p.m. If you need to change this appointment, please notify our office within 48 hours prior to your appointment.

The items you need to bring with you to your appointment are:
(List the items provided on Pages __ through __.)

We look forward in meeting and talking with you on July 5, 2006. If you should have any questions, please do not hesitate to call my virtual bankruptcy assistant, Jane Doe, at 262-555-1212.

The First Appointment

When the client arrives for their initial consultation, first impressions count!! Make sure you offer them coffee or a beverage and direct them to a private conference room where the attorney will meet with them. It is important to allow clients to get comfortable in their surroundings. If you move them to several different locations they tend to get confused and are not relaxed. Your goal is to help the clients relax so they will feel that you truly care about them. When they feel this way they will be more helpful (as well as calmer) in providing you with the crucial financial information you need to provide to your attorney for his or her review and analysis for their bankruptcy petition.

Think about it for a moment. How would you feel if you walked into work one day and you lost your job? Or what if your child was involved in a car accident and there was no insurance to pay the high medical bills? Although not all clients seeking to file bankruptcy are in desperate situations like these, the large majority of debtor(s) filing bankruptcy have experienced some sort of traumatic event that led up to them going through the trouble to locate an attorney to file bankruptcy.

In addition, you also will normally find the debtor(s) are very nervous and scared when they meet with the attorney or virtual bankruptcy assistant for the first time. They normally are afraid they will say the wrong thing and the bankruptcy court will take everything they own, sit them out of the street and declare them homeless. (This may sound extreme, but many first-time filers feel this way.) Remember that many of them have spent the last several months beating themselves up emotionally for being in this situation. They also had to face the fact they are unable to pay their creditors and they have suffered through the harassment calls and other embarrassment brought on by collection methods utilized by aggressive collection agencies. Therefore, show some compassion and try to understand that most debtor(s) are *not* at their best when they come to see a bankruptcy attorney for the first time.

Meeting with the Bankruptcy Attorney

After the clients have been offered a refreshment and seated in a private conference room, the attorney may come in and briefly talk with the clients. Meeting with the clients first will enable the attorney to decide if he or she will be taking the case. There is no need to waste money and time by having you or a member of the office staff go through the entire interview process, only to find out that the client(s) are not serious about filing or are ineligible to file. Also, the attorney can determine if extensive litigation will be required for these clients by meeting with them briefly and be able to provide the clients with a more accurate fee rate for representing them.

After the Attorney Meets with the Clients

Once the attorney has completed this brief meeting, he or she will normally turn the interview over to the bankruptcy assistant to obtain the information he or she needs to advise the clients properly. Here are some intake interview tips and techniques to help you as a bankruptcy assistant when conducting the interview:

- Introduce yourself to the debtor(s) and ask them what questions they may have. Of course, a bankruptcy assistant cannot provide legal advice and your attorney will train you on what information you can and cannot provide. If the debtor(s) do ask a question that requires legal advice, make sure you have a note pad to write down their questions for review by the attorney after they have completed the Client Intake Forms.

Tip for Not Violating Unauthorized Practice of Law: If the answer to a question is of a general nature (such as *Where is the bankruptcy court located?* or *Where do I sign my name?*) you can answer general information questions. Any other questions, regardless if they seem harmless could be a violation of unauthorized practice of law. Questions like: *Can I keep my car?* or *Will I lose my home?* or *Will I be filing a Chapter 7 or Chapter 13,* are all examples of questions ONLY an attorney can answer.

- Next, provide the debtor(s) with a set of Client Intake Forms. As previously mentioned, I developed a set of very client-friendly intake forms for you to use at https://www.713training.com/intake_forms/.

Or you may choose to mail a set of the Client Intake Forms to the client(s) or make the forms available for download from a website *prior* to the intake interview. This way the forms are already completed by the debtor(s) before they arrive and this step will save them time at the attorney's office.

- If the client(s) are filling out the Client Intake Forms in the attorney's office, explain that you will give them time to properly complete the forms and you will return to check on them in a little while. Also let them know how to get in touch with you if they have a question (i.e., have the receptionist buzz you, etc.) Just don't leave them sitting in the room for hours. Watch the clock. Check on them in about 30 minutes. (Also remember to tell them where the bathroom is.) On the average, most client(s) take approximately 30 to 45 minutes to complete the forms in the office. Use your best judgment, keeping in mind that you do not want the client(s) to think you forgot about them.

- If the client(s) feel in any way that you forgot about them, you may find they will walk out and go someplace else. When they do go someplace else, they will probably complain about the service at the law firm to others. So you can see that a simple thing like *checking on the client(s)* so they don't think you forgot about them can save you time, money and bad publicity. You will find that *little things* like these courtesies are essential when dealing with client(s) regardless of which type of business you work in.

- Make sure you give the clients privacy by closing the door to the conference room where you have them seated. Most clients are embarrassed about filing bankruptcy plus they need to be free from distractions in the office so they can properly complete the Client Intake Forms or talk with the bankruptcy assistant and attorney in confidence.

- After the Client Intake Forms have been completed by the client(s), the trick is not to *quickly glance* over the forms. Instead, you should take the time in the initial client intake to go through every page (with pen in hand) and make notes, verify any illegible handwriting or ask questions about any missing information the client did not fill in. Since the client(s) are sitting in the same room with you at this point, this is an excellent opportunity to get this missing information since it is fresh in their minds.

Although it may appear that this procedure would take more of your time, it is actually a method that will save you a great deal of time in the long run. Therefore, it is worth the investment of 10 to 15 extra minutes now to save you and your attorney many hours of wasted time throughout the case. That's because if you spend the time in the intake interview to get all of the pertinent information to draft a well-detailed bankruptcy petition, you will reap many timesaving benefits. Some of those benefits include:

- Reduce the filing of additional Amendments where a mistake was uncovered after the case was filed; and

- Virtually eliminate the need to file skeleton petitions and putting yourself on an automatic *time rush* to file the remainder of the petition by a certain date.

Reviewing the Client Intake Forms for Completion

To begin, always obtain a copy of the client's picture ID or driver's license that provides the client(s) social security number. Do not solely rely on a social security card as identification because there is no photo on it to identify the person. Then, compare the social security number from the picture ID with the information the client wrote on the Client Intake Forms. You would not believe how many people write down the wrong social security number or even the wrong name. Wrong information on the Voluntary Petition could result in a dismissal of the case and at the very least will cause you to prepare an Amendment that must be filed in the bankruptcy court to correct the petition. Why not just check the ID at this time so you can avoid these problems from occurring?

The best way to start reviewing Client Intake Forms for completeness is to initially scan each page for lines within the forms that are not filled in or that are illegible. When you find a missing line, you have the opportunity at that moment to ask the client for the missing information. If you wait until later to fill in the missing information, it may take several days before you can contact the client again and the subject will not be as *fresh* on the client's mind as it would be in the intake interview. You will find this crucial step to be one of the best ways to save yourself many headaches and problems as the bankruptcy case progresses.

Reviewing the Debt Sheets

Next, thoroughly review the debt sheets. After you have done a few, you will develop a *trained eye* to pick up on information that needs further explanation. But for beginners, look at the name of the company and see if you know what the debt is for. Naturally, JC Penney is a department store credit card and Capital One is probably a credit card, but Joe and Sons could be a debt for almost anything.

Here is the way to identify credit cards by their account numbers:

- An American Express credit card account begins with the number 3 and there are only 15 digits in the number.
- Visa, Mastercard and Discover cards all contain a total of 16 digits:
  - A Visa credit card account begins with the number 4.
  - A Mastercard credit card account begins with the number 5.
  - A Discover credit card account begins with the number 6.

With training from your attorney you should attempt to identify the types of debts these debtor(s) have. This is important because **every debt** must be recorded on the proper schedule within the bankruptcy petition. I have seen many petitions that have been filed where secure debts that should have been listed on Schedule B were listed as unsecure debts on Schedule F. When this happens, the attorney or virtual bankruptcy assistant has just created an unnecessary time loss of one or two hours, depending on the asset associated with the secure debt. Or, it could result in something as drastic as the debtor(s) risk losing their personal or real property. If this happens, the debtor(s) can sue the attorney and probably win in court.

One big mistake I have made in the past is assuming a debt is *unsecure* when a client describes the debt as a *personal loan.* Sometimes you need to ask the client to provide a copy of the contract they signed when they obtained this personal loan because many of them do not understand the difference between a *secure* and an *unsecure* loan. However, many personal loans are actually secure loans while others may be a line-of-credit that is connected to the mortgage on their home. In both situations a personal loan would turn into a secure debt and would need to be listed on the petition in relationship to the proper asset it is connected to.

As you can see by reviewing the debt sheets at the initial intake interview, you not only are provided with the ability to identify the *unsecure* debts but also to identify the *secure* debts. One tip an attorney taught me was to place the letter *S* beside debts that were secure and *U* by the unsecure debts for quick identification on the debt sheets. This helps the attorney to be able to quickly scan the debts and be aware of any possible litigation that could occur.

Pending Lawsuits

Make it a point to ask the client(s) if they have experienced a repossession, foreclosure notice, complaint for a money judgment, lawsuit, recent divorce or traffic tickets within the past year. Obtain copies of the actual court documents for your attorney to review. This step is very important because a court document contains important facts and clues that most clients overlook and quite often the entire case can be affected by just one document. Additionally, any lawsuits, repossessions, etc. must be recorded on the Statement of Affairs within the bankruptcy petition and you need the court location, case number and other pieces of data that most clients do not know how to provide.

In addition, it is also important to do a search online through the county courthouse where the debtor(s) have resided. For the search you will need the debtor(s) full names as well as the maiden name of the wife (if applicable.) This step is necessary even though the clients provide you with legal documents of all their pending lawsuits. Why? Because often there are very old debts the debtor(s) may have forgotten. It is your job to find all the debts that a debtor(s) owes in order to protect your attorney from being charged with a violation. Citations and fines for attorney violations were added when the new bankruptcy law went into effect. Therefore, it is important that you do everything within your power (also known as *due diligence*) to make sure the bankruptcy petition is 100% complete and lists every debt the debtor(s) are responsible for.

Titles and Deeds

It is vitally important for you to obtain copies of all motor vehicle titles, mortgages, deeds and proof of insurance on these assets. In many bankruptcy courts, the trustee will ask for a copy of the *recorded* mortgage and deed, which can only be obtained from the Recorder's Office. Homeowners do not normally have a copy of the *recorded* copy of their mortgage and deed; they only have a copy before it was recorded. The Recorder's Office will charge the homeowner(s) a small copy charge to obtain a time and date-stamped copy but you can also obtain copies on the county courthouse website.

How to Do Online Courthouse Records Search

At the time this book is being written almost 85% of all the courts have an online searchable database. Unfortunately, every one of them operates in a different way so it is up to you to take the time to familiarize yourself with your local online courthouse.

How do you find the website for your courthouse? Go to any search engine such as Google at http://www.google.com and type in the search words: *your county name* and *state courthouse.* For example, if I want to find the Franklin County courthouse in Ohio, I would type in the search words *Franklin County Ohio courthouse.* If the debtor(s) local courthouse is online, a link should appear near the top of the search engine. If you do not locate the local courthouse, look in the local Yellow Pages and get the telephone number. Call the courthouse and find out if they have a website or when they plan to have one.

You might want to say something like: *Hello. My name is Susie Homemaker and I work for bankruptcy attorneys. Do you have an online search where I can locate public information such as mortgage and judgment liens, criminal records, etc.?* Once the courthouse is aware that you are a professional seeking information for attorneys they will be more inclined to help you. When you obtain the website link to the courthouse, make sure you bookmark it immediately and do not lose it. Also, do not make the mistake of asking the clerk at the courthouse to teach you how to use the website. It is up to you to learn the search feature on your own. The courthouse employees are not to be used for technical support.

Why Are These Documents Necessary?

All of the court documents we have covered so far in this chapter will be extremely useful to you when the bankruptcy petition is being prepared. One of the most helpful pieces of information for me personally was the property description on the deed and the exact make, model and year of the motor vehicle on the title. Believe it or not, I have encountered many situations where a client will write down the wrong year and even the wrong model of their vehicle on the Client Intake Forms. This makes it impossible to obtain a correct market value of the vehicle. Without a correct market value listed on the petition, the attorney may be charged with a citation for not obtaining the correct information.

Paycheck Stubs

If you are involved in the client intake interview, always make copies of the client(s) paycheck stubs for the attorney's file. First of all, this will help to establish the client's identity and provide you with actual proof of their salary. Additionally, it is difficult for the average client to figure their average monthly salary. This is because the majority of employees are paid either weekly or bi-weekly. Let's say that Jack is paid $250 per week. If you ask him how much he earns in a month, he will say *$1,000.* But he is wrong. This figure would be correct if Jack was *always* paid four times every month, but some month's Jack will receive five paychecks instead of four. In addition, people who are paid bi-weekly normally receive two checks a month, but there are some months where they will be paid three times.

Therefore, you may have to do a little math to determine the correct monthly figure to place on Schedule I of the bankruptcy petition or your bankruptcy software may automatically calculate the figure for you.

Continuing with the example of Jack, if we used the $1,000 figure as his base salary per month, we would be basing this figure solely on the fact that Jack is paid four times a month for 12 months. But 12 x 4 = 48. As we all know, there are 52 weeks in a year, not 48. Therefore, that extra money needs to be factored into Jack's pay and then averaged out over a 12-month period. I know this sounds complicated, but the example below will make it easy for you to figure the average monthly salary for our fictional debtor named Jack:

If Jack is paid $250 weekly, do the following math:
$250 per week X 52 weeks = $13,000 per year
$13,000 ÷ 12 = $1,083.33 per month of average income

If Jack is paid $500 bi-weekly, do the following math:
$500 bi-weekly X 26 weeks = $13,000 per year
$13,000 ÷ 12 = $1,083.33 per month of average income

In other words, find out how much Jack earns for the entire year, then divide by 12 to get the average monthly salary. As you can see, Jack's original answer that he earned $1,000 per month is incorrect. He really earns $1,083.33 per month.

Meeting the Credit Counseling Requirement

Almost all of the debtor(s) filing bankruptcy are required to meet the Credit Counseling Requirement under the new bankruptcy law. There are exceptions to this rule, such as not residing in an area where credit counseling is not available; but debtors you encounter who meet these exceptions will be rare. In most cases, the debtors will be required to complete the Credit Counseling Requirement before their case can be filed in court. To locate the approved credit counseling agencies for your area visit the Department of Justice website at
http://www.usdoj.gov/ust/eo/bapcpa/ccde/cc_approved.htm

Additionally, there are a host of approved credit counseling services online that offers debtor(s) the option of completing the credit counseling requirement at home from their computer. One website is located at http://www.cccsatl.org/index.asp?pg=titlepg_BK_options or call CCCS toll-free at 1-866-672-2227. You can find many more by typing in the search words: *pre-petition bankruptcy education* from any search engine. However, be sure to check with your attorney to make sure online credit counseling is approved by the state before debtor(s) are referred to the online services.

The Second Credit Counseling Requirement

Before a bankruptcy case can be discharged, the new bankruptcy law requires the debtor(s) to complete a second *exit-type* credit counseling class. This class is known as the *Post-Petition Pre-Discharge Financial Management Course* and the Executive Office of the United States Trustees has stated the course must take a minimum of two hours to complete. These are also offered online through the CCCS website provided above or go to any search engine and type in the search words: *post-petition bankruptcy education* to find many more.

Recognizing Debtor(s) Who May Be Hiding Assets

As a virtual bankruptcy assistant, you will find that some debtor(s) may try to hide their assets during the initial intake interview or anytime during a telephone interview. It is important for you to listen to everything the debtor tells you so you can analyze whether there are additional debts or assets that need reported on the petition. While this skill will take some time before you are really good at it, you will get better with every petition you work with.

Why do debtor(s) hide certain assets? Even after the purpose of exemptions are explained to them in terms they can understand, the debtor's normally never understand that all or a portion of their assets are protected under allowable exemptions. Instead, their next question will most likely be: *What if my income were to change during my bankruptcy or if I were to gain assets (like purchasing a car.) Would that mess everything up?*

The client can normally be put at ease by explaining the purpose of Amendments without committing unauthorized practice of law. I might say something like: *If you file a bankruptcy petition in court today and you accepted a new job next week, an Amendment could be filed with the court to provide your new income information.* Of course, most debtor(s) will not understand what the word *amendment* is, so you might want to say: *An Amendment is a piece of paper filed with the court to change or update information on a piece of paper previously filed with the court.* By taking this extra step, I found that the client will normally open up and supply me with more crucial information about their current financial situation. This, of course, would result in a more complete and well-detailed bankruptcy petition and less work on the attorney as well as myself.

> **Note:** Notice in my answers above I only provided general information. I did not refer to any specific case or discuss the client(s) bankruptcy with them; so therefore I stayed within the parameters of unauthorized practice of law regulations.

Because the reluctance of revealing assets is one of the main problems I encountered from debtor(s), I developed the Client Intake Forms in an effort to assist me in catching many of the problem areas. For example, asset information is essential because if an asset is overlooked now and you don't find out about it until the 341 Hearing, it will cost you a lot of extra work and delay the client's bankruptcy discharge. So save yourself some time and make sure you obtain all the information on the debtor's assets at the initial intake interview. This includes often overlooked items like anticipated tax refunds, uncollected back child support, wedding rings valued at $200 or more, 401K plan, 401K loans, money in bonds, stock, trust accounts and whole life insurance policies that have a cash value among many others.

Let me give you an example of how unrevealed assets can hurt a debtor. John Doe has lost his job and is $35,000 in debt. He goes to the bankruptcy attorney and the bankruptcy assistant never asks John how much money he has in his bank account or if he has any bonds. The bankruptcy assistant spends about 45 minutes of time with John and the attorney spends about 15 minutes with him. Another hour is spent by the bankruptcy assistant drafting the bankruptcy petition, $299 is spent filing the petition with the court and money is spent making copies and serving secure creditors. At the 341 Meeting, John brings in copies of his bank statements and it is revealed that John has $22,000 in his savings account. In addition, John tells the trustee that he also has $40,000 in Series EE government bonds.

What a shock to the attorney! All the work, time and effort he just put into John's case is lost. The attorney may have no choice at this point but to file a Motion to Dismiss. If the case is allowed to continue, the trustee may require John to pay $35,000 to the court for distribution to his or her creditors since he has the money to pay all his creditors in full. Besides, if the case were allowed to continue, creditors would be filing Objections, proofs of claim and other documents alleging fraud. What a mess! And this could have been avoided if John had only been asked about his savings account and bonds during the initial intake interview.

Other Questions the Debtor(s) May Ask

How will my credit be affected by filing bankruptcy?

Since the debtor(s) are already behind in paying their bills, their credit is already affected. Filing a bankruptcy may actually be a debtor(s) first step in repairing a bad credit situation. When a creditor finds a bankruptcy on a debtor(s) credit report, it shows them that all prior credit problems have been resolved. The question then becomes: *Is the debtor creditworthy?*

Because every creditor is different and each one treats bankruptcy with a different set of rules for determining creditworthiness, there are still many exceptions to granting credit. Normally a creditor likes to see how well debtor(s) are paying their bills during the first year or two after filing bankruptcy before they extend new credit to them. So although a bankruptcy appears on a debtor(s) credit report for ten (10) years, most debtor(s) only find it to be a problem for a couple of years after filing provided everything else looks good on their current credit report.

In addition, there are thousands of creditors who extend credit to people who have recently filed bankruptcy. The interest rates are normally higher, of course, but debtor(s) can obtain credit easily with one or more of them. One of the best ways to build credit after bankruptcy is to obtain a *secured* credit card. (This also teaches the debtors how to start living without credit cards.) A *secured* credit card is one where money is deposited into a bank and the bank issues a credit card using the deposit as collateral. After the debtor(s) have demonstrated their ability to make timely payments, their credit line may be increased without any additional deposit of more funds. Eventually, the secure credit card could qualify as an unsecured one.

However, the fact remains that one of the main reasons for filing bankruptcy is to get *out* of debt -- not back into it. Urge debtor(s) to take responsibility for their own financial spending and saving so they never need to file bankruptcy again. Once a debtor experiences the total freedom of paying for items and owning those items free and clear, they will be able to take control of their lives and in the process will discover they have more disposable income. (One of the best books I recommend to help people in these situations is the New York Times bestseller: *The Laws of Money, The Lessons of Life* by Suze Orman, ISBN: 07432-45172)

Before credit cards existed the only assets the average American went into debt for was an automobile for transportation and a home for their family to live in. Everything else was be purchased out of the monthly income, or saved for and purchased in full. The main reason Americans are in debt way over their heads today is because they want it *now* and don't have the patience to wait.

If I am married, does my spouse have to file bankruptcy?

The attorney will provide the debtor(s) with his or her recommendation whether a husband and wife should file bankruptcy separately or together, based on their particular circumstances. However, it is not required that a husband and wife file bankruptcy together, just like it is not required that a husband and wife file their taxes together. However, the spouse that does not file bankruptcy will not receive the benefits of bankruptcy. In other words, if the non-filing spouse is jointly liable on certain debts, he or she will remain liable for those debts if the filing spouse filed for a Chapter 7 bankruptcy. He or she will also remain liable for any amount not paid for in the filing spouse's Chapter 13 plan. On the other hand, the non-filing spouse will not have bankruptcy noted on his or her credit report.

Additionally, if one debtor is married but living separately from their legal spouse, a joint bankruptcy petition can still be drafted indicating two separate living expenses for each person at two separate addresses.

Also, if the debtor(s) live in Arizona, California, Idaho, Louisiana, Nevada, New Mexico, Texas, Washington or Wisconsin (community property states), most of the property is equally owned by both the husband and wife regardless of the name of the person on the title or mortgage.

Will bankruptcy stop a wage garnishment?

Yes, some of the money garnished from a debtor(s) paycheck may even be returned to them if the wage garnishment is deducted after the bankruptcy petition has been filed. Of course this all depends on how much was garnished and when it was garnished. The attorney is the only one qualified to address this question.

Stopping a wage garnishment occurs because whoever is garnishing the debtor(s) paycheck is now being paid (or their debt is being discharged) through the bankruptcy petition they file. As soon as the clerk file-stamps the bankruptcy petition, the debtor(s) will have immediate protection under the United States Bankruptcy Court. This protection also includes wage garnishments. (Also review Page 64 for more information about the *bankruptcy stay* and wage garnishments.)

What if I owe the IRS back taxes? How will bankruptcy help me?

Under the new 2005 bankruptcy law, unsecured taxes that first became due three years or more before the filing of a bankruptcy can be discharged. This is providing the tax returns were non-fraudulently filed. For taxes owed that are less than three years old, relief is still available under the bankruptcy law. However, the measure of relief is based upon the following factors:

- the type of taxes owed;
- the age of the tax;
- whether a tax return was properly filed, and
- the chapter of bankruptcy debtor(s) filed under.

How much does it cost to file bankruptcy?

The court currently charges a $299.00 filing fee to file a Chapter 7 bankruptcy petition and $274.00 to file a Chapter 13. This fee is standard in all 50 states.

When does a bankruptcy take effect?

When the court receives the bankruptcy petition and assigns a case number, the *bankruptcy stay* is immediately in effect. The court will normally send a notice of the debtor(s) bankruptcy filing to all of the creditors listed on the Creditor's Matrix generally within five days after filing of the petition. That is why it is so vitally important to obtain complete addresses and zip codes of all creditors listed in the bankruptcy petition. The court will send a copy of a notice to all creditors which will allow them the opportunity to file an Objection, Proof of Claim or Motion for Relief from Stay. If the addresses are inaccurate or missing, the creditor will not be properly notified and they could file an Objection to the Bankruptcy Discharge based on this fact alone. (Also review Page 62 for more information on the filing process.)

I feel so guilty not being able to pay my bills. Am I a bad person because I need to file bankruptcy?

Debtor(s) often need reassurance of the fact that they are not *bad* people just because they decide to file for bankruptcy. Before the 20th Century, if a person was bankrupt, creditors stepped in, sold everything the person owned, split the money between them, put the bankrupt person out in the street and made a public mockery of them. If they did not have any property to cover the repayment of their debt, they were sent to debtor's prison. These are the reasons why some people feel that bankruptcy is a *bad* thing to do. But that was the procedure over 200 years ago! The economy has changed, employers have changed, life is more complicated, interest rates are higher than they have ever been in history, unemployment is high and people do tend to get in major debt because of all the tempting offers of no-hassle credit.

These factors, as well as others, could cause a *good* person who was responsible and financially secure to suddenly consider filing bankruptcy. Not one of us is immune from the world's problems. So when a person finds it necessary to file for bankruptcy, urge them not to look back. Encourage them to meet the problem head on, clean up the situation and move on with life. I tell many debtor(s) that they should be glad the United States has set up a governing body to protect people so society as a whole can continue to grow and prosper without the heavy burden of debt. Most countries do not have the fair bankruptcy laws that we do in the United States.

What about filing bankruptcy on bad checks I wrote at check-cashing agencies? Can I include them in my bankruptcy?

First of all, debtor(s) need to include *all* the debts they owe in their bankruptcy petition regardless of whether they intend to continue paying them or not. However, most debtor(s) consider a check that bounced at a check cashing agency to be treated the *same* as a bad check written at the corner grocery store or for a utility bill. An attorney taught me that when someone walks into the check cashing agency and writes a *postdated* check in order to receive a cash advance, the clerk at the check cashing agency is fully aware of the fact that the check they received is *postdated.* This is much different from writing a check to someone who accepts the check in good faith that the monies are available for immediate payment. However, if someone goes to several check cashing agencies in order to obtain cash advances against the *same* payroll check they are committing fraud because all of their *postdated* checks amount to *more* than their payroll check will cover on the date of the *postdated* check. In a situation like this, the attorney needs to be alerted at once.

As far as including the debt on the bankruptcy petition, bad checks written to check cashing agencies are listed as a non-priority unsecure debt with a description of *check deficiency* on Schedule F. Also, you should ask the debtor(s) if there are any pending judgments or collection letters associated with this *check deficiency.* Additionally, you should find out if the bank (where the checks were written on) charged them additional bank fees and/or if any bank accounts were recently closed voluntarily or involuntarily by the debtor(s.) Additional bank fees can be listed on Schedule F and the recent account closing should be listed on Item 11 of the Statement of Affairs.

Will I lose any of my personal belongings or household goods when I file bankruptcy?

If the debtor(s) are filing a Chapter 13 bankruptcy and paying back their creditors 100% of the debt owed to them, the trustee at the bankruptcy court will *not* take any of their personal belongings or household goods and sell them to pay the outstanding debts.

If the debtor(s) are filing a Chapter 7 bankruptcy, they could lose any personal belongings or household goods if any of the following are true:

- The debtor(s) do not totally own their personal belongings or household goods free and clear of any liens. (Example: furniture and appliances purchased at a rent-to-own store.) In this case, if the debtor(s) want to keep the item(s), they can *reaffirm* the debt if they have enough money per month to continue paying the bill or the attorney may determine the market value of the item(s) are much less than what is currently owed to the creditor and negotiate a settlement amount. Otherwise, the debtor(s) may want to consider surrendering the item(s), which does not necessarily mean it will be repossessed. This is an area that requires the advice of the attorney so never give debtor(s) a specific answer to this question without consulting with your attorney first.

or

- If the personal belongings or household goods are not covered by an exemption, that item could be sold by the trustee and distributed to the creditors. However, you will find that most average consumers filing a Chapter 7 normally do not have more than one motor vehicle, television set, computer, stove, refrigerator and some miscellaneous costume jewelry and these items are all normally exempted in the bankruptcy petition.

How is my leased vehicle treated in bankruptcy?

A leased vehicle is treated as an executory contract and the monthly payment is included on Schedule J along with the normal monthly expenses if the debtor(s) intend to keep the vehicle. A car lease and a purchase can be compared to the difference between a home rental and mortgage. I was trained to record an amount of $1 as the market value on any leased vehicle recorded on Schedule B and Schedule G of the bankruptcy petition. A *purchased* vehicle carries a market value listed in the Kelly Blue Book or NADA on Schedule B.

Some of the personal belongings and furniture I have belong to an ex-roommate. Should I list these in my bankruptcy?

Yes, the value of these items will be recorded on the Statement of Affairs in the bankruptcy petition as *one* amount. All items in the debtor(s) possession at the time the bankruptcy petition is filed must be listed regardless of who the owners of the item(s) are. The main issue here is *why* the debtor(s) are holding these items. Could there be a potential lawsuit because the ex-roommate owes them money? If this is the case, you must ask the debtor(s) to provide information as to how much money this person owes them and if a lawsuit has been or will be filed in the near future. Any anticipated future monies need to be listed on Schedule B regardless if the debtor(s) expect to receive any compensation or not.

Understanding Creditor Harassment

As previously discussed, by the time the debtor(s) come into the office of a bankruptcy attorney they have normally endured weeks and months of collection calls and creditor harassment. Let's face it. No one wants to receive a call from a collector who demands a payment *right now.* One tactic many of them use is to scare debtor(s) into providing them with their credit card number so they can deduct the amount owed to them from a checking or savings account at regular intervals. You should urge debtor(s) never to give out their credit card number or bank routing number to anyone over the phone. If the debtor(s) do decide to pay a creditor in this manner prior to filing bankruptcy, they should demand a written statement be faxed to them which they will fill out and return with their confidential, sensitive information. The statement should contain the amounts to be deducted from the debtor(s) bank account and the dates they will deduct the payment. This is the only way to document the collector will deduct the proper amount on the dates the debtor(s) verbally agree to.

Another reason debtor(s) should not provide credit card or bank routing information over the phone is because anyone could call the debtor(s) up, pretend to be a collector and obtain this information. Then this person or company could steal the money in a debtor(s) bank account virtually overnight. And even if the collection agency is legitimate, the debtor(s) should still request something in writing. The creditor could still deduct more money than they verbally agreed to. The situation would then boil down to the debtor(s) word against the collection agency and the debtor(s) will probably never get any money back for the additional money deducted from their account especially since they owe this amount to the creditor anyway.

Why Are Some Collectors So Cruel?

Most collectors are paid on commission which means that their salary is determined by the amount of money they collect. The majority of collectors could care less if the debtor(s) eat or live in a house without electricity. Their only concern is scaring the debtor(s) into paying their bill so the collector will receive a commission check on the amount of money he or she collects. This *commission based* collection method helps to fuel an intense, competitive environment which often results in hostile collection methods. In addition, most debts turned over to a collection agency by a creditor are purchased for a lower amount than the debt actually is for. In fact, some debts are purchased for as low as 10¢ on the dollar which results in even more hostile collection methods to collect the full amount of the debt since the collection agency will make a 90% profit. For example, suppose Sears sold a debt to a collection agency for $200 but $2,000 was the total amount the debtor(s) owed. The collection agency would want to use every method available to them to collect the $2,000 because $1,800 of the amount would be pure profit for their collection agency.

Credit Card Collectors Are a Rare Breed

From my experience, the worst collectors are ones that are collecting on credit card debts. But keep in mind that a credit card is normally an unsecure debt. By that, I mean that if the debt is not paid the credit card company cannot come to the debtor(s) house and take anything they own to satisfy the debt. To further illustrate, if the debtor(s) used a Visa credit card to purchase a television set, Visa cannot come and take the item(s) unless the debtor(s) signed a document putting the television up for collateral and obtained a personal secured loan. However, if the debtor(s) are renting to own their television and don't pay the bill, the rent-to-own store has the right to repossess the item because a contract was signed at the initial purchase, providing the rent-to-own company with the option of repossessing the item(s) if the debtor(s) did not pay the bill or filed bankruptcy.

Although unsecured creditors cannot repossess property, they can file and obtain a judgment against the debtor(s.) This judgment would give them the ability to garnish a debtor(s) paycheck, bank account or place a lien on their real or personal property. The only choices debtor(s) have against a money judgment is either filing bankruptcy or paying the debt in full now or later.

Will Credit Cards Ever Be Paid Off?

If someone makes the minimum monthly payment on their credit cards, statistics show the debt will not be fully paid for 20, 30 or more years. That is because credit card companies add on so many interest fees, over limit fees, late fees and other hidden charges they legally can get away with. Also, the debtor(s) signed a contract when they first obtained the credit card allowing the credit card company to add these charges but most people don't read it. Other companies will send debtor(s) a statement in the mail (normally printed in tiny six-point type) explaining their right to add on hidden charges. However, most people throw this information in the trash when they receive it, which is what the credit card companies are counting on.

It is really a shame that many collectors have actually aided in forcing people to file bankruptcy that would otherwise have been more than happy to pay their bills. Back in the old days when credit cards first began making their evil way into the lives of consumers (circa 1970s), you could charge a purchase to a credit card and interest was calculated on the amount you originally borrowed. Today, companies will add interest on top of interest, daily charges, over limit fees and anything else they can drum up to get a few extra dollars from debtor(s.) When they do this to millions of people, you can understand why credit card companies and banks get rich off the common working class of people in today's world. And people who continue applying for credit cards are feeding these greedy companies.

For instance, I knew a debtor who had a credit card with only a $200 limit. Because she had bad credit, the company issued this unsecure credit card with this low limit. However, each month she had to pay a $6.00 service fee for the right to carry this high-interest credit card. One month when the company added the $6.00 fee, it pushed her balance up to $200.16. And because she owed 16¢ more than her credit limit allowed, the company charged the client an additional $30 over-the-limit fee and another $6.00 service fee as well as a late fee compounded daily for each 24-hour period the account remained over the limit. In my opinion, this is legal robbery. About the only way to stop this behavior is not to carry these types of credit cards in the first place or pay them off and cancel your account as soon as possible.

Collection Agencies for Medical Bills

Most hospitals have their own collection agencies where accounts are transferred to for collection. Unfortunately, these collectors can be just as mean, hateful and uncooperative as credit card collectors. However, by requesting an itemized statement from the hospital, debtor(s) may find that their insurance has already paid a portion of the bill and they may not owe as much as they are led to believe. After working in the personal injury area of law for several months, I encountered many situations where hospitals were double-billing the insurance company as well as the debtor(s) for the same charge. Again, the itemized statement should prove to be beneficial. The debtor(s) can then contact their insurance company to find out exactly how much of the bill was paid and the remaining amount will be the actual amount the debtor(s) owe.

After the debtor(s) determine the amount they owe the hospital, they may want to make an appointment with the hospital's billing department and attempt to negotiate a settlement to reduce the amount of the total bill on their own. However, most people just file bankruptcy on the total amount the hospital claims is owed and they do not do any further research to uncover the truth.

Other Outstanding Loans

Most creditors are happy to negotiate a lower amount on the total amount the debtor(s) owe because it is better for them to get some money (rather than nothing) if the debtor(s) file a Chapter 7 bankruptcy. But always remember that collectors and creditors never have the debtor(s) personal interest at heart and they often never follow through with verbal promises made over the phone. To protect yourself, make sure you get written documentation of the conversation for your attorney.

The Virtual Bankruptcy Assistant's Interaction with Collectors

Once the debtor(s) have retained the bankruptcy attorney to represent them, the debtor(s) should be instructed to refer all future collection calls to their attorney's office. When the collector calls the attorney's office, the only information that needs to be provided to the collectors is the case number of the bankruptcy petition filed by the debtor(s.) Keep in mind that if the collector was listed on the bankruptcy petition, they will probably already be notified of the filing. I found that some collectors are too lazy and do not want to update their information with the bankruptcy court's notification. Instead, they would much rather call the attorney's office and get the information versus getting up from their station, walking to the mail room and getting the case number from the bankruptcy notice.

Remember though that a law firm is not required to provide a collector with a copy of any portion of the bankruptcy petition. All creditors have the ability to request copies of bankruptcy petitions from the bankruptcy court because a bankruptcy filing is public information. But since the collector will be required to pay a copy charge and wait on the court to send them the information, they would rather waste the attorney's time and get them to send a free copy. Unfortunately, if this is done for every collector you will spend a large majority of your time being nonproductive for your attorney. So, don't give creditors more information than what is required by law.

Chapter 5

Drafting the Bankruptcy Petition

Drafting the Bankruptcy Petition

This chapter of the book will walk you through the initial training in the preparation of a bankruptcy petition. However, if you have never drafted a bankruptcy petition before, you will need to purchase the multi-CD training video entitled, *How to Draft a Bankruptcy Petition* from my website at www.713training.com. This video will walk you through, step-by-step, every Form and Schedule of an entire bankruptcy petition. Plus, I provide much more detail within the CDs including additional tips and techniques.

The CDs are intended to be used in conjunction with this book. Simply insert the CDs into your computer. The CDs are filmed directly on the computer screen so you can follow along with every mouse click and duplicate exactly what I am doing. You can pause the video, perform the task, then start the CD again and move on to the next Form or Schedule of the bankruptcy petition.

Regardless if you have the multi-CD training videos or not, below is the information you need to get started using this chapter to self-train yourself in the drafting of a bankruptcy petition:

1. Download a FREE demo version of Best Case Bankruptcy Software at:
http://www.bestcase.com

At this stage of your training you do NOT need to purchase the registered version of any bankruptcy software program. Instead, download the free demo (which works exactly like the registered version) and use it to work through this chapter so you can see exactly how a bankruptcy petition is drafted.

Only until you begin marketing your services to attorneys (and have received your first petition to draft) do you need to actually purchase the registered version of Best Case software. Or, you may choose to select another software program from the links provided on Page 279.

2. After you install Best Case and open it up to use for the first time, you will need to go through the Setup Wizard to select a Jurisdiction (such as Southern District of Ohio) and law firm information. Feel free to use filler information for these areas such as *Angie Lawyer* for the name of the law firm and *123 Main Street* as a street address. The information you enter here is only for demonstration purposes, so you can pretty much enter anything you want. However, you must enter something in these areas for Best Case to be set up properly.

3. Beginning with the Voluntary Petition on Page 113 of this chapter, read the information and input data into the bankruptcy software. Work through every form and follow the instructions provided.

The Importance of Drafting a Detailed Bankruptcy Petition

One time I worked for a law firm that placed absolutely no importance on the accuracy and completeness of the bankruptcy petition. Their viewpoint was to get the clients in, process them as quickly as possible and make as much money as quickly as they could. They figured that if they made a mistake on the bankruptcy petition or left out important information, an Amendment could be drafted later.

However, when I was hired as a consultant to help this particular law firm with their tremendous workload, I quickly determined why their workload was so tremendous. I found that the staff as well as the attorney were spending large amounts of time and money preparing and filing Amendments and dealing with hundreds of phone calls from the court as well as the client(s) simply because the petition was not drafted correctly in the beginning.

The law firm was spending almost every minute of their workday *putting out fires* dealing with emergencies and they naturally had a high employee turnover rate. How can anyone work for a long period of time in an atmosphere like this anyway? That is why I have decided to dedicate an entire chapter of this book to the subject of properly drafting a bankruptcy petition.

Before publishing the following information regarding most of the forms that make up a bankruptcy petition, I had a bankruptcy attorney review it for accuracy. But remember, the following material is still written from the perspective of a paralegal so do not confuse the following information as legal advice.

The Means Test

Prior to October 17, 2005 debtor(s) had the ability to choose whether to file a Chapter 7 or Chapter 13 bankruptcy petition. But after years of fraud and abuse, the Bankruptcy Abuse Prevention and Consumer Protection Act of 2005 (BAPCPA) was enacted to help prevent this behavior. One of the changes this new law brought about was the introduction of the Means Test.

The Means Test is used to determine which chapter a debtor(s) can file under by comparing the debtor(s) income to their state median income levels. The debtor(s) no longer have the ability to decide for themselves. The purpose of the Means Test is to make Chapter 7 available to those who really need it. For those who have disposable income available, they are now required to pay back a portion or all of their debt to creditors; where under the old law they might not have had to.

The actual Means Test can be very simple to pass if the debtor(s) fall below their median state income level. If the debtor(s) are below the median income level for their state, the debtor(s) can file a Chapter 7 bankruptcy. Debtor(s) who exceed the median income level may still be able to file a Chapter 7 but they must complete several more steps in the Means Test before that determination is made. If the debtor(s) fail the Means Test, they are not prohibited from filing bankruptcy. However, debtor(s) who fail the Means Test cannot file a Chapter 7.

Below are some web site links to help you advance your knowledge about the Means Test:

- Median Income by States
  http://www.usdoj.gov/ust/bapcpa/bci_data/median_income_table.htm

- Means Testing Information (provided by the US Trustee Program)
  http://www.usdoj.gov/ust/bapcpa/meanstesting.htm

We also will cover more information about the Means Test later in this chapter under the subheading: *Form 22A: Statement of Current Income/Means Test* which begins on Page 148.

The Credit Counseling Requirement

Another new addition to the bankruptcy law that became effective with the changes implemented on October 17, 2005 was the credit counseling requirement. Your job as a virtual bankruptcy assistant is only to check the proper box on the Voluntary Petition relating to this requirement. However, for the attorney and debtor(s) the credit counseling requirement is more detailed and time consuming.

Within 180 days (6 months) of filing bankruptcy, the debtor(s) must have completed a credit counseling course in an effort to educate them and hopefully prevent future bankruptcy filings. This new requirement can be met in a variety of ways, such as:

- internet credit counseling;
- phone credit counseling;
- group counseling; or
- individual counseling through a court approved agency.

Note: To locate the court approved agencies for all 50 states, visit: http://www.usdoj.gov/ust/bapcpa/ccde/cc_approved.htm

The maximum amount an agency may charge for the credit counseling service is $50.00 and this fee is set by the federal government. After the credit counseling sessions are completed, the debtor(s) receive a Certificate of Completion which is filed with the bankruptcy petition.

But as with most things in life, there are exceptions to every rule. Under Section 109(b) of the Bankruptcy Code this requirement can be waived if any of the following exceptions apply:

- Exceptions for disabled and incapacitated persons;
- Exceptions for persons who are in combat duty;
- Exceptions for persons where counseling is not available; and
- Exceptions for exorbitant circumstances or if the debtor(s) are denied service

Form 1: Voluntary Petition

The Voluntary Petition is the first (3) three pages of the bankruptcy petition. It contains the name, address, venue, attorney's name and other important information about the debtor(s) and the bankruptcy petition. One important thing to remember on the Voluntary Petition is to make sure the *husband* is listed as the main *debtor* and the *wife* is listed as the *co-debtor.* Of course this only applies to a husband and wife filing bankruptcy together. If only one person is filing bankruptcy, they are naturally the main and only *debtor.* (See sample below.)

(Official Form 1) (10/05)

United States Bankruptcy Court District of Colorado	**Voluntary Petition**
Name of Debtor (if individual, enter Last, First, Middle): **Doe, John Richard**	Name of Joint Debtor (Spouse) (Last, First, Middle) **Doe, Betty Ann**

The Voluntary Petition is also where you will list information about any prior bankruptcy the debtor(s) has filed within the past eight years. This crucial piece of information is necessary because the bankruptcy attorney may not be able to represent the debtor(s) if they filed a Chapter 7 within the past eight years or a Chapter 13 within the past six years. The attorney may be forced to recommend alternatives or turn the debtor(s) away completely until the proper time period has elapsed when they are eligible to file bankruptcy again.

On October 17, 2005, the bankruptcy law changed to also include the following additional information on the Voluntary Petition, as required by BAPCPA:

- A Chapter 15 option was added on Page 1 of the Voluntary Petition for *Recognition of a Foreign Main Proceeding* and *Recognition for a Foreign Nonmain Proceeding;*

- A credit counseling checkbox was added on Page 2 of the Voluntary Petition under the area titled: *Certificate Concerning Debt Counseling by Individual/ Joint Debtor(s);* and

- A statement by the debtor(s) who is currently residing as a tenant was added on Page 2 of the Voluntary Petition under the area titled: *Statement by Debtor Who Resides as a Tenant of Residential Property.*

Involuntary Petition

Most virtual bankruptcy assistant's working with Chapter 7 and Chapter 13 debtor(s) may never encounter an Involuntary Petition. An Involuntary Petition is normally used in Chapter 11 business filings but as a virtual bankruptcy assistant you still need to know they do exist. An *involuntary* petition is exactly what it says it is. The debtor(s) did not *voluntarily* decide to file bankruptcy; instead, their creditors forced them to file bankruptcy *involuntarily.* Among other things, the Involuntary petition lists the names of the creditors who petitioned for the debtor to file bankruptcy as well as the amount of money the debtor(s) owe them.

Involuntary petitions are normally handled by law firms specializing in Chapter 11 bankruptcy filings. If you do encounter one in your lifetime and the attorney requests that you draft one for him or her, you need to contact the bankruptcy software company who developed the software you are using (i.e. Best Case, etc.) to obtain the proper forms. The Involuntary Petition form differs slightly from the Voluntary Petition form.

Application to Pay Filing Fee in Installments

The Application to Pay Filing Fee in Installment form is also rarely used because most attorneys require the debtor(s) to pay the full filing fee before their bankruptcy petition is filed. However, in rare hardship cases the attorney may ask you to draft an Application to Pay Filing Fee in Installments. On this document you need to provide the dates and the amount of money the debtor(s) will pay the court. For instance, if Jane wishes to pay her $299 Chapter 7 filing fee in installments, she may pay $74.75 when the petition is filed on March 1, $74.75 on March 15, another $74.75 on March 30 and the final $74.75 filing fee on April 15.

The Application is also accompanied with an Order for the judge to sign. But even if the Order has not been signed by the judge when the installment payments are due, the debtor(s) still needs to continue making the payments on or before the dates they agreed to on the Application in order to avoid a possible dismissal of their case.

Form 6: Summary of Schedules

Most bankruptcy software programs will automatically prepare the Summary of Schedules based on the information entered into the other forms and schedules of the bankruptcy petition. However, if you are constructing this document by hand it will contain the totals of all the debts broken down into the sections designated on the Summary of Schedules. In other words, the Summary of Schedules is an overview of the entire debt picture of the debtor(s) presented in numerical form.

When the new bankruptcy law was enacted the Summary of Schedules was updated to include a new page titled: *Statistical Summary of Certain Liabilities.* This page totals the debts for the following:

- Schedule E - Domestic Support Obligations;
- Schedule E – Taxes and Certain Other Debts Owned to Governmental Units;
- Schedule E – Claims for Death or Personal Injury While Debtor was Intoxicated
- Schedule F – Student Loan Obligations;

- Domestic Support, Separation Agreement, and Divorce Decree Obligations Not Reported on Schedule E; and
- Schedule F – Obligations to Pension or Profit-Sharing and Other Similar Obligations

These totals are calculated for statistical purposes and are required by 28 USC, Section 159.

Schedule A

Schedule A provides all the information pertaining to *real* property the debtor(s) own. One of the most common mistakes a virtual bankruptcy assistant makes is not understanding the difference between *real* and *personal* property. As previously discussed, *real* property is anything that is attached to *God's green earth.* Normally this is a home or piece of ground with or without a home attached to it.

The confusion occurs when a debtor lives in a mobile home which is still sitting on wheels. In this case, the mobile home is considered *personal* property not *real* property since the mobile home is not actually attached to *God's green earth.* Only unless the wheels have been removed from the mobile home and it is permanently attached to *God's green earth* does the mobile home become *real* property.

The following is an example of a property description I used for Schedule A:

Primary residence located at 123 Main Street, Anytown TN, described as 1,800-square-foot home situated on 1.2 acres of ground with 4 bed-rooms, 2 baths, attached 2-car garage and 800-square-foot outbuilding.

Also, if you have a copy of the deed you can add the legal property description but it is not necessary. The sample above includes all the pertinent information to describe the property, and it is normally sufficient for the bankruptcy petition.

You will also need to provide the name and address information of the mortgage company(s), the appraised value of the home, the amount owed to the mortgage company(s), the date the mortgage was obtained, how much the monthly payments are, if the debtor(s) are behind in their payments and which months (if any) they are behind.

Schedule B

Schedule B contains *everything* else that is an asset of the debtor(s) that is *not* attached to *God's green earth.* This includes the following items:

- Cash on hand
- Checking, Savings or other financial accounts, certificates of deposit
- Security deposits with utilities, landlords and others
- Household goods and furnishings
- Books, pictures and other art objects; collectibles
- Wearing apparel
- Furs and jewelry
- Firearms and sports, photographic and other hobby equipment
- Interests in insurance policies
- Annuities
- Interests in an education IRA or under a qualified state tuition plan
- Interests in IRA, ERISA, Keogh, or other pension or profit-sharing plans
- Stocks and interest in businesses

- Interests in partnerships or joint ventures
- Government and corporate bonds; other negotiable and non-negotiable instruments
- Accounts receivable
- Alimony, maintenance, support and property settlements
- Other liquidated debts owing debtor including tax refunds
- Equitable or future interests, life estates, etc.
- Contingent and non-contingent interests of an estate of a decedent
- Other contingent and unliquidated claims of every nature
- Patents, copyrights and other intellectual property
- Licenses, franchises and other general intangibles
- Customer lists or other compilations containing personally identifiable information
- Automobiles, trucks, trailer and other vehicles
- Boats, motors and accessories
- Aircraft and accessories
- Office equipment, furnishings and supplies
- Machinery, fixtures and equipment and supplies used in business
- Inventory
- Animals
- Crops growing or harvested
- Farming equipment and implements
- Farm supplies, chemicals and feed
- Other personal property of any kind not already listed

Although every bankruptcy petition is unique because every debtor(s) situation is unique, after preparing thousands of bankruptcy petitions over the course of my career I have found the items I normally use over and over again for most debtor(s) on Schedule B are:

- Cash on Hand;
- Checking, Savings or Other Financial Accounts, Certificates of Deposit;
- Security Deposits with Utilities, Landlords and Others;
- Household Goods and Furnishings;
- Wearing Apparel;
- Furs and Jewelry;
- Interests in Insurance Policies
- Alimony, Maintenance, Support and Property Settlements;
- Other Contingent and Unliquidated Claims of Every Nature; and
- Automobiles, Trucks, Trailers and Other Vehicles.

Also, if the debtor(s) are filing bankruptcy before July 15, you will need to find out if they received or anticipate receiving a tax refund. Why July 15 and not April 15? Because if the debtor(s) received a tax refund on April 15 and file bankruptcy before July 15 of the same year, they received their refund ninety (90) days prior to filing. All income must be disclosed on the bankruptcy petition if it was received within the past ninety (90) days. The information is recorded on Schedule B under *Other liquidated debts owing debtor including tax refunds.*

When you ask the debtor(s) to provide you with the amount of their tax refund, the next question they will normally ask is: *Are they going to take my tax refund?* Of course as a virtual bankruptcy assistant you cannot provide them a direct answer without receiving permission from your attorney, but you should make them aware that there is a possibility all or a portion of the tax refund could be used to help pay some of the creditors they owe money to. But even if this happens, help the debtor(s) to look at the positive side. If they are asking the court to relieve them of a great deal of debt, isn't it worth giving up one tax refund check to possibly become debt free? If I could give up my $2,000 tax refund to excuse

$60,000 worth of debt I would consider it a benefit — not a loss. However, the attorney will need to provide the debtor(s) with a definite answer when faced with this situation. Your job is to provide general information and never to answer specific questions relating to a debtor(s) case. Doing so places you in the position of providing legal advice, which is against the law.

The following are examples of descriptions I personally use for some of the common items previously mentioned on Schedule B. This will help you when entering the information on the bankruptcy petition. Of course, you need to obtain approval from the attorney you are working for to make sure there are not additional requirements imposed by your local bankruptcy court.

Cash on Hand (Property Type: 1)

- Cash on Hand = $22.08

The figure stated here should be the amount of cash the debtor(s) have in their pocket after they pay their attorney. Because some debtor(s) pay their attorney in cash (perhaps due to a closed bank account) they may come into the office with $1,200.00 but if the attorney fee is $1,100.00 you would only record $100.00 as Cash on Hand.

Checking, Savings or Other Financial Accounts, Certificates of Deposit (Property Type: 2)

- Checking Account No: 12345678, My Bank, Anytown USA

Again, the amount you record for this asset should be the amount left in the checking or savings account *after* the debtor(s) have paid the monthly debts listed on Schedule J of their bankruptcy petition. This includes mortgage or rent, taxes, utilities, food, clothing, etc. If the debtor(s) also have a savings account, Christmas club or other type of bank account, each account should be listed separately.

Security Deposits with Utilities, Landlords and Others (Property Type: 3)

- Security deposit with present landlord, The Landlord Company, Anytown USA for the rented residence located at 123 Main Street, Anytown USA.

- Security deposit with My Electric Company, Anytown USA. Deposit to be returned to debtor(s) approximately May 2007.

Household Goods and Furnishings (Property Type: 4)

Prior to the year 2000, attorneys lumped all the household goods and furnishings into one category and provided one total market value for this item on Schedule B. However, bankruptcy courts began requiring a more detailed inventory. While some attorneys still continue to try and lump everything together without providing any detail of the household goods and furnishings, you will discover that most trustees in the bankruptcy court will reject the filing and demand an Amendment to Schedule B be filed that provides the level of detail as in the sample that follows:

Household goods and furnishings consisting of: stove ($75); refrigerator ($50); washer/dryer ($150); microwave ($50); cooking utensils, flatware, cookware ($40); living room furniture ($150); bedroom furniture ($175); dining room furniture ($275); dressers/nightstands ($40); television ($75); VCR ($50); DVD ($25); stereo and compact disks ($75); miscellaneous household repair tools ($60); and lawnmower ($30)

Other items like books, collectibles, firearms and other similar items should be listed under their proper category under Schedule B with a complete description. However, for computers and other office equipment that is solely for the personal (not business) use of the debtor(s) can be listed under Property Type 4 or Property Type 28. Your attorney will normally allow the household goods exemption for these items since the computer and printer as being used as household goods and furnishings. But remember to ask the debtors how the computer equipment is being used. If they are using it for business purposes (any enterprise where an income is generated), make a note of this information on the Attorney Summary Page and ask the attorney which exemption he or she wants you to use.

Wearing Apparel (Property Type: 6)

- Wearing apparel and personal effects for two adults and one child

It is important to state the number of people for which the total amount was determined for the amount listed under *wearing apparel.* This should also match the number of people listed in the bankruptcy petition. For example, the total market value of wearing apparel for two adults and one child might be $750.00.

Next, you go to Schedule J and make sure two adults and one child are included in the bankruptcy petition to maintain consistency within the document. If you are drafting a bankruptcy petition for a single person or a married person filing without their spouse, the amount of wearing apparel should only be listed for the individual and not the non-filing spouse since they are not filing.

Also notice on Schedule J, the amount the debtor(s) listed as their monthly expense for clothing. Make sure it is consistent with the declared value for all the wearing apparel listed on Schedule B. For example: I was drafting a bankruptcy petition one time and the debtor claimed that all her clothing (including coats, shoes, socks, etc) was worth only $200. Yet, for her monthly expenses she stated she needed $500 per month for clothing. This is inconsistent. If this lady was actually spending $500 per month for clothing, she would certainly have more than $200 worth in her possession at the time she is filing bankruptcy. This inconsistency could become a major problem for your attorney as well as the bankruptcy court. But rather than change the figure, you need to provide all the information to your attorney on the Attorney Summary Sheet so he or she can make the decision about which figure needs changed.

Furs and Jewelry (Property Type: 7)

- Wedding rings ($350); miscellaneous costume jewelry ($75); men's watch ($25)

If the debtor(s) have been married they will most likely have a wedding ring. Although I have known some debtor(s) who claim they threw their wedding ring into the river after getting a divorce; the majority of people do have wedding rings. In my personal experience, I have found that some trustees will specifically look for this asset to be listed on Schedule B especially if the debtor(s) are married. If they find this detail omitted they will have cause to suspicion the accuracy of the rest of the data provided in the bankruptcy petition.

Interests in Insurance Policies (Property Type: 9)

- Term life insurance policy, provided by employer, payable only upon death. Beneficiary: Mary Jones; Relationship: wife

and/or

- Whole life insurance policy, The Insurance Company, Johnson City TN, Beneficiary: Mary Jones; Relationship: wife

Alimony, Maintenance, Support and Property Settlements (Property Type: 17)

- Uncollectible child support from ex-spouse of debtor wife, John Doe, 123 Main Street, Anytown USA

This recording of an asset under the Property Type: *Alimony, Maintenance, Support and Property Settlements* is not for those who are paying alimony or child support. It is for debtor(s) who are owed alimony or child support. In most cases I found that there was a large amount owed in back child support and that amount was normally uncollectible. Therefore, I used this data for the example provided above.

Other Contingent and Unliquidated Claims of Every Nature (Property Type: 21)

- Fraudulent transfer of funds by spouse currently separated from debtor. Spouse (Mary Jones, 1812 Divorce Way, Kenosha WI 53142) allegedly transferred $15,000 from debtor(s) checking account without debtor(s) knowledge, which had been designated to pay creditors.

This property type can be used for a wide variety of reasons, but the example above is often used when the debtor is going through a divorce or separation from their spouse. If the non-filing spouse has taken money from the debtor without their knowledge, this information should be recorded on Schedule B of the bankruptcy petition. There is a possibility that the bankruptcy court may initiate a claim against the spouse to collect the money, which will then be disbursed to the creditors. Therefore, make sure you always include the name and address of the non-filing spouse under Additional Notify for this asset so they can be included on the Creditor's Matrix and notified of the claim.

Automobiles, Trucks, Trailers and Other Vehicles (Property Type: 25)

- 1997 Pontiac Thunderbird, Mileage = 85,000, Condition = Good
  or if the car is junked or not running, you would type in:
- 2001 Kia Rio, Mileage = 27,800, Condition = Junked

It is important to obtain a copy of the title for every motor vehicle the debtor(s) own so you can make sure the year, make and model are correct. Debtor(s) often make errors when providing this information on their Client Intake Forms due to stress or just from *not thinking.* And because the information on Schedule B concerning motor vehicles is so crucial to the bankruptcy case – it is your responsibility to make sure this information is accurate and there are no errors.

Next, you need to go online and obtain a current Kelly Blue Book or NADA market value and record this figure in the proper area on Schedule B for this asset. For vehicles that are not running or junked, you may want to talk with your attorney and ask them to provide you with a figure to record on Schedule B for this asset. As a virtual bankruptcy assistant, you would be violating UPL (unauthorized practice of law) if you attempted to *guess* at the value of a piece of property owned by the debtor(s.) Leave that decision up to your attorney.

Determining Market Values for Items

The amount you enter into Schedule B for all the items the debtor(s) have in their possession at the time they are filing their bankruptcy petition should be a *market* value. This is *not* the replacement value of the item(s) but rather the value of the property at the time the bankruptcy is filed. (Remember, a repossessed car no longer in the debtor(s) possession is not listed on Schedule B because it is no longer an asset.)

For assets like clothing, household goods, jewelry, computers, etc.; getting the debtor(s) to provide you with a market value is often a difficult task. However, as a virtual bankruptcy assistant you cannot estimate the value for them. But you may want to say something like: *If I purchased a television set today for $200, I would probably only get $50 or $75 if I pawned it at the pawn shop, or sold it in a yard sale.* Or: *If I had to sell my clothing at a yard sale, a t-shirt would bring about 25¢ and a pair of jeans only $1 or $2.* These examples should help the debtor(s) get a better idea of the type of value they need to list as the market value on their bankruptcy petition for the items in their possession. But, you will find that some debtor(s) like to *brag* and think the *Lazy Boy* chair their parents gave to them 15 years ago is worth a million dollars, but it may not be worth more than $25 or $30 at a yard sale.

I remember one situation where a lady claimed she had a diamond ring worth $15,000. The exemption allowance for furs and jewelry in the state she resided in was $800. This meant there would have been $14,200 in *unexempt* equity which may have resulted in $14,200 being paid to the bankruptcy court for distribution to her creditors. I brought this matter to the attorney's attention and he called the debtor to explain the problem. The lady continued to claim this diamond ring was really worth $15,000 so the attorney told her to take the ring to a pawn shop and find out the market value. The lady was very upset when the pawn shop owner gave her a price of $350. It turned out the diamond was only 1/4-caret and even if she had purchased it at an expensive jewelry store the current retail value was only about $800.

The attorney was very happy that he had saved the debtor $14,200, but she was still unable to understand why. So she became very upset with the attorney. She claimed he made her feel like her jewelry was worthless even though her husband gave her the diamond ring when they first fell in love.

But this is only one exception to the rule. Normally, I found that most debtor(s) *underestimate* the market value for the assets they own. Many of them had the preconceived notion that someone was actually going to come to their home and do a physical inventory so they tried their best to underestimate the market values. However, some people will overestimate the market value and the attorney or trustee may order an appraisal. This is one good reason why providing a full description of the assets on Schedule B is extremely important.

Obtaining market values for automobiles and other motor vehicles should be looked up in either *Kelly Blue Book* or *NADA*. However, if you have never looked up a value for a motor vehicle before you may be confused as to which listed price you should use. For example, the different values listed in *Kelly Blue Book* are:

- The amount the vehicle could be sold for if taken to a dealer
- The amount the vehicle could be sold for privately
- The amount the vehicle could be sold for if a dealer sells to another dealer

When you visit the *Kelly Blue Book* web site at http://www.kbb.com or the *NADA* web site at http://www.nadaguides.com in order to obtain the market value for a motor vehicle, your attorney may have you use the *Private Party* value since dealer prices are normally unsteady.

It is also important to print out the web page showing the market value of the motor vehicle and place it in the client's file. This provides documentation as to the actual market value and will save your attorney time if asked to provide this documentation to the trustee during the 341 Meeting.

What is a Cram Down?

In some situations, you may find a motor vehicle is worth substantially less than the amount owed on the loan. For instance, Joe may owe $12,000 on a car that is only worth $8,500 in the NADA guide. Be sure to bring any situation like this to your attorney's attention immediately. If the debt is more than 30 months old before the petition is filed, there may be the possibility the debtor(s) are eligible for a *cram down* so he or she can pay back the market value of the vehicle rather than the total amount owed to the creditor in their Chapter 13 plan.

For example, Joe owes $12,000 on a car with a market value of $8,500. If Joe purchased this car and made the debt more than 30 months before filing his Chapter 13 bankruptcy petition, Joe may only need to pay back $8,500 instead of $12,000. This saves Joe $3,500. So, as you can see, a *cram down* can potentially save the debtor(s) hundreds or even thousands of dollars. However, under the new bankruptcy law, a *cram down* is not permitted for other secured debts involving personal property within one (1) year of filing bankruptcy.

Schedule C

Schedule C contains the information for exemption allowances for the items that were listed as assets on Schedule A and Schedule B. The attorney will either provide you with this information to place on Schedule C or your bankruptcy software program may automatically select the proper exemption automatically for you when you click on the **Exemption tab** within your software program.

There are two different types of exemption allowances an attorney may use on Schedule C of the bankruptcy petition: *federal* exemptions and *state* exemptions. Some states are required to use the federal exemptions, other states are required to use the state exemptions, while other states allow the attorney to choose between the two. However, no petition may contain *both* federal and state exemptions; it must be either one or the other. To find out if your state uses federal or state exemptions or if the attorney has the option of choosing which one is the most beneficial for the client, go online to *Bankruptcy Action's* website at http://www.bankruptcyaction.com/bankruptcyexemptions.htm.

If the state exemptions are used, you will find that the exemption allowance for each item will differ from state to state. For instance, in Wisconsin the current state exemption allowance for household goods for an individual filing bankruptcy is $5,000 but in Ohio it is only $1,500 to $2,000 depending on whether the debtor(s) own a home or not.

State exemption allowances not only change from state to state but they are increased and decreased by the court often without prior notice. It is important for the attorney and virtual bankruptcy assistant to keep up-to-date on changes in exemption allowances. One way to do this is to keep your bankruptcy software updated. One feature I love about Best Case software is that when I start up the program it automatically tells me if there are any updates. Then Best Case will download and install them for me automatically. This ensures that I am always working with the most up-to-date bankruptcy forms and schedules.

One new area that was added to Schedule C when the new bankruptcy law went into effect was the checkbox for the homestead exemption. This box is checked if the debtor has a homestead exemption that totals $125,000 or more. However, some states do not allow the homestead exemption allowance. Check with your attorney to find out if it is allowable in your state before checking this box on Schedule C.

The interesting trivia about the homestead exemption cap is that it actually became law on April 20, 2005 when President George Bush signed the reform legislation. Most of the other provisions of the new bankruptcy law did not go into effect until October 17, 2005.

Under the new law, the debtor(s) may exempt up to $125,000 of interest in a homestead that was obtained within a 1,215-day period prior to filing bankruptcy. However, the calculation does not include any equity that was rolled over during that period of time from one house to another within the same state. For debtor(s) who have violated securities laws or engaged in certain criminal conduct, the cap is $125,000 regardless if there is a higher state law allowance. And if the homestead was obtained through any type of fraudulent conversion of nonexempt assets during the 10-year period before the filing of the bankruptcy petition, the homestead exemption is reduced by the amount of the fraud.

Schedule D

Schedule D provides a list of the creditors that have secure claims, the description of the claim and the market value. This information is pulled from the data provided on Schedule A and B of the bankruptcy petition. In most bankruptcy software programs, any lienholder listed on Schedule A and B is automatically inserted on Schedule D. Therefore the virtual bankruptcy assistant rarely needs to enter information into this form but it is always a good idea to look over the information to double-check your accuracy on Schedule A and B.

Schedule E

Schedule E provides a list of the creditors who hold unsecured *priority* claims. What does this mean? It is a debt for something that the debtor(s) do not physically have in their possession (unsecured), but the debt is a priority debt that must be paid back in full. These include common debts for personal and property taxes, unpaid child and spousal support, fines, student loans, etc. You can easily see that debts of this nature do not have any physical tangible item attached to them, which is why they are classified as unsecure but they receive priority over the repayment of other debts.

One common debt that appears on Schedule E quite frequently are unpaid taxes. These taxes may be property taxes, city taxes, state taxes or federal taxes. If the debtor(s) owe federal taxes, you must always notify these two additional parties because it is a federal debt:

Department of Treasury
Internal Revenue Service
Washington DC 20001

US Internal Revenue Service
1111 Constitution Ave NE #3000
Washington DC 20002

The new bankruptcy law adjusted the Domestic Support Obligations to be the first priority of the other priority unsecured creditors. Additionally, a new property type for *Claims for Death or Personal Injury While Debtor Was Intoxicated* was added. Most bankruptcy software programs will include the subtotals of these property types under the proper area of the Summary of Schedules – but you may want to double-check if you are not using Best Case software.

Schedule F

Schedule F contains all the debt information for unsecured *non-priority* claims. These debts are normally for credit cards, medical bills, repossessed motor vehicles, loans from family and friends that are not attached to personal or real property, bank overdraft fees, check deficiencies, unsecured personal loans, etc. For credit card debts I used the following format on the *date incurred* line of the bankruptcy petition:

- 1998, Last Used: 10/2001

Remember when we previously covered the problem of debtor(s) using their credit cards 90 days prior to filing bankruptcy? If the last date they made a purchase on their credit card was 90 days or less, you also need to provide the credit card usage information in the *description* area of Schedule F for this debt. An example would be:

- My Bank Visa Card
  Recent usage: 10/2005 = $75.00, Purpose: Groceries
  Recent usage: 11/2005 = $420.00, Purpose: Paid rent
  Recent usage: 12/2005 = $180.00, Purpose: Paid utilities

Providing this level of detail on Schedule F will aide your attorney in saving time at the 341 Meeting, plus the trustee's job much easier. If the credit card company should file an Objection to deny the money the debtor(s) spent 90 days prior to filing their bankruptcy petition, this information will greatly aide the trustee in making the determination whether to allow the claim made by the credit card company or disallow it. Of course, the debtor(s) should have receipts or other documentation to verify the money was actually spent on these allowable expenses in case they are requested.

Schedule G

Schedule G contains information about executory contracts and unexpired leases. Even if you listed a debtor(s) car on Schedule B as a car lease, the information needs repeated on Schedule G. The most common information I have found listed on Schedule G for debtor(s) are cell phones. Here is an example of the description I normally use for this Schedule in relation to a cell phone contract:

- 2-year cellular phone contract beginning 02/2005, Mnthly Pymt = $49.95; or

- Month-to-month cellular phone contracting beginning 02/2005, Mnthly Pymt = $49.95

I also listed the expense on Schedule J of the bankruptcy petition to allow for the payment in the monthly budget. If the debtor(s) were rejecting the contract and no future monthly payments would be made, I left the expense off Schedule J because the debtor(s) would no longer be paying this bill.

Schedule H

Schedule H provides a list of co-debtors who are associated with any of the debts the debtor(s) owe. Normally it is filled in automatically as you enter in information on Schedule A and B. If a husband and wife are filing a bankruptcy petition together, they are not considered to be the co-debtor for each other. However, if the wife's mother co-signed for her daughter and husband to get a car, home or other secured asset, the wife's mother would be listed as a co-debtor on Schedule H.

Often, I have found that debtor(s) will tell me their car is titled in their name when in actuality their wife or boyfriend co-signed for them on the loan. It is not a bad thing that a debtor had to obtain a co-signer in order for them to get a loan on their car. The bad thing is not reporting this information properly on Schedule H and clearly linking it to the specific asset.

Schedule I

Although every Form and Schedule within the bankruptcy petition is extremely important, Schedule I is one of the most crucial documents as it is also linked to the Means Test. As a virtual bankruptcy assistant you will input the current monthly income data on Schedule I that is provided by the debtor(s) on their Client Intake Forms. However, you also need to take the extra step and compare the data to the current and previous six (6) months of paycheck stubs to ensure accuracy.

Paycheck stubs (or other verification of income) should have been gathered at the client intake interview by the attorney or the staff. If you are working at your home office, you may need to call the attorney and request this information be faxed to you so you can compare the figures with the information provided by the debtor(s) for Schedule I if necessary.

Reviewing Schedule I will help you to identify additional information you may need to list in other areas of the bankruptcy petition. For instance, if the debtor(s) have listed a deduction from their paycheck for a 401K plan, you need to list the 401K as personal property on Schedule B. However, under the new law the debtor(s) 401K (valued up to $1 million dollars) will be exempt and will never be subject to claims by the creditors regardless of what state the debtor(s) reside in. If the debtor(s) have recently lost their job, they will be required to rollover the 401K and not permitted to cash it in when filing bankruptcy.

You should also find out from the debtor(s) if they have any outstanding loans against their 401K when you discover they have one. If they do, this creates another secure debt and a lienholder is attached to the 401K asset listed on Schedule B. If the 401K loan is deducted from their paycheck by the employer, it is considered a wage garnishment and needs to be listed under Item 4(b) of the Statement of Affairs.

Remember any income reported on Schedule I needs a separate year-to-date total of the monies received also listed under Item 1 or Item 2 of the Statement of Affairs. We will cover this under the Statement of Affairs on Page 138.

Schedule J

Schedule J is another one of the crucial documents within the bankruptcy petition. It provides details on the average monthly budget of the debtor(s.) Debt payments listed on Schedule F of the bankruptcy petition are normally never listed on Schedule J because Schedule J is for listing basic living expenses of the debtor(s.) Of course, the monthly payments for necessary living expenses (previously listed on Schedule A, B, E and G of the bankruptcy petition) should be included if the debtor(s) are *not* surrendering the item(s.)

Under the new bankruptcy law however, attorneys are no longer permitted to adjust the monthly budget figures to whatever amount they want in order to qualify the debtor(s) for a Chapter 7. Instead, the government has established guidelines for monthly expenses such as utilities, living expenses and transportation expenses. Below are the links to the IRS where you can locate these figures:

- National Standard for Housing and Utility Expenses
  http://www.irs.gov/businesses/small/article/0,,id=104696,00.html

- National Standards for Living Expenses
  http://www.usdoj.gov/ust/bapcpa/bci_data/national_expense_standards.htm

- National Standards for Transportation Expenses
  http://www.irs.gov/businesses/small/article/0,,id=104623,00.html

Reviewing other items listed on Schedule J will help you to identify additional information you may need to list in other areas of the bankruptcy petition. For instance, if the debtor(s) have listed an amount they pay for life insurance, you should list the life insurance policy as an asset on Schedule B. A *whole life* policy carries a cash value and the debtor(s) could borrow money against it. A *term life* policy is only payable upon death and carries no market value on Schedule B.

In addition, if the debtor(s) list an amount for medical expenses on Schedule J you need to verify that this is not the same amount reported on Schedule I for medical insurance deducted from their paycheck. (You cannot list the same expense twice. This would be a double deduction.) Also, cell phone contracts, monthly payments to student loans, fines and taxes also need listed on Schedule J since they are necessary expenses the debtor(s) are obligated to pay. The only exception I found to this rule is for student loans. If one or both of the debtor(s) are still enrolled in college and the student loan is in deferment until they graduate, of course there would be no monthly payment to list on Schedule J for this expense since the student loan is not being paid at this time from the monthly budget.

Balancing Schedule I and Schedule J

As a virtual bankruptcy assistant you are not permitted to adjust figures and balance out Schedule I and J without the supervision of your attorney. Instead, you should enter in the information provided by the debtor(s) on the Client Intake Forms. When you are finished you would then deduct the total amount of monthly expenses on Schedule J from the total amount of income on Schedule I. If this figure is a negative number (less than $0 dollars) you should alert your attorney at once because this indicates there is a problem.

What happens if your attorney files a bankruptcy petition that shows there are more expenses than income? Because it is impossible to pay out more money than what is available, secure creditors may argue the debtor(s) do not have enough money to maintain the minimum monthly payments which could result in the debtor(s) losing their home, cars or other valued assets. Therefore, making sure that the final figure is not less than $0.00 will help to ensure this problem does occur.

Normally, when you end up with a negative number after subtracting the expenses on Schedule J from the income on Schedule I, the debtor(s) have probably not reported their income and monthly expenses properly. I ran into many situations where a divorced woman would file bankruptcy and report that she had no income. However, the woman would also report that she paid certain monthly expenses. This would be impossible to do. A person cannot pay money for something if they don't have any money. Often, in circumstances like these, I discovered the woman was living with another person who was paying the expenses for her. In this case, the amount of money the roommate or other person was paying would become income for the debtor in order to show how she was able to pay her basic living expenses.

Declaration Concerning Debtor's Schedules

The Declaration Concerning Debtor's Schedules Form is a signature page the debtor(s) sign. The debtor(s) state: *under penalty of perjury that the information provided in the bankruptcy schedules is true and correct to the best of their knowledge, information and belief.*

Form 7: Statement of Affairs

The best way to learn what information goes on the Statement of Affairs is to print out the forms and review them. You can do this from your bankruptcy software program.

The Statement of Affairs often can be viewed as a summary of the bankruptcy petition. Some information provided in the petition is carried over into the Statement of Affairs, while some of the information is only intended to be listed on the Statement of Affairs and not within the actual Forms and Schedules of the bankruptcy petition. The most common items on the Statement of Affairs that I encountered are listed below along with a sample description for several of them:

1. Income from employment or operation of a business

This is where I recorded the year-to-date income for each debtor separately as well as the income earned from employment or operation of a business within the past two years. Here is the format I used when recording information under this Item of the Statement of Affairs:

- AMOUNT SOURCE (if more than one)
$2,263.47 Husband's income year-to-date 2006 = $2,263.47
Husband's income 2005 = $38,697.16
Husband's income 2004 = $9,760.02

- $0.00 Wife's income year-to-date 2006 = $0.00
Wife's income 2005 = $1,649.37
Wife's income 2004 = $12,339.04

- $682.00 Wife's self-employment income year-to-date 2006 = $682.00
Wife's self-employment income 2005 = $0.00
Wife's self-employment income 2004 = $0.00

2. Income other than from employment or operation of a business

This is where I recorded the year-to-date income of each debtor separately as well as the income earned within the past two years that was *not* earned from employment or operation of a business. Here is the format I use when recording information under this Item of the Statement of Affairs:

- AMOUNT SOURCE

  $920.00 Husband's unemployment income year-to-date 2006 = $920.00
  Husband's unemployment income 2005 = $0.00
  Husband's unemployment income 2004 = $0.00

3. Payments to creditors

This is the section where I would list any payments made by the debtor(s) within 90 days prior to filing their petition that they paid to any one creditor of $600 or more. But pay attention to the information you list on this Item of the Statement of Affairs. If the debtor(s) have paid several creditors you may want to ask them where they obtained the money to pay these debts. Perhaps the debtor(s) obtained a cash advance on their credit card to pay them — which is an important piece of information your attorney needs to know. Or, maybe they used a retirement fund or a relative loaned them the money. However, if any debts listed in this section are not paid in full at the time of the bankruptcy filing, make sure the figure you provide in the *Amount Still Owing* section of this Item match the amount due this creditor on the Schedules of the bankruptcy petition. Here is the format I use when recording information under this Item:

NAME AND ADDRESS OF CREDITOR:
The Mortgage Company
123 Main Street
Anytown USA 12345

DATE AND AMOUNT OF PAYMENTS:
12/26/2005 $1,400.00

BALANCE OWED:
$102,439.77

4. Suits and administrative proceedings, executions, garnishments and attachments

Item 4(a) of this section of the Statement of Affairs is where I would provide the required details in which the debtor(s) are or were a party within one year prior to filing their bankruptcy petition.

Item 4(b) of this section of the Statement of Affairs is where I would provide the required details about any property that has been attached, garnished or seized under any legal or equitable process within one year prior to filing their bankruptcy petition.

5. Repossessions, foreclosures and returns

Under this Item of the Statement of Affairs I provided the necessary information relating to repossessions, foreclosures and/or property transferred through a deed in lieu of foreclosure or returned to the seller within one year prior to the filing of the bankruptcy petition.

8. Losses

When I drafted petitions for an attorney in Nevada I used this Item in the Statement of Affairs quite frequently. This is where I recorded information about losses due to fire, theft, casualty or gambling within one year prior to the filing of the bankruptcy petition. And from my experience, almost everyone in Las Vegas, Nevada who filed bankruptcy had losses due to gambling.

9. Payments related to debt counseling or bankruptcy

Under this item of the Statement of Affairs I would provide information about the payments made to the bankruptcy attorney or law firm in relation to this case. Also, if the debtor(s) previously paid any monies to any other attorneys or credit counseling centers relating to their debts, that information also needs to be recorded under this Item. Below is an example:

Recipient: **Credit Counseling Center or Law Firm Name**
Address: **123 Main Street, Anytown USA, 99999**
Date of payment, Name of payor if other than debtor: **03/2005**
Amount of money or description and value of property:
$1,500.00 paid for attorney representation in this bankruptcy case
or
$50.00 paid for required debt counseling requirement

What if the debtor(s) paid money to a debt counseling service (not the one required by the court to file bankruptcy) but a debt counseling service that distributed money received from the debtor(s) and disbursed to the creditors prior to filing bankruptcy? You would still list the credit counseling agency information but in order to get the *value of the property* to enter into Item 9 of the Statement of Affairs you need to determine the amount the debtor(s) actually paid for the service (not the money that was used to pay their bill.) Normally, when I asked debtor(s) how much they paid to a credit counseling center they provided me with an amount that included the amount also paid toward their debts. For example: A debtor told me he had paid $120 per month for a period of eight months to the credit counseling center. I asked him: *How much of that $120 was paid to your creditors and how much was the administrative fee charged by the credit counseling center?* Often I received an answer like *$20 per month (or some other small* *amount).* Since the debtor was in the program for a total of eight months ($20 x 8 = $160), I then listed the $160 as the monies paid to the credit counseling center under this section of the Statement of Affairs.

11. Closed financial accounts

Under this Item of the Statement of Affairs I would provide information about any closed financial accounts within one year prior to the debtor(s) filing bankruptcy. Many times I could look at the debt sheets and when I found debts that occurred because of a bounced check (check deficiency) I would ask the debtor(s) if there were any closed bank accounts. I found it often to be the case that when a check bounced, debtor(s) rarely paid the check or the bounced check fees and the bank automatically closed their account.

You may wish to record the closed account like this:

Type and number of account and amount of final balance:

- **Checking Account No: 4279, Final Balance Paid to Debtors = $0.00**

Amount and date of sale or closing:

- **$280.00 bank fees, Closed 05/2005**

15. Prior address of debtor

All addresses the debtor(s) have lived at within the past three years prior to filing their bankruptcy petition should be provided under this Item of the Statement of Affairs. I recorded the dates as well as the complete address for all residences as in the following sample:

Address: **18187 River Drive, Apt 4, Rush CO 80833**
Name Used: **John and Betty Doe**
Dates of Occupancy: **02/2002 to 10/2004**

16. Spouses and former spouses

This is one of the new additions to the Statement of Affairs since the year 2000. I found that some debtor(s) get a little nervous when I attempted to obtain this information. Most divorced people wanted to forget about past relationships and may became defensive about this question. My attorney trained me to let the debtor(s) know this question is essentially for identification purposes. Their ex-spouse is normally never contacted unless the ex-spouse is listed as a co-debtor or other interested party on the debts listed in the bankruptcy petition. Besides, you will find out if the debtor(s) were recently divorced, which could mean they received assets in the divorce settlement. If this possibility could exist, notify your attorney at once.

18. Nature, located and name of business

This Item in the Statement of Affairs can become confusing until you learn what qualifies as a business in your state. For instance, if someone had an internet business where they bought and sold items on EBay – most attorneys would not consider this a type of business to be listed on Items 18-25 of the Statement of Affairs. However, some attorneys may consider an internet home business a legitimate business and they may want you to fill in this information. So check with your attorney if you encounter debtor(s) who own a business of any kind and get instruction whether to proceed with filling information into this area of the Statement of Affairs or not.

Summary of the Statement of Affairs

Although I did not cover every single Item listed in the Statement of Affairs, the information I did provide are for Items I normally use on a frequent basis. Of course, you should still print out a copy of the Statement of Affairs form and review it so you will be able to accurately complete the Statement of Affairs for your attorney to review and revise. You may also find that as you are recording information on the Statement of Affairs you may have left something out of the bankruptcy petition and be able to correct it at this initial drafting stage.

Double and triple-checking your work as you progress through the drafting of the bankruptcy petition is essential and extremely necessary. Get into the habit of cross-checking figures and information you enter to make sure they match up on other areas of Forms and Schedules of the bankruptcy petition. This habit will save you, your attorney and the debtor(s) a great deal of time and expense because you will catch everything in the beginning and not after the petition is filed when changes are harder to make.

Form 8: Chapter 7 Individual Debtor's Statement of Intention

This document provides a list of all the secure creditors that were entered on Schedule A and Schedule B of the bankruptcy petition and provides their statement of intention regarding the repayment of the debt. This form is not used in a Chapter 13 bankruptcy because in a Chapter 13 the debtor(s) are making an attempt to pay all or most of their debts — not just the secure ones.

The choices for the debtor(s) Statement of Intention on Form 8 are:

- Property to be surrendered
- Property is claimed as exempt (avoid lien)

- Property will be redeemed pursuant to 11 U.S.C. Section 722
- Debt will be reaffirmed pursuant to 11 U.S.C. Section 524(c)
- Debtor will retain collateral and continue to make regular payments
- Debt to be reaffirmed for fair market value
- Do not list

Your attorney will be able to provide you with the correct statement for the Chapter 7 Individual Debtor(s) Statement of Intention, but this list is provided to give you an idea as to the selections available.

Normally for secure debts like homes and motor vehicles you would select the option of *Debt to be reaffirmed pursuant to 11 U.S.C. Section 524(c)* if the debtor(s) are going to keep their home and motor vehicles. If they are not going to keep the assets you would check *Property to be surrendered.* However, always make sure to review these with your attorney for approval. Always double-check and make sure that every asset with a debt attached to it has a stated intention from the list above if you are drafting a Chapter 7.

Compensation Statement of Attorney

The Compensation Statement of Attorney is a form detailing the attorney fees as well as the filing fees. This figure should match the attorney fee information you provided on Item 9 of the Statement of Affairs. Often the attorney may forget to provide you with this information so you may need to call the office and obtain the figures for this Form. Or better yet, ask for this information when you first accept the work from the attorney.

The format I used under Item 9 of the Statement of Affairs to provide for the attorney fee was:

Recipient: **Fill in the name and address of the attorney**
Date of payment: **(Month and year payment made to attorney)**
Amount of money or description and value of property:
$1,300.00 paid by debtor for representation in this bankruptcy case

Verification of Creditor's Matrix

This one page cover sheet is signed by the debtor(s) and verifies that the Creditor's Matrix is true and correct to the best of the debtor(s) knowledge.

Creditor's Matrix

Every bankruptcy court normally has a special format they require for the Creditor's Matrix so be sure and check the local rules. Or, if you are using Best Case software, the matrix will be formatted automatically for you to the specifications of the bankruptcy court. The Creditor's Matrix is nothing more than a name and address list of all the creditors, co-debtors, collection agencies and other parties listed in the entire bankruptcy petition. This list is used to mail out the notices to the creditors that the debtor(s) are filing bankruptcy as well as serving other internal court functions.

Form 21: Statement of Social Security Number

This form complies with Rule 1007(f) of the Bankruptcy Code which requires debtor(s) to submit a statement under penalty of perjury that they have or do not have a social security number and what that number is. This form is necessary because Rule 1005 requires that the caption of the bankruptcy petition only include the last four digits of the debtor(s) social security number. Form 21 provides the necessary information for the clerk to include the debtor(s) full social security number on the notice of the Creditor's Meeting as required under Rule 2002(a)(1.)

Creditors in a case, along with the trustee and United States trustee or bankruptcy administrator, will receive the entire social security number on their copy of the notice of the Creditor's Meeting. The copy of the notice that goes into the court file for public use will only show the last four digits of the social security number.

Form 22A: Statement of Current Monthly Income/Means Test

Most bankruptcy software programs fill in most of the information on this form when you enter in the other information on the Forms and Schedules of the petition. However, just like the Statement of Affairs, you should print out this form and read it thoroughly so you will know the type of information it contains. (Also, complete the training provided in Chapter 6 of this book which begins on Page 159.

With regard to the Means Test Form, it will help you to better understand current monthly income if you do not view it as *current* or *monthly* or *income.* Rather current monthly income for the Means Test is an **average** of the amount of income earned by the debtor(s) for the **previous six (6) months** including the current month. This total is then compared to the median income for the state and the Means Test is applied to determine if the debtor(s) are eligible to file a Chapter 7 or Chapter 13 bankruptcy.

Whether debtor(s) are allowed to file a Chapter 7 will depend on several factors. If the debtor(s) household income is greater than the state median income for a family of the same size, the creditors, the court and/or the bankruptcy trustee may request that the court dismiss the case due to *abuse* unless the debtor can verify their monthly expenses justify the filing of a Chapter 7 case.

If the debtor(s) adjusted gross income is above the state median income the Means Test then requires another set of calculations to determine if the debtor(s) can afford to file a Chapter 13 and whether that payment will be substantial enough to satisfy the creditors. In order to make this determination a calculation is made starting with the gross income and deducting allowed expenses. If the debtor(s) are left with $100 or more in disposable income this amount is repaid to the creditors. In most cases, the debtor(s) will have to repay a minimum of $6,000 over a period of up to five (5) years through a Chapter 13. If debtor(s) find they fall into this category, their attorney can argue against dismissal of their Chapter 7 or conversion to a Chapter 13 if they can demonstrate *special circumstances* in relation to additional expenses or adjustments to their current monthly income. But even if the income falls below the state median, the court may still dismiss the case for abuse.

The new Chapter 13 bankruptcy law also provides a way for calculating the payment amount for the debtor(s) in their Chapter 13 plan. The monthly disposable income (total income minus allowable expenses) is multiplied by 60 to arrive at the total amount that must be repaid to unsecured creditors. For example, if the debtor(s) monthly disposable income is $100, they must pay $6,000 to unsecured creditors in the Chapter 13 plan. Under the old law, an amount (determined by the attorney) was offered in the Chapter 13 plan and this amount was not always based on the ability to pay. This is one reason why this area of the law was changed so unsecured creditors could be assured of recouping some of their lost monies.

Form 22C: Statement of Current Monthly Income and Disposable Income Calculation

This form must be filed with all Chapter 13 bankruptcy petitions. The mathematical calculations on this form are similar to those in the Means Test and the bankruptcy software should automatically fill it in for you.

Discharge of a Bankruptcy

Before a bankruptcy can be discharged, the new bankruptcy law requires debtor(s) to complete a **mandatory debtor or education course** in personal financial management. This course must be approved by the U.S. Trustee and a list is normally provided to the debtor(s) for them to choose a provider from.

Once the debtor(s) complete this education they will receive an action plan with a certificate. These documents are then filed with the bankruptcy court in order to facilitate the discharge.

If you are interested in finding out more about the debt counseling requirement, a teleconference recording is available on the 713Training.Com website:

1. Sign up for a username and password at https://www.713training.com/administrator/signup.php

2. Once you login, click on *2006 Teleconferences*

3. Listen to the March 9, 2006 teleconference where Richard Mauk was the special guest. Mr. Mauk is a bankruptcy attorney that started his own court-approved debt counseling agency at http://www.cfefa.org/ and he explains the entire process in great detail.

How to Be Alert to Potential Problems as You Draft the Bankruptcy Petition

1. Divorced debtor(s) who report no income

As previously stated, I have personally encountered situations where a divorced woman will fill out their Client Intake Forms, write down that she has no income but report she pays rent, utilities and other living expenses. My first question is: *How can you pay these debts if you have no income?* I often found out it is because they have a live-in partner or roommate who pays the bills for them. It is perfectly okay if a live-in partner is paying the bills while the debtor is unemployed or living on other types of government assistance but the information needs to be reported properly.

In a situation like this, I will list all the normal living expenses on Schedule J. On Schedule I under *other income* I recorded the amount the live-in partner contributes to pay these bills. This will balance out Schedule I and J of the bankruptcy petition and will satisfy the trustee's possible question as to how monthly living expenses are met with no income.

2. Self-employment income of debtor(s)

Another problem you might encounter is when debtor(s) do not list their small business income simply because they didn't file income taxes on the amount they earned. Although we all know it is illegal to not file income taxes if you are earning any type of income, some people still do not report this income because they are barely making enough money to label their enterprise a business.

But what happens if the debtor(s) are no longer able to pay their bills and file bankruptcy? If they report this self-employment income on their bankruptcy petition, will the Internal Revenue Service come knocking down their door and haul them to jail? Very unlikely! All the debtor(s) need to do is go to the IRS website at http://www.irs.gov and download the tax forms for the last two years, fill them out and file their taxes from previous years if they have not done so.

Besides, it is very rare that debtor(s) will owe very much tax if they had a small home business that never made any money. It is very common for home businesses to make less money than they earned, resulting in little or no actual business income. By providing the IRS with a list of their allowable business expenses (which normally offsets the income they actually made) the debtor(s) will normally not be responsible to pay any exorbitant amount in taxes for those years they didn't file. Even if the debtor(s) are required to pay taxes on their self-employment income, the IRS provides an option of making payments on the past due amount. If this type of payment arrangement is made, this figure would then be listed on Schedule E and included in the bankruptcy petition as a priority debt.

3. *Fines, tickets and payments for crimes*

Some people would rather just pay their fines and not reveal this information in a bankruptcy petition. If the fine has been paid in full, it is no longer a debt and does not need to be listed on the petition. However, if all or a portion of the fine is still owed, include these debts as a priority unsecured debt on Schedule E. Then, additional money can be added to the debtor(s) Schedule J allowing them enough money each month from their income to pay those fines. In other words, fines are an allowable monthly expense just like other priority debts.

4. *Amounts owed for uncollected or back child support*

I often found that most people do not want to reveal how much money they are owed by an ex-spouse in back child support. For some reason, the majority of people think the court is going to try and take this money away from them. However, under the new bankruptcy law, all child support is fully exempted.

NOTE: Another excellent change made by the new bankruptcy law is that a bankruptcy will not be discharged if the debtor(s) owe any back child support. Hopefully this will aide in helping ex-spouses to get the money they so richly deserve if their ex-spouse happens to file bankruptcy.

Other Unrevealed Assets and Liabilities

Every time you draft a bankruptcy petition you will learn something new. That is one reason I always found working in debtor bankruptcy so exciting. Every person will bring about a new set of circumstances and over a period of time you will gain the skill of being able to relive the life of a debtor based on the information they provide you.

Also, as you draft petitions you will discover many more situations where debtor(s) are nervous about revealing their assets and/or the bills they owe. I found that in most cases it is not because the debtor(s) are trying to intentionally commit fraud, but rather they do not understand how revealing all their assets and liabilities could actually be a benefit to them. They also normally have no idea of the freedom filing bankruptcy can provide in helping to relieve the heavy burden of debt because their knowledge about bankruptcy was obtained from their friends who are not attorneys.

It will take experience to recognize the pattern of how people think and react in order to more easily identify unrevealed assets and liabilities. I remember when I first started working in bankruptcy; it never entered my mind that anyone would not list all their debts on the debt sheet. I thought that anyone filing bankruptcy would be more than happy to list their debts, especially since they thought the debt would possibly be discharged.

But after I started drafting bankruptcy petitions I discovered many situations where there was a large amount of income left on Schedule I after I deducted the expenses listed on Schedule J. I alerted the attorney and he would contact the debtor(s.) We often found that some people had purposely not listed an automobile or other asset as a debt because they wanted to keep paying for it. We even found some people not reporting certain credit card debts because they wanted to keep *something back* in case of an emergency.

When you learn how the brain of *John Q Public* thinks about bankruptcy, you will be better able to watch out for unrevealed assets and omissions that could have a dramatic impact on the case. But in the beginning when you are less experienced, the best advice I can give you is to question everything. If a piece of information doesn't make sense, write it down and find out the answer. No question is stupid. It is always better to provide the attorney you are working for with more information rather than not enough. And by alerting the attorney you are working for to matters like these, you will become a very valuable asset to the law firm and never need to worry about being unemployed.

Hands-On Workbook Available

Need more training? I developed a separate workbook entitled: *The Virtual Bankruptcy Training Workbook,* ISBN: 09761591-8-X which is available online at http://www.713training.com/workbook/. This workbook is the only one of its kind available at this time. You can use it for self-training in the drafting of a well-detailed bankruptcy petitions.

Using the Client Intake Forms provided in the workbook — you take the information and transfer it to the proper areas in your bankruptcy petition software. After entering the information, print out your draft copy of the completed petition and compare it with the final version included in the workbook. This helps you to immediately recognize your problem areas so you can correct them and learn from your mistakes. Also included are several quizzes along with the correct answers so you can self-test your bankruptcy petition preparation knowledge.

Chapter 6

The Means Test
Training Course

(with computer screenshots)

The Means Test Training Course

What is the Means Test?

Prior to October 17, 2005 the Means Test did not exist in bankruptcy. Instead, the debtor who was filing bankruptcy was permitted to choose whether they wanted to file a Chapter 7 or Chapter 13. Even if the debtor had more income than expenses left over at the end of the month, he or she could still choose to file a Chapter 7 because it was their right as an American citizen. Although the court could dismiss the Chapter 7 after it was filed if there was an excessive amount of money left over to pay debts, the creditors also had the right to object and prevent a Chapter 7 filing after being approved by the Trustee.

Multiply this scenario by hundreds of thousands of people and you have a world filled with mounds of paperwork, as well as loss of time and money for the courts, debtors, attorneys and creditors. These and many other scenarios are what led to the bankruptcy law being changed on October 17, 2005.

Under the new law, instead of allowing the debtor(s) to decide which type of bankruptcy they want to file, the government developed a Means Test. The Means Test will tell the attorney if the debtor can file a Chapter 7 or a Chapter 13 -- not the other way around.

There are two different forms for The Means Test:

1. **Form 22-A** - Statement of Current Monthly Income/Means Test
   This is the Means Test form filed with a Chapter 7

2. **Form 22-C** - Current Monthly Income/Disposable Income
   This is the Means Test form filed with a Chapter 13

The legal definition for the Means Test is:

A formula that uses predefined income and expense categories to determine whether a debtor whose current monthly income is higher than the median family income for his or her state should be allowed to file for Chapter 7 bankruptcy.

The Means Test looks similar to a tax form. You can print out a sample of a Means Test from your bankruptcy software so you will know exactly what the form looks like. Unfortunately many people give it a glance and are immediately intimidated by it. One article I read on the web was written by an attorney. He said The Means Test was a very complicated and hard to understand document. I suppose his statement could be true if he was preparing the document by hand -- but who does that these days? Today we have software programs that do all the complicated compilations for us. All we need to do is enter the figures in the proper areas and the bankruptcy software does 95% of the rest.

The learning curve is in knowing where to place the numbers correctly on the Means Test. Just like tax preparers need to know which line to enter information on when preparing a 1040 tax return, a virtual bankruptcy assistant needs to know which line to enter figures on the Means Test in order for the software to do the correct calculations.

So let's get started learning how .....

Understanding The Purpose of The Means Test

The purpose of the Means Test is to make Chapter 7 debt relief available to those who really need it. For those people who have disposable income available, they are now required to pay back a portion or all of their debt to the creditors; where under the old law they might not have had to.

The actual Means Test can be a very simple test to pass if the debtor(s) fall below their median state income level. If the debtor(s) are below the median income level for their state, the debtor(s) can file a Chapter 7 bankruptcy. Debtor(s) who exceed the median income level may still be able to file a Chapter 7 but they must complete several more steps in the Means Test before qualifying. If the debtor(s) fail the Means Test, they are not prohibited from filing bankruptcy. However, debtor(s) who fail the Means Test cannot file a Chapter 7.

Below are some links to help you advance your knowledge on the Means Test:

- **Median Income by States**
  http://www.usdoj.gov/ust/eo/bapcpa/bci_data/median_income_table.htm

- **Means Testing Information** (provided by the US Trustee Program)
  http://www.usdoj.gov/ust/eo/bapcpa/meanstesting.htm

How Schedule I is Relational to The Means Test

Although every Form and Schedule within the bankruptcy petition is extremely important, Schedule I is one of the most crucial documents as it is also linked to the Means Test. As a virtual bankruptcy assistant you will input the data provided by the debtor(s) from their Client Intake Forms. However, you also need to take the extra step and compare the data to the current and previous six (6) months of paycheck stubs to ensure accuracy. Paycheck stubs (or other verification of income) should have been gathered at the client intake interview by the attorney or the law office staff. If you are working at your home office and you do not have the information, you may need to call the attorney and request this information be faxed to you so you can compare the figures with the information provided by the debtor(s) on the Client Intake Forms. A mistake at this point could cost $1,000s so be very precise with your calculations now to avoid major problems down the road.

Also, don't worry about calculating numbers by hand. Most bankruptcy software programs have a built-in calculator for determining the average income for the debtor(s) over a period of six (6) months. Unlike the old days where we had to drag out a calculator and mathematically figure the amounts by hand, software programs like Best Case are a great time saver.

Be sure to note that prior to the BAPCPA law going into effect, the average income recorded on Schedule I of the bankruptcy petition reflected the **current monthly** amount the debtor(s) earned. But the new law extended this period of income reporting to a full six (6) months regardless if it matches the present income or not. In other words, if a debtor earned an income of $5,000 per month prior to filing bankruptcy but he lost his job and only earns $500 per month now, the $5,000 per month would still be calculated into the average monthly income including the current $500 per month income.

However, if initially the debtor(s) fail the Means Test when basic income information is entered, additional calculations can be performed that may help to qualify them for a Chapter 7. You can somewhat compare this to the difference between a Tax Form 1040EZ and a Tax Form 1040. You can claim more deductions on a Form 1040 compared to the Form 1040EZ.

Perhaps it will help you to better understand current monthly income if you do not view it as *current* or *monthly* or *income.* Rather **current monthly income** is an average of the amount of income earned by a debtor for the previous six (6) months including the current month. This total is then compared to the median income for the state and the Means Test is applied to determine if the debtor(s) are eligible to file a Chapter 7 or Chapter 13 bankruptcy.

Whether debtor(s) are allowed to file a Chapter 7 will depend on several factors. If the debtor(s) household income is greater than the state median income for a family of the same size, the creditors, the court and/or the bankruptcy trustee may request that the court dismiss the case due to *abuse* unless the debtor can verify their monthly expenses justify the filing of a Chapter 7 case.

If the debtor(s) adjusted gross income is above the state median income the Means Test then requires another set of calculations to determine if the debtor(s) can afford to file a Chapter 13 and whether that payment will be substantial enough to satisfy the creditors. In order to make this determination a calculation is made starting with the gross income and deducting allowed expenses. If the debtor(s) are left with $100 or more in disposable income this amount is repaid to the creditors. In most cases, the debtor(s) will have to repay a minimum of $6,000 over a period of up to five (5) years through a Chapter 13. If debtor(s) find they fall into this category, their attorney can argue against dismissal of their Chapter 7 or conversion to a Chapter 13 if they can demonstrate *special circumstances* in relation to additional expenses or adjustments to their current monthly income. But even if the income falls below the state median, the court may still dismiss the Chapter 7 case for *abuse* and the debtor may need to file a Chapter 13.

What Are the Differences Between Schedule I and J and The Means Test?

Although Schedule I and J of the bankruptcy petition are linked to the Means Test, Schedule I and J do have some major differences:

1. Schedule I provides the debtor(s) current income and the Means Test averages out the debtor(s) income over six (6) months.

2. The Means Test excludes all Social Security income, making this income totally exempt (which is good news for the debtor.)

3. The monthly expense categories on Schedule J are different on the Means Test.

4. Schedule J lists the debtor(s) actual monthly expenses while the Means Test uses IRS standards for some expenses and the actual amount for others.

5. Schedule J of the bankruptcy petition allows the attorney more flexibility in listing other types of expenses. However, the Means Test does not allow an unlimited amount of other expenses.

Now, let's move on and actually practice drafting a Means Test.

Getting Ready to Learn

The following tutorial for Means Test training includes screen shots from my particular bankruptcy software program, Best Case. If you use another software the screens should be similar enough that you can still follow along. If you want to download a free demo of Best Case and practice along with this tutorial, you can get a copy at http://www.bestcase.com

The General Tab

The first screen in the Means Test is the General information screen (as illustrated in Screenshot 1.) This form is basically self-explanatory. In most software programs, if you have already entered the debtor(s) information on the Voluntary Petition and Schedule I and J, most of the information on this screen will be filled in for you automatically. But you still need to double-check the following:

1. Debtor Location

This should be the COUNTY and STATE the debtor(s) reside in.

2. Part I: Exclusion for Disabled Veterans

This box is only checked if instructed by your attorney. Otherwise, leave this box unchecked.

3. Martial Status

In most consumer cases you will check either *A* or *D*. *A* is for an unmarried debtor and *D* is for married debtor(s) filing a joint bankruptcy petition. You would only check choices *B* and *C* if the descriptions provided apply. In other words, choice *B* is for a married debtor who is filing bankruptcy without his

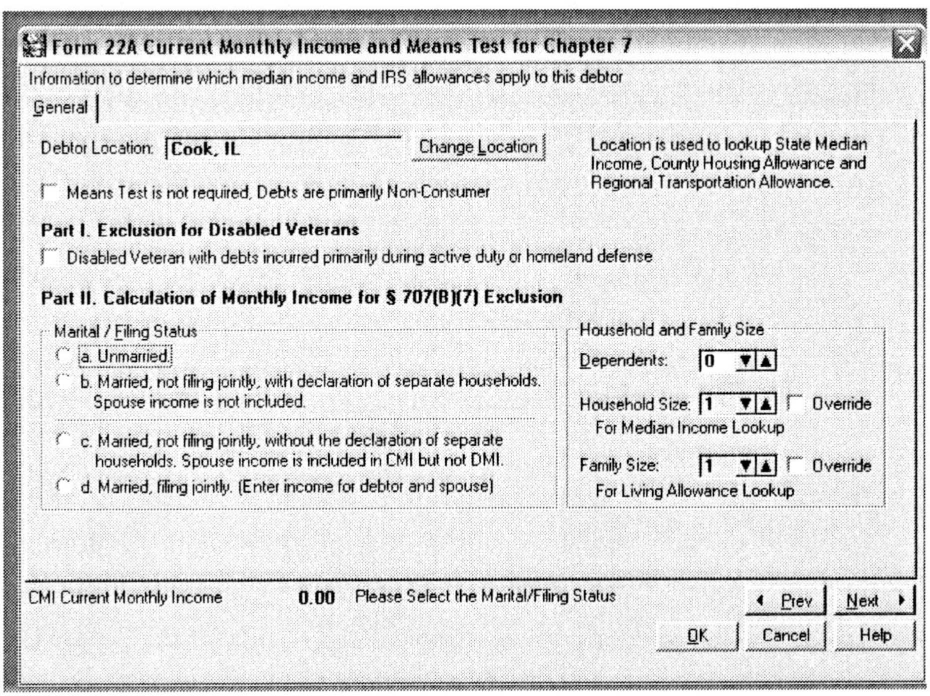

Screenshot 1

or her spouse. Also, choice *B* is only for married couples who are living in two separate households. Choice *C* is just the opposite. It is for married couples who do NOT live in separate households but only one spouse is filing bankruptcy.

4. Household and Family Size

If you have already completed Schedule I for this debtor in your bankruptcy software, this information should already be filled in for you. But if not, type in the correct numbers for the total number of dependents, the total household size and total family size in the proper areas.

The Income Tab

Now we move on to the crucial information. The data you enter on The Income Tab (Screenshot 2) will be the first determination about whether or not the debtor(s) can file a Chapter 7 or a Chapter 13 bankruptcy. Make sure you check and recheck your figures to make sure everything is precise and accurate. A mistake could be detrimental to the lives of the debtor(s) at this point so take your job very seriously. **Don't rely solely on the figures the debtor(s) filled in on the Client Intake Forms.**

The following are some tips to help you enter the correct information on **The Income Tab** (Screenshot 2):

Wages, Salaries, Tips, Bonuses, Overtime, Commissions

Start with the total the debtor(s) earned (before taxes) for the past six (6) months. If the debtor(s) have worked for the same employer during the past six (6) months, this figure should be easy to obtain from a recent paycheck stub. Locate the year-to-date total, divide by the number of months the debtor was paid this year and you have the calculation for the average monthly income. The following is an example:

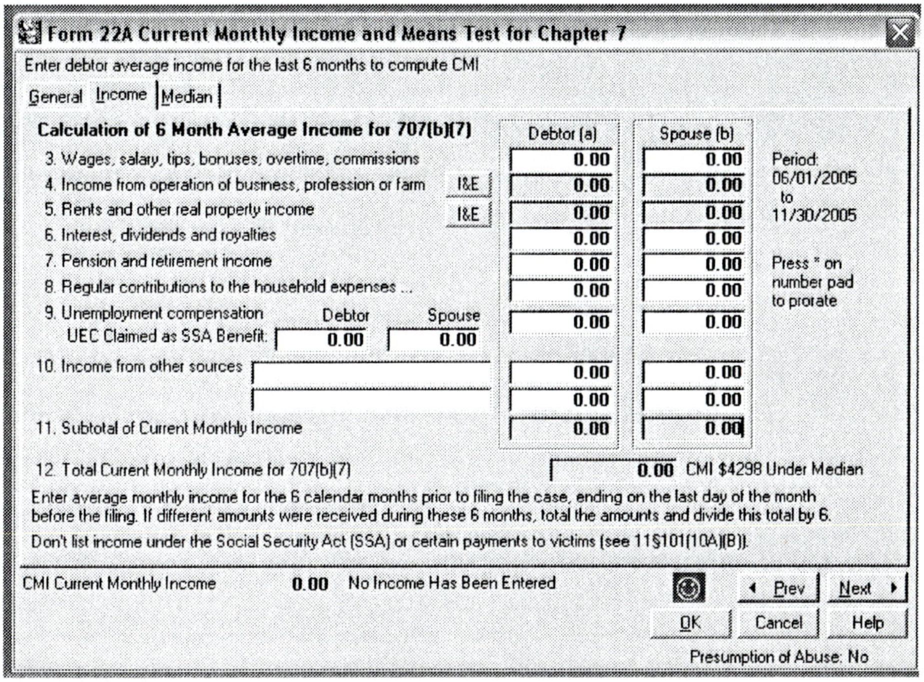

Screenshot 2

Year-to-date income on paycheck stub $17,500
The month is August (the 8th month) so divide
$17,500 by 8 = ... $2,187.50
($2,187.50 is the average monthly income)

Income from operation of business, profession or farm

Income from operation of business, profession or farm applies to any income that was not earned through an employer, such as income earned from a small business, independent profession or income earned from farming. Start with the total earned income for the past six (6) months and divide by six (6) to find the money average for this category.

Rents and other real property

The calculation for **rents and other property** does NOT apply to rent the debtor(s) are **paying** to a landlord where they reside. This is income **earned** by the debtor(s) from property they own and rent out to others.

Interest, dividends and royalties

The **interest, dividends and royalties** income includes interest earned from bank accounts as well as any number of other interest bearing accounts. It also includes dividends from stocks that were paid to the debtor(s) during the past six (6) months as well as royalties.

Pension and retirement income

The **pension and retirement income** is income the debtor(s) earned during the past six (6) months in a pension or retirement plan. It does NOT include Social Security. You may need to help the debtors separate these two figures. Often, debtor(s) may tell you they receive $1,000 in retirement when $800 may be from Social Security and only $200 is the actual retirement income from the previous employer they worked for.

Regular contributions to the household expenses

If a debtor is married, is filing an individual bankruptcy petition, and their spouse earns an income, the spouse's income is used to pay some or all of the household living expenses. **Regular contributions to the household expenses** is the income you would enter on this line of the Means Test. However, if both debtor(s) are filing bankruptcy together, this line would not be used.

Unemployment compensation

The tip here is to make sure the unemployment compensation the debtor(s) receive is not a benefit received under social security. As mentioned earlier, SSA benefits are excluded from the Means Test.

Income from other sources

This calculation would be income received from any other source not already listed. One example of **income from other sources** would be a family member, such as a mother living with her children and the mother pays for her portion of the utilities and telephone expenses.

After entering these figures, the bankruptcy software program will tell you if this debtor is eligible to file a Chapter 7 or not. If the debtor's income falls below the state median, you are finished with the Means Test. However, if the debtor's income is above the state median, you will need to continue and enter in additional calculations.

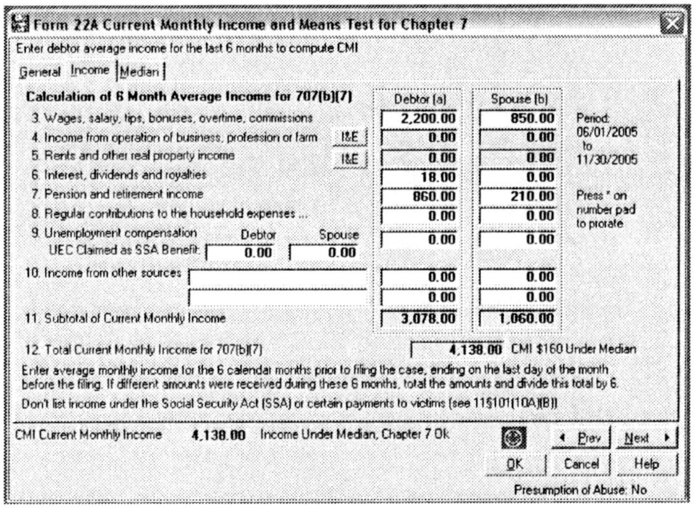

Screenshot 3

Note: Screenshot 3 shows an example of a debtor with a income that falls BELOW the state median and qualifies to file a Chapter 7:

Screenshot 4 shows a sample of two debtor(s) who are $1,774 over the median income and bankruptcy *abuse** is therefore presumed. At this point you should notify your attorney. Allow the attorney to instruct you whether to proceed with the Chapter 7 Means Test or draft a Chapter 13 for the debtor(s) instead. If instructed by your attorney, you would complete the Means Test for a Chapter 13.

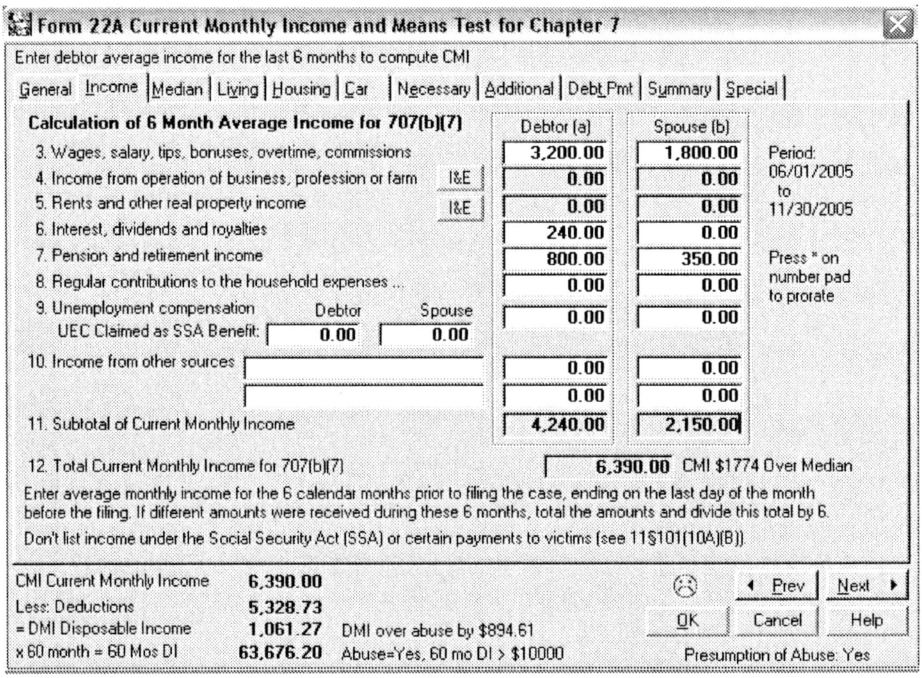

Screenshot 4

Note: Try not to become alarmed with the use of the word *abuse.* In this case it is referring to the 2005 Bankruptcy Abuse Prevention and Consumer Protection Act (BAPCPA) itself. So use this term only within the confines of discussions between you and your attorney. Avoid using it when working directly with the debtor(s) as it can be taken the wrong way and they may become defensive.

The Median Income Tab

Screenshot 5 shows the Median Income screen. The Median Income screen is the information you would provide to your attorney in order for him or her to know how this particular debtor should be advised in the filing of their bankruptcy. This screen also contains other important information you should be aware of such as:

Median family income

This is the amount of **median family income** designated by the federal government. The attorney can use it to determine how much the debtor(s) are over their allowance.

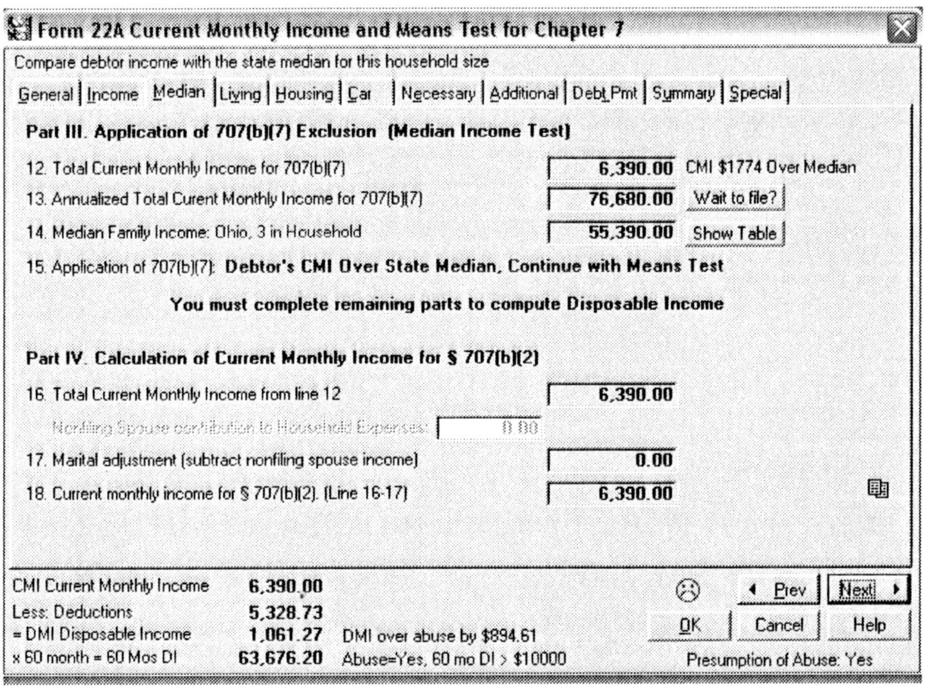

Screenshot 5

The **Wait to File** button (located on the far right of Line 13) may also be helpful to the attorney because it shows how much less the debtor would need to earn per month if they waited from one to six months to file bankruptcy.

Also the **Martial Adjustment** line of this form is useful if the debtor is married, not living separately from their spouse, but the spouse is not filing bankruptcy with his or her spouse. This adjustment will remove the portion of the spouse's income which is not used to pay for household expenses.

The Living Tab

Most bankruptcy software programs will automatically enter in the IRS standard allowances for living expenses on this particular screen (see Screenshot 6), including the allowable clothing, food, housekeeping, personal care and miscellaneous living expenses. For these items you will need to leave these totals at the IRS standard amounts no matter what the actual amounts are that are listed on Schedule J of the bankruptcy petition. Remember, you are working with the Means Test which is qualifying the debtor(s) for a particular Chapter of bankruptcy they are eligible to file under. The actual Schedules within the bankruptcy petition will provide the factual information on this particular debtor.

The only adjustment you may be required to make on this particular screen (as a virtual bankruptcy assistant) would be to select the proper income bracket the debtor(s) fall under. You do this by selecting the proper box under the **Income Level Source for IRS Living Allowance.** The IRS has eight (8) different income brackets for determining allowance expenses. The amount the debtor(s) are allowed to spend on these living expenses is determined by his or her income bracket and family size.

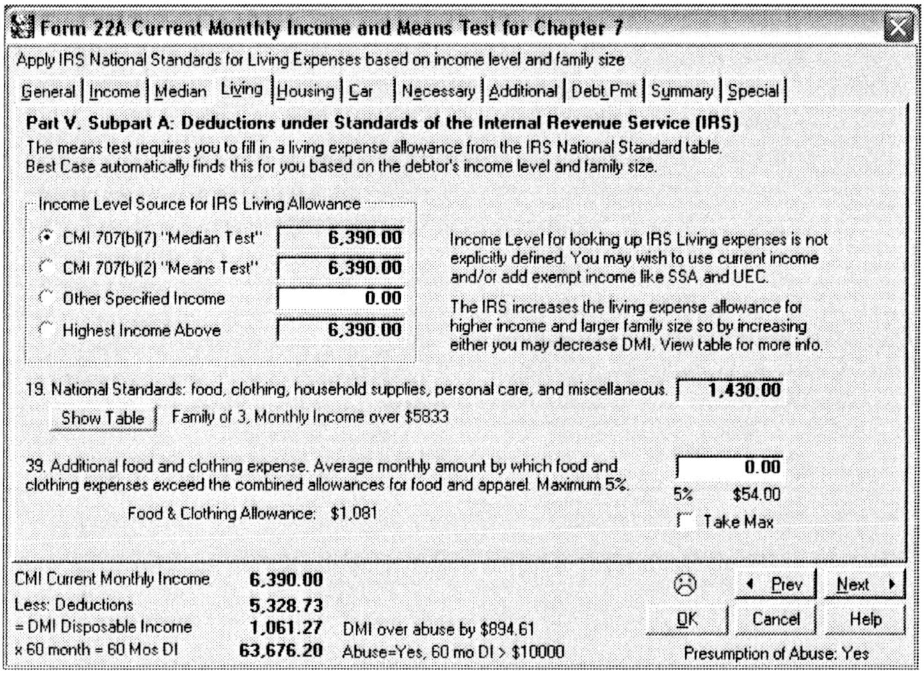

Screenshot 6

The Housing Tab

In Screenshot 7, Line 20A is the IRS Housing and Utilities allowance for **non-mortgage** expenses. You cannot adjust this figure. It is determined by the county in which the debtor(s) reside as well as the size of their family.

Line 20B is the IRS Housing and Utilities allowance for **mortgage and rent** expenses. While the IRS does not allow for adjustments on the Means Test for non-mortgage expenses, the BAPCPA law does provide that the FULL mortgage or rental expense is necessary for the debtor(s) to maintain their property. Therefore, this amount may be adjusted.

In the Screenshot 7 example, the IRS allowance is $913.00. If the debtor(s) mortgage payment is only $740.00, the $740.00 figure will be used on

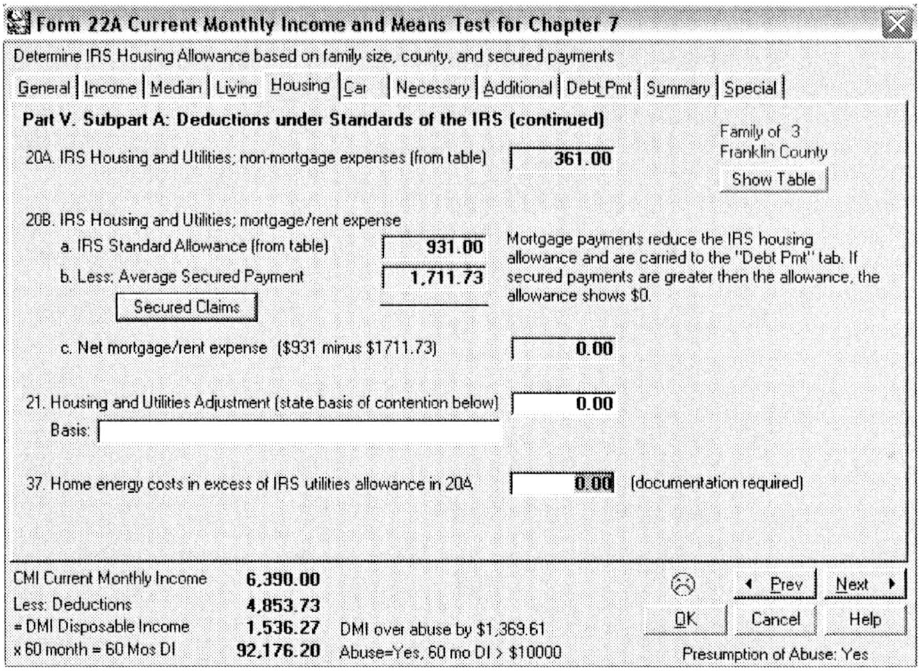

Screenshot 7

the Means Test. However, if the debtor(s) mortgage payments are more than $913.00, the Means Test calculation will show $0.00 on Line C under 20B.

To make this calculation in Best Case software, you would click on the **Secured Claims** button under Line 20(B)(b.) Select the debt for the mortgage payment (of course you should already have filled in Schedule A and B of the bankruptcy petition before doing this.) Next, you will see another screen where you fill in the required information such as the mortgage and escrow payments, total amount of payments the debtor(s) are behind, number of months left to pay off the mortgage, etc. Once this screen is completed Best Case fills in the rest of the information on the Means Test for you automatically.

On Line 21 of Screenshot 7 you will find the line for Adjustments. This line should be filled in only when directed by your attorney. While the IRS has split expenses into two categories: (a) non-mortgage; and (b) mortgage for purposes of the Means Test, the attorney may contend that the IRS allowance does not allow the debtor(s) to deduct the full amount to which they are entitled. In this case, the attorney may enter a housing and utility allowance on Line 21 and provide his or her basis for this contention in the text box area provided.

Line 37 is relatively easy to complete. If the debtor(s) can provide documentation that they pay more than the allowance the IRS provides for utility expenses, the adjustment can be entered on this Line of the form. The documentation could be copies of utility bills over a six (6) month period or copies of canceled checks payable to the utility company.

The Car Tab

In Screenshot 8 you will see the figures I entered for a hypothetical debtor. Your figures of course will be different.

Line 22 asks you to select the number of vehicles the debtor(s) pays transportation expenses for. The software should automatically calculate the IRS allowance. The IRS has two types of allowances; (1) an allowance for operating costs; and (2) an allowance for car payments. The operating allowance is based on the region of the country where the debtor(s) live. The allowance for the car payments is based on the national average and the number of vehicles the debtor(s) own or lease. At the present time that average is $475.00 for the first car and $338.00 for the second.

But what if the debtor(s) pay more than $475.00 per month for their car payment? No problem. The new BAPCPA law allows the debtor(s) to deduct the entire payment regardless of what the IRS limits are. This is because the new law

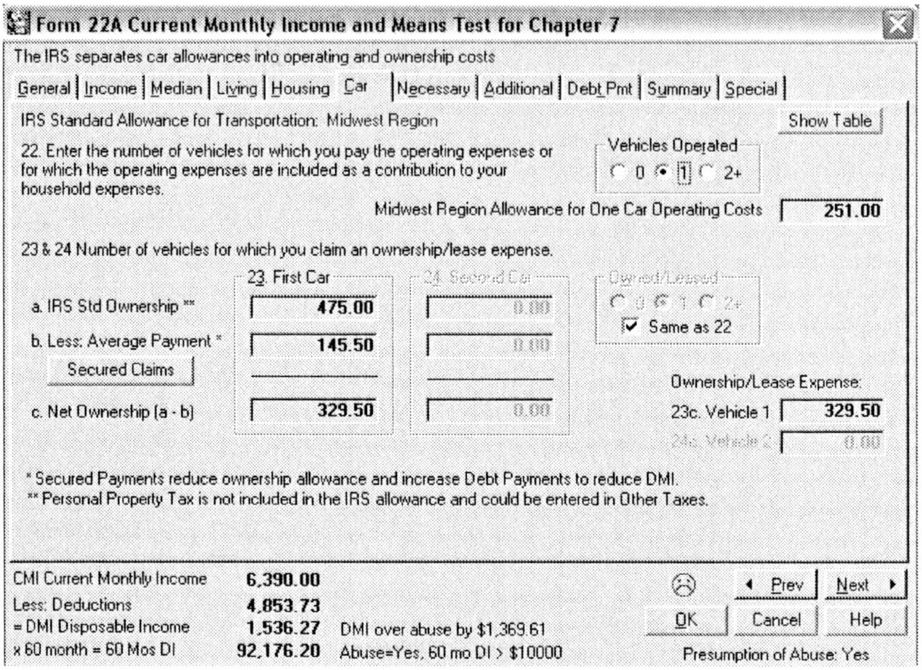

Screenshot 8

states that debtor(s) are *allowed to deduct from disposable income, all secure payments contractually due in the next 60 months, even if the payments exceed the IRS allowance.* However, because the debtor(s) are not permitted to *double-dip* (a term used by the court) as the amount of car payments increase over the national average, the debtor(s) IRS transportation allowance will be reduced.

What if the debtor(s) car payments are **less than** the national average which is currently $475.00? Good news! The debtor(s) still get credit for $475.00 in the Means Test and will be able to reduce their disposable income by the difference between the car payments and the allowance.

For example; suppose John Doe pays $194 per month on his 2003 Kia Rio car. He still has 45 months left to pay on the car.

$194 x 45 = $8,730

The car ownership allowance is currently $28,500 (60 months x $475) so John Doe is far below the IRS allowance. If we subtract $8,730 from $28,500 we obtain a result of $19,770 for 5 years or $3,954 per year. John Doe is able to take the $19,770 reduction from his disposable income even though he is not really paying out this money. Because of this reduction, some people may be able to qualify for a Chapter 7 when they normally would not.

Another fact you need to remember about the Means Test is that car payments are averaged out over a period of 5 years or 60 months. Most bankruptcy software programs has a built-in calculator that will provide this figure once you enter in the amount of the car payment and the months remaining to pay the car off. In other words, John Doe paid $194 per month for his car and he had 45 months left to pay it off. For the Means Test, the $194 needs to be averaged out over 60 months instead of 45 months. The calculation would look like this:

$194 x 45 = $8,730
$8,730 divided by 60 = $145.50
$145.50 is the monthly average for the Means Test

What if the debtor(s) do not own a car? They will then receive a public transportation allowance. Most bankruptcy software programs will fill in this allowance for you automatically and in most cases, you do not need to enter any additional information.

What if the debtor(s) own a car but their car is paid off? They will still receive the standard IRS ownership allowance. Even if the car is leased, the debtor(s) still receive this standard ownership allowance regardless of the amount of the lease payments and the remaining months left to pay on the lease.

The Necessary Tab

In Screenshot 9 you will see a screen for **necessary expenses.** You simply enter the total **monthly** expenses for these items. These expenses include:

Taxes

Federal, FICA, Medicare, state and local taxes, personal property tax

Because you entered the gross salary of the debtor(s) before taxes were taken out in Screenshot 1, here is where you enter them again so they are properly deducted and reflect the true *take home salary* of the debtor(s.) You also can include personal property taxes with this calculation such as taxes on cars, etc. But you CANNOT include real estate taxes since these are considered to be part of the Housing Expenses - not Personal and Necessary expenses.

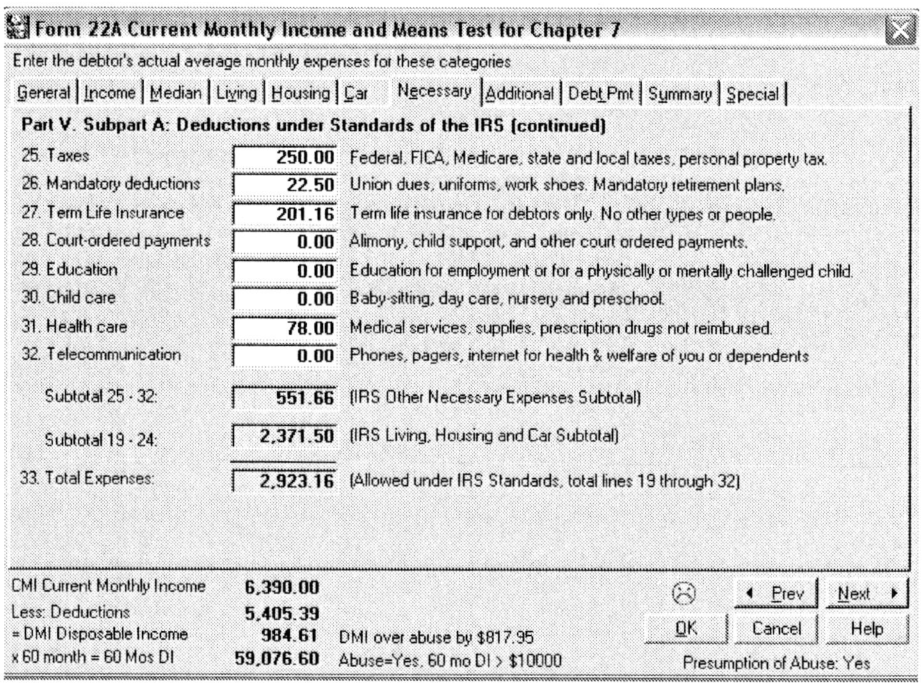

Screenshot 9

The remaining expenses should also be entered in based on monthly averages. These remaining expenses are:

Mandatory deductions
Union dues, uniforms, work shoes. Mandatory retirement plans.

Term Life Insurance
Term life insurance for debtor(s) only

Court-Ordered Payments
Alimony, child support and other court-ordered payments

Education
Education for employment or for a physically or mentally challenged child

Child Care
Babysitting, day care, nursery or pre-school

Health Care
Medical services, supplies, prescription drugs not reimbursed

Telecommunication
Phone, pagers, internet for health and welfare of debtor(s) or dependents

The Additional Expenses Tab

Screenshot 10 shows a sample of the Additional Expenses screen. As you will see, it is self-explanatory. The allowable Additional Expenses such as health and disability insurance, care for the elderly, chronically ill or disabled, etc. are listed for you. But if any of their expenses fall under Items 37, 38 and 39, the debtor(s) will need to provide documentation to the Trustee that verifies these expenses are reasonable and necessary.

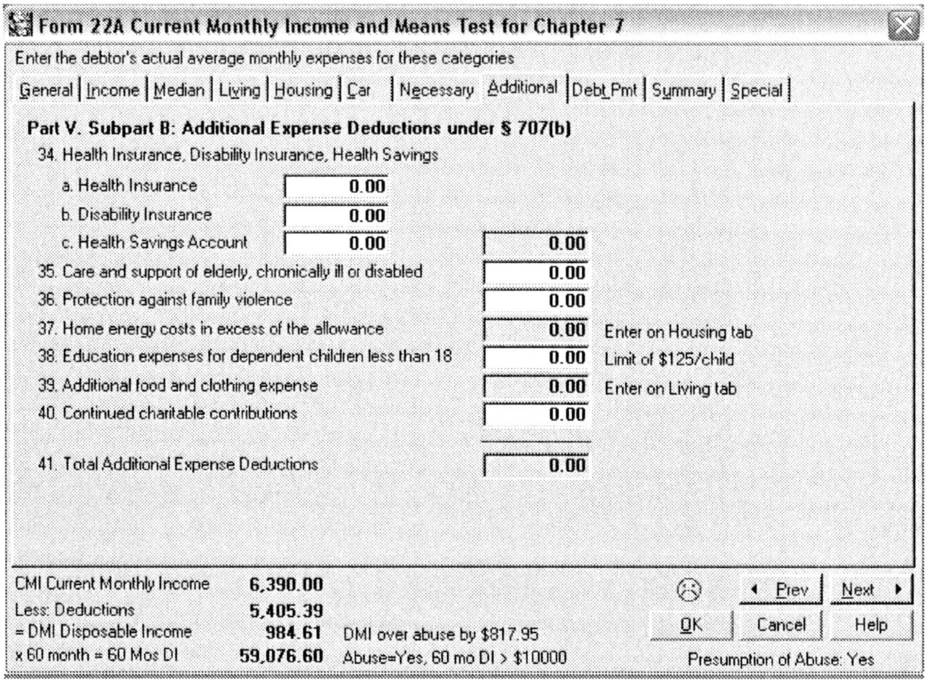

Screenshot 10

The Debt Payment Tab

In Screenshot 11 you will find the screen where you enter debt payments that are deducted from the debtor(s) income. I have typed in a few numbers to use as an example on Screenshot 11, but remember that your figures will be different.

The new BAPCPA code allows the debtor(s) to deduct the following types of debt payments from their disposable monthly income:

- Secure debts that will be due and payable within the next 60 months. This figure is then divided by 60. Normally these are expenses such as the mortgage, car payments and secure debts and they are included on Schedule D of the bankruptcy petition.

- Past due payments owed on secured real or personal property that are necessary for the debtor(s.) This total figure is then divided by 60. Again, these payments are normally for expenses such as the mortgage, car payments and other secure debts.

- Priority claims are also divided by 60. Priority claims are listed on Schedule E of the bankruptcy petition.

- Administrative expenses that are projected in a Chapter 13 case. How would you know what the projected payment could be in a Chapter 13 case? You wouldn't. Your attorney needs to provide you with this information. Best Case will perform the calculation (as most software programs do) but the attorney will need to provide you with the projected monthly Chapter 13 plan payment as well as the multiplier for the debtor(s) particular district. Some software programs even have the multiplier built-in, but you still need to obtain direction from the attorney you are working for to make these calculations.

As previously mentioned, most bankruptcy software programs fill in the information on Screenshot 11 automatically for you when you enter the information in the actual bankruptcy petition. This does not mean that you should ignore the information provided above; but instead, make sure you understand where the figures come from and how they are calculated whether the computer does them for you or not. Knowing more than the computer knows is what makes you a professional with a higher level of skill than the average person. This unique quality is what sets you apart from the crowd and enables you to become more successful in your business.

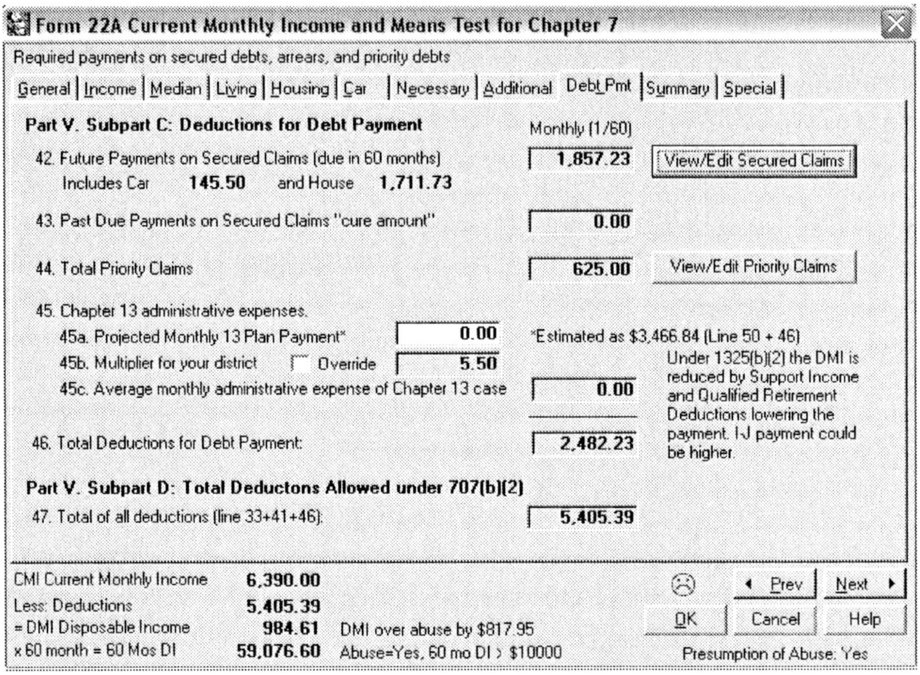

Screenshot 11

The Summary Tab

In Screenshot 12 you will find the information included on the Summary Tab of my Means Test software program. Of course these figures are only hypothetical. The Summary screen is exactly what its name implies - a Summary screen. This screen provides you with the final calculations in determining whether the debtor(s) may file a Chapter 7 or a Chapter 13 bankruptcy petition.

As you can see, this screen lists the debtor(s) income as well as the allowable deductions. These figures are then calculated using a 60-month projected plan. If the disposable income (income left over after expenses are paid) for the next five (5) years is less that $6,000, the debtor(s) can file a Chapter 7.

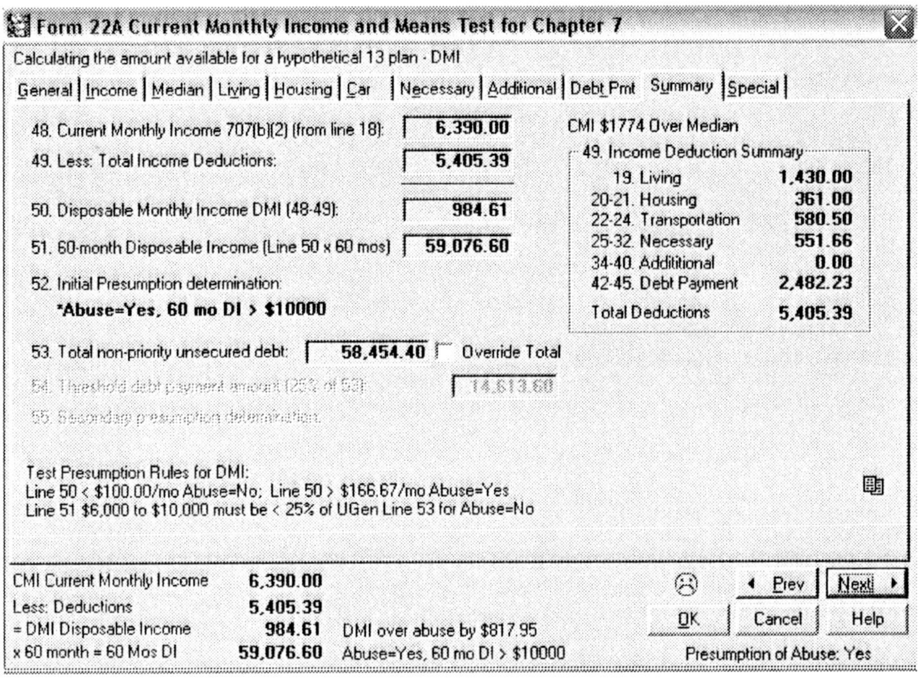

Screenshot 12

However, if this disposable income figure is $10,000 or more, the debtor(s) may or may not be eligible to file a Chapter 7. Only your attorney will be able to make this determination based upon other factors.

But what happens if the debtor(s) five-year disposable income is between $6,000 and $10,000? Then the Means Test will look at the amount of unsecured non-priority debt (Schedule F.) If there is enough income left over to pay at least 25% of these unsecured non-priority debts, the debtor(s) will probably need to file a Chapter 13.

Just remember (regardless of whether you know or not) if a debtor is eligible to file a Chapter 7 or Chapter 13 bankruptcy, it is a violation of unauthorized practice of law to tell the debtor. The only one who has the authority to tell any debtor(s) which chapter of bankruptcy to file will be the attorney, or if the attorney asks you to relay this information to the debtor. In this case you would say something like: *Mr. Debtor, Attorney Jones asked me to inform you that the Means Test revealed that you are not eligible to file a Chapter 7.* In other words, always make the consumer debtor aware of who is providing the information so they will know the difference between actual legal advice and your non-attorney opinion.

The Special Tab

The final screen in the Best Case software Means Test is the Special Tab as shown in Screenshot 13. As shown on this screen, the debtor(s) may list any additional allowable expenses that have not been provided for previously in the Means Test. What are these allowable expenses? This is a question but can be answered by 11 USC, Section 707(b)(2)(A)(ii)(i) of the Bankruptcy Code:

> *The debtor's monthly expenses shall be the debtor's applicable monthly expense amounts specified under the National Standards and Local Standards, and the debtor's actual monthly expenses for the categories specified as Other Necessary Expenses issued by the Internal Revenue Service for the area in which the debtor resides, as in effect on the date of the order for relief, for the debtor, the dependents of the debtor, and the spouse of the debtor in a joint case, if the spouse is not otherwise a dependent. Such expenses shall include reasonably necessary health insurance, disability insurance, and health savings account expenses for the debtor, the spouse of the debtor, or the dependents of the debtor. Notwithstanding any other provision of this clause, the monthly expenses of the debtor shall not include any payments for debts. In addition, the debtor's monthly expenses shall include the debtor's reasonably necessary expenses*

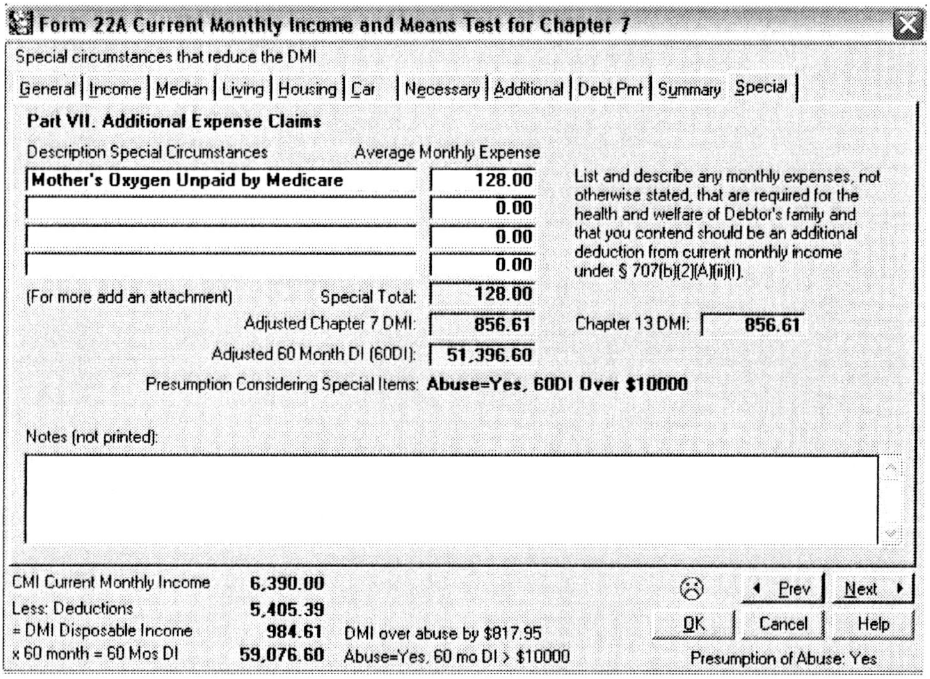

Screenshot 13

incurred to maintain the safety of the debtor and the family of the debtor from family violence as identified under section 309 of the Family Violence Prevention and Services Act, or other applicable Federal law. The expenses included in the debtor's monthly expenses described in the preceding sentence shall be kept confidential by the court. In addition, if it is demonstrated that it is reasonable and necessary, the debtor's monthly expenses may also include an additional allowance for food and clothing of up to 5% of the food and clothing categories as specified by the National Standards issued by the Internal Revenue Service.

And what is the definition of **Necessary Expenses** according to the National Standards issued by the Internal Revenue Service?

> *Necessary Expenses are the allowable payments you make to support you and your family's health and welfare and/or the production of income. This expense allowance does not apply to business entities. Our Publication 1854 explains the National Standard Expenses and gives the allowable amounts. We derive these amounts from the Bureau of Labor Statistics (BLS) Consumer Expenditure Survey. We also use information for the Bureau of the Census to determine local expenses for housing, utilities, and transportation.*
>
> Ref: http://www.irs.gov/businesses/small/article/0,,id=104598,00.html

To research more, request Publication 1854 from the IRS. Go to the main website at http://www.irs.gov/ and type *Publication 1854* in the search box. There is no charge for this publication and you can download it from the internet in PDF format. However, remember to keep your attention focused on gathering the proper information for your attorney and leave the rest of the *legalities* up to him or her. There are times when arming yourself with too much information can become confusing during training.

Means Test Summary

- The Means Test is simply a way to determine if the debtor(s) have enough income to file a Chapter 13 or don't have enough income and are eligible to file a Chapter 7.

- If the debtor(s) have a low income, passing the Means Test will probably be very quick and easy. You will simply enter a few figures into the software and you are done.

- When the debtor(s) have enough income left over to pay all or a portion of the debts you will need to enter in additional calculations for the Means Test to determine if these debtor(s) can file a Chapter 7 or not.

- Most bankruptcy software programs fill in the majority of the Means Test calculations for you if you have filled in the information on the Forms and Schedules of the actual bankruptcy petition.

Additional Means Test Study Materials

Once you learn how to properly prepare a Means Test for your attorney, your skills will be in high-demand. Working in law firms for many years I know that attorneys do not enjoy doing mundane work such as drafting bankruptcy petitions and calculating Means Test figures. They normally give this work to their secretary, paralegal or someone else in the office. But if you harness the knowledge of understanding the Means Test, you will have a high-level skill that many people working in the legal offices do not have at this time. In other words, this skill will put you far above the competition and it will be a skill in high-demand by attorneys nationwide.

My first suggestion is to download a free demo copy of Best Case software at http://www.bestcase.com and practice using the training in this chapter. Fill in some bogus figures and play with different calculations to see how the Means Test calculates figures.

Next, advance your knowledge with the following materials:

Article from U.S. Department of Justice
http://www.usdoj.gov/ust/eo/bapcpa/meanstesting.htm

NARCA Legislative Alert - Senate Bill 256 - Summary
http://www.collectlaw.com/lawsandarticles.htm

Summary of the BAPCPA of 2005
http://abiworld.net/newsletter/financialadvisors/vol2num3/summary.html

Chapter 7 Means Test Questions and Answers
http://www.nacba.org/ubb/chicagofaqc73.asp

Free Bankruptcy Ezine to Subscribe To and Read Previous Issues
http://www.bankruptcymedia.com/bkfinder/pastissues.html

Bankruptcy Books, Software and Periodicals
http://www.bankruptcybooks.com/

You can also do your own research online regarding bankruptcy but be sure the books you purchase are updated for the new BAPCPA law. Because many books take up to a year before they are available for purchase you may run into many of them and purchase the wrong material.

But remember not to not allow yourself to become so overwhelmed with Means Test research that it takes you away from your focus as a virtual bankruptcy assistant. While it is good to know how the Means Test calculations are done and the type of information you need to type in the software for the Means Test to perform an accurate calculation, I suggest you leave the study of the actual bankruptcy law to the attorneys and paralegals. Unless your desire is to one day become an attorney, deep study of the bankruptcy law is not a requirement for a virtual bankruptcy assistant to do their job.

Chapter 7

Advanced Tips and Techniques for
Virtual Bankruptcy Assistants

Advanced Tips and Techniques for Virtual Bankruptcy Assistants

In the first part of this chapter I will cover the procedure for signing up with PACER, the Chapter 13 Network and paralegal organizations. Next, I will cover some of the frequently asked questions from virtual bankruptcy assistants who are new to this field. Finally, I will end the chapter with an overview of the commonly used bankruptcy pleadings you may encounter as a virtual bankruptcy assistant working in the debtor arena. In addition, I will include information about foreclosure procedures and repossessions so you will have a better idea of how to handle questions from debtor(s) who are faced with these situations.

Signing Up with PACER

PACER, (which is an acronym for *Public Access to Court Electronic Records*), headquartered in San Antonio, Texas, is the national online case system. To sign up to access the system go to http://www.pacer.psc.uscourts.gov/register.html. Registration is free and you do not need to be an attorney to request a username and password.

PACER enables you to search the bankruptcy court's website for case information and important deadline dates as well as keeping up-to-date on any Objections that may be filed against the debtor(s.) Keeping attorneys updated on Objections that are filed by the creditors against the debtor(s) is an added service you can provide as part of your virtual bankruptcy assistant services. All you do is log in to your PACER account, do a search for the debtor(s) by last name and look at the case history. If you find an Objection that has been filed, you can click on the link and view the actual court document. Print this out and fax it to your attorney (or call them on the telephone) and ask for further instruction. Once the attorney gets comfortable with your work, he or she may have you draft an Answer to the Objection. Normally this requires you to pull up a template (provided by the Attorney) and you fill in the pertinent details about this case. If you find yourself in a situation where the attorney has asked you to draft an Answer to an Objection, do not hesitate to let them know that this is your first pleading so they can walk you through the simple process. If you don't speak up and ask for training in this crucial area, you could embarrass yourself by guessing.

Signing Up with the Chapter 13 Network

The Chapter 13 Network is another online case lookup system but your attorney must register in order to obtain a username and password. Once the attorney obtains a username and password, they will provide it to you so you can use the Chapter 13 Network to work with their clients. This web search system will allow you to obtain more detailed information on debtor(s) who have filed a Chapter 13 bankruptcy petition compared to the information available on PACER. You also can look up payments made by the debtor(s) as well as payoff amounts and other pertinent information. Like PACER, the Chapter 13 Network will also save you a great deal of time.

To sign up, your attorney must obtain a username and password from the U.S. Trustee of his or her local bankruptcy court. The Chapter 13 Network is a service hosted by Bankruptcy Software Specialists, LLC. BSS is the nation's leading provider of Bankruptcy Software and Services to Chapter 13 Trustees and the Chapter 13 Network website can be accessed online at www.13network.com/.

Joining a Paralegal Organization

Should you join a paralegal organization? Some virtual bankruptcy assistants do not know they can join their local paralegal and bar association even if they are not a paralegal. Instead, you would join as an *Associate Member.* Your yearly membership fees will be less but you will not be able to vote or sit on the Board. And since most virtual bankruptcy assistants are not interested in voting or becoming Board Members anyway, joining as an *Associate Member* makes perfect sense. This way, you get the benefit of the meetings, training classes and networking opportunities at a lower membership fee. Also, at this time of this writing, you need to be aware that paralegal regulations are being debated among the different organizations in all 50 states. You should know about this existing controversy in order to make a decision whether to join an organization at this time or not.

To give you a little history lesson: Back in 1979 when I started working for attorneys, I do not remember the term *paralegal* existing. As far as I know, there also was no formal training offered for paralegals back then. Instead, our job titles were either *secretary* or *legal secretary.* We typed dictation from handwritten notes and only a small number of us actually got involved with cases and aided our attorneys in the capacity paralegals do today.

As the legal secretarial field grew, our job duties were increased and we were given more responsibility by our attorneys. Debtor(s) appreciated the money they saved by paying the paralegal hourly rate for routine duties that the attorney used to perform. Attorneys also appreciated delegating these routine tasks to legal secretaries under their direction so they could concentrate more on their legal strategy and other higher-level legalities of the case.

Around the beginning of 2000, I began hearing the paralegal organizations discuss whether the job title of a legal office staff member (who was performing more responsible duties) should be considered a *paralegal* or *legal assistant.* At first, I paid no attention to these rumors because I could have cared less what my job title was. I just wanted to receive fair pay for the level of duties I performed regardless if my attorney called me a *secretary* or not.

On the surface, the subject sounded like a silly waste of time to many paralegals I interviewed. Even if a decision was reached to use the job title *paralegal* instead of *legal assistant* do you really think attorneys will use the word? I don't think so. Do you really think personnel departments will reprint all their job descriptions if they have the words *legal assistant* inserted instead of *paralegal* in the job title? I don't think so. Unless the job title of *paralegal* pays more or less in your law firm compared to the job title of a *legal assistant*, who really cares? In fact, in some law firms the attorneys still refer to their paralegal/legal assistant as a *secretary* but the work they perform is the same as a paralegal/legal assistant.

It was at this time that I decided to investigate and find out what was at the root of this matter. In my mind, the issue did not make sense. I knew there had to be more to it than just deciding on a job title. To begin, I first asked myself, *Why, all of a sudden, is there an interest in a specific job title?* Paralegals and legal assistants have been around since the first attorney passed the bar over 200 years ago. I finally discovered the answer: Paralegal regulation is at the core of this entire movement. Since paralegals were trying to pass laws regulating paralegals, they wanted one job title. Two job titles would only complicate the issue.

The Major Paralegal Organizations

At this time there are three national organizations for paralegals:

1. The National Federation of Paralegal Associations (NFPA); http://www.paralegals.org/
2. The National Association of Legal Assistants (NALA); http://www.nala.org/
3. International Paralegal Management Association http://www.paralegalmanagement.org/

This poses an interesting problem. Let's suppose the term *legal assistant* was chosen over the word *paralegal.* Would one of these organizations close down, or would they merge into one? Wouldn't a drastic change like this effect thousands of paralegals across the United States, some negatively and some positively? What would be the result of all these changes?

I then turned my research to the non-legal *secretarial* world. As you know, in the non-legal world there are job titles such as: *executive assistant, administrative assistant, secretary* and *office manager.* All have specific job descriptions and most are paid a different salary based on their level of responsibility. Only in the legal world do we have two words that describe the same job: *paralegal* and *legal assistant.* It is interesting to note that at http://www.legalstaff.com, Legal Assistant Management Organization is listed under *paralegal* organizations. For those of you supporting the need to waste time arguing about this issue, shouldn't this be a warning flag for you?

So if paralegal regulation is at the core of this problem and the words *paralegal* and *legal assistant* are only necessary to form one job title for regulation purposes, why is there so much controversy over the issue? Let's examine the issue about paralegal regulation.

California paralegals were the first to experience a state law regulating paralegals; however at the time of this writing the state of Washington is opposed to paralegal regulation and feels that regulating paralegals will interfere with the lower fees the general public pays for simple document preparation. While those in favor of paralegal regulation state: *The driving force behind a legislature to take action to license a profession is the health, welfare and safety of the public. . . .*
I personally believe the mission goes much deeper than that.

I called and interviewed 16 California paralegals about the difference in their jobs before and after the new paralegal regulation laws went into effect. Only two of the paralegals said it made no difference in their current jobs, but 14 said they were very disappointed concerning how paralegal regulations had interfered with simple jobs they used to perform. In bankruptcy for instance, some California paralegals were actually prevented from doing a simple client intake interview, which costs the attorney more time and increases the legal fee the debtor(s) pay. Many jobs that once were performed by paralegals and billed at the paralegal rate now must be performed by the attorney and billed at the higher attorney rate. As you can see, what may have begun as a way to *protect the general public* has resulted in higher legal fees and less job interaction for the paralegal/legal assistant.

How Can You Find the Paralegal Regulations for Your State?

Because the regulations for paralegals differ from state to state and they change almost overnight, locating the regulations for your state may be an impossible task. The best way to find out more about paralegal regulations in your area is to visit the websites of the national paralegal organizations. Dig into the websites and locate the contact information for the specific chapter in your area and contact your local paralegal organization.

In some instances you may need to join the organization to obtain copies of the current paralegal regulations and in some cases, the local organization will be happy to mail you a copy. But in other situations, the regulations may still be at the initial stage of development. By joining an organization in your area right now, you could have a voice in changing minds of decision-makers about certain paralegal regulations you disagree with.

Aside from possibly having a voice in the changing paralegal regulations, these organizations are also an excellent resource for keeping you up-to-date on legal issues that affect the paralegal. So I urge you to join a chapter in your area and network with other paralegals to improve your skills and knowledge.

Frequently Asked Questions from Virtual Bankruptcy Assistants

QUESTION: Can you tell me what you are advising virtual bankruptcy assistants regarding the new forms the attorney have to sign, certify and disclose as to the fee certification and *sharing of fees?* I am seriously thinking of starting this type of business but this one thing really bothers me. I do not want to find out *down the line* that it is something that can no longer be done. I have been drafting bankruptcy petitions for many years. I asked an attorney regarding this issue. He concurred that it would be the same as *fee sharing* which is prohibited by law. He suggested I talk to the U.S. Trustee in our District about it but I wanted to bounce it off you first. Thank you for your time and response. -- Carol

ANSWER: Thank you so much for submitting this question. I had an attorney in Michigan raise this same question back in 2001 when I was operating my virtual bankruptcy assistant service. Regardless of how much I explained to him that his client(s) do not pay me. Instead, they pay the attorney and the attorney pays me for a clerical service; he still was not convinced. However, when he checked with the Michigan Trustee as well as the actual interpretation of the law as to what the term *sharing fees* actually meant - he found that hiring an independent virtual bankruptcy assistant is the same as hiring a temporary office worker or an independent court reporter.

Where the violation of *sharing fees* would come into play between an attorney and a virtual bankruptcy assistant would be if the virtual assistant solicited clients to hire and retain the attorney, then the attorney would share his or her attorney fee with the virtual assistant based on the referral. Simply assisting an attorney in any type of office related duties and getting paid as a clerical worker has no relevance to *sharing fees.*

QUESTION: If I am a freelance virtual bankruptcy assistant, would I be required to obtain such documents like the deeds or car titles, etc., or would I just be responsible for completing the bankruptcy forms as thoroughly as possible, taking the information from the client intake forms? --Emma

ANSWER: My first thought is *why* would you want to skip a very important task that rarely takes more than 10 minutes of your time? Also, why would you jeopardize the bankruptcy petition and the information it contains? Going online to the county website and doing a simple search for judgments, foreclosures, etc. is essential in finding hidden debts in order to protect the debtor as well as your attorney from possible litigation and/or additional paperwork later down the road. Additionally, you need to obtain a current market value of all vehicles for Schedule B of the bankruptcy petition and this information is easily and quickly located on the Kelly Blue Book or NADA websites. In other words, you cannot draft a thorough bankruptcy petition without the information you obtain from an online search of your local courthouse records.

You have the ability to run your business in any way you want Emma. But if you continue to only do half of your job and draft petitions for attorneys that cause them headaches and additional work, you will lose business and gain some very unsatisfied attorney customers.

QUESTION: Will the new bankruptcy law prevent people from filing bankruptcy? --Lori

ANSWER: Of course not. This rumor was started before the new law went into effect and during the time that negotiations were still being made before implementation. According to Steven Rhodes, a Chief United States Bankruptcy Judge, he states in an article dated September 20, 2005: *...although the means test was undoubtedly intended to be the primary substantive change in Chapter 7, the early analyses of those who have studied it in depth suggests that it may not have much substantive impact on the availability of Chapter 7.*

(Ref: http://www.fbamich.org/index.cfm?location=154&ParentID=156)

So for those of you who heard the rumor that Chapter 7 filings would become obsolete, please understand that it was only a rumor. Although it is too early to tell the exact percentages of increase in the filings under the new law compared to the old law - rest assured that Chapter 7 filings will still alive and well and it is in your best interest to continue your training in this arena.

QUESTION: I cannot believe it. I am listed in the Nationwide Bankruptcy Directory on the www.713training.com website and today I received a call from an attorney in another state. The attorney asked me if I could draft some petitions for her under the old law because her office filed several skeleton petitions prior to the law change and they only have 30 days to get the rest of the petition filed. I told her that I only drafted petitions under the new law. Was I wrong for turning work away? --Farah

ANSWER: Yes dear - you were very wrong. You should NEVER turn work away from your business. Business owners should always remain flexible and customize their services to the needs of their customers. As you are aware, there are very minor changes in the new bankruptcy forms compared to the old ones so you already have the knowledge to draft petitions under the old law. You could easily have made $1,000s of dollars helping the attorney to clean up during the transition. I urge you to call the attorney back and try to help them. Then remember never to turn down work in your field of business again.

QUESTION: Are you experiencing any major problems with the bankruptcy petitions under the new bankruptcy law? --Barbara

ANSWER: I have currently processed two bankruptcy petitions that have been filed in court under the new law. But the other four bankruptcy petitions are being held because the attorney did not instruct the client(s) to go through the required credit counseling. I highly urge anyone who prepares bankruptcy petitions for attorneys to NOT start a petition until the credit counseling requirement has been met. If you do, and it takes 30 days or more for the client(s) to complete the class, you will have to go back and update all the numbers. Rather than risk missing one and making a mistake, do not start the petition until the client has completed the credit counseling class.

Do You Have More Questions?

The virtual bankruptcy assistant field is not for everyone. That is why I encourage you to ask as many questions as you want before you decide whether to start a virtual bankruptcy assistant service or not. Below are links on the 713Training.Com website that can help provide more answers to your questions:

- **The Free Teleconference Ezine**
  https://www.713training.com/subscribe.html

- **Weekly Bankruptcy Teleconferences**
  http://www.713training.com/teleconference/

- **Power Marketing Seminars**
  http://www.713training.com/seminars/

- **Free Online Help Form**
  http://www.713training.com/help.html

Outline of Some Commonly Used Pleadings

What is a pleading? It is a document filed with the court to request an action be taken or an answer to a request made by the opposing party. As a virtual bankruptcy assistant you may never be asked to draft pleadings. But as mentioned before, if the attorney you are working for gives you more responsibility, you may be asked to draft a pleading. Therefore, it would be a good idea to understand the most common ones used in consumer bankruptcy filings.

Of course, it would be impossible for me to cover every type of pleading you may encounter working in the debtor area of bankruptcy law. Not only do pleadings vary in style and language, they also must be customized to fit the unique situation of the debtor(s.) As a virtual bankruptcy assistant you should ask the attorney which pleading he or she wants you to draft and they should provide you with a template to use. Make sure you save this template for future use and begin compiling your own pleading files that are in compliance with the state and federal laws for the attorneys you are working for.

After drafting the pleading, do not be upset if the attorney returns it to you with several changes. I have found that the attorney always made changes to the pleadings I drafted before they were filed with the court — so don't worry if your pleadings are not perfect the first time. Besides, as a virtual bankruptcy assistant you are only permitted to prepare a *draft* not a *final* document. It is much easier for an attorney to have a draft to start with rather than preparing a pleading from scratch. If you learn how to do a good job in this area, you could earn an excellent second income from pleading preparation alone.

Below are some of the pleadings I drafted when I worked as a bankruptcy paralegal and some tips I learned for preparing them.

Answer to Trustee's Motion to Dismiss

This pleading was drafted if the bankruptcy trustee decided to dismiss the bankruptcy case for any reason. The attorney would file an Answer to this Motion if he or she had good cause to disagree with the Trustee. For instance, my attorney had a debtor who was in a Chapter 13 Plan and she was behind on her payments. The trustee filed a Motion to Dismiss and my attorney contacted the debtor. We found out that the debtor had lost her job but now had the money to pay back all the arrearages in the plan plus her regular Chapter 13 plan payment. I drafted an Answer to the Trustee's Motion to Dismiss that explained the amount the debtor was willing to pay in order to bring her Chapter 13 plan payments current. The Answer was filed and the trustee withdrew his Motion.

Amendment to Schedule F

I could quote the exact wording in this pleading because I drafted so many of them. As you already know, Schedule F of the bankruptcy petition lists all the unsecure debts. What will often happen is that the debtor will go home and a new bill will arrive in the mail they forgot to include in their bankruptcy petition. If the bankruptcy petition has already been filed but the bankruptcy hearing has not occurred, you would draft an Amendment to Schedule F to add on the additional debt to the bankruptcy petition. (See Page 202 for a sample of an Amendment to Schedule F.)

SAMPLE

UNITED STATES BANKRUPTCY COURT
SOUTHERN DISTRICT OF OHIO
EASTERN DIVISION

In Re:	:	Case No. 06-12345
	:	Chapter 7
John Jay Debtor	:	Judge Smith
SSN: 123-45-6789	:	
	:	
Mary Sue Debtor	:	
SSN: 234-56-7890	:	
Debtor(s).	:	

AMENDMENT TO SCHEDULE F
CREDITORS HOLDING UNSECURED CLAIMS

The Debtor Amends Schedule F to add the following creditor, as described below:

CREDITOR	DESCRIPTION	AMOUNT
My Hospital 123 Main Street Dublin OH 43016	Medical bill Date of debt: 02/2006	$2,017.65

Respectfully submitted,

____

Angie Lawyer (068773)
Attorney for Debtor(s)
Street Address
City, State, Zip
(000) 000-0000

continued

SAMPLE (continued)

CERTIFICATE OF SERVICE

The undersigned certifies that a copy of the foregoing was served upon (Trustee's name and address goes here); (other parties of interest and their attorney's name and address goes here) U. S. Trustee, (address of your local U.S. Trustee); this _____ day of ____________, 20___, by regular, postage pre-paid, U.S. Mail.

____
Angie Lawyer (068773)
Attorney for Debtor(s)

If the 341 hearing has already occurred and this is a Chapter 13 case, the Amendment to Schedule F would serve as the exhibit to an Amendment to the Chapter 13 Plan. (This is the procedure we used in Ohio so check with your attorney to make sure you follow the procedures required by that state's bankruptcy court.)

Motion for Relief from Stay

A Motion for Relief from Stay (hereinafter referred to as "MFRS") is filed by a creditor who is asking the bankruptcy court to lift the bankruptcy stay so they can repossess the item(s) the debtor(s) owe them for. When I worked for a brief period of time in the creditor bankruptcy arena, we cranked these pleadings out by the hundreds. As soon as we received a Notice from the bankruptcy court that a debtor filed bankruptcy we immediately drafted a MFRS and filed it with the bankruptcy court.

A copy of the MFRS was mailed to the debtor(s) attorney and answered normally within 28 days. In some cases, a creditor may file an *expedited* MFRS which will force the debtor(s) attorney to answer these pleadings within a few days. Therefore, the best thing to do when a virtual bankruptcy assistant is aware a MFRS was filed in a case - is to make it top priority. If the attorney delays in his or her Answer to the Motion, the debtor(s) could lose their home, cars, household goods or whatever secure item(s) they possess.

Make sure you look at the *due date* for the Answer and mark it on your attorney's calendar if this is part of your job. I suggest that you increase the Answer date by three days on the calendar so you can always make sure the MFRS is answered before the actual due date. For instance, if the Answer to the MFRS is due by June 15, mark it as due on your attorney's calendar by June 12. This way, if another emergency comes up you still have time to file the Answer on June 13.

Some MFRS's do not need to always be answered. For instance, if the debtor(s) are surrendering their home, car or other possessions, the creditor will still file a MFRS so they can repossess the item(s.) This is common procedure. A copy should be mailed to the debtor(s) so they will have a copy for their files. In your cover letter to the debtor you may want to explain that this document is a common procedure that creditors follow in order to repossess their item(s.) Since the debtor(s) have decided to surrender the property, a response from the attorney may not be necessary. However, if the debtor(s) are still residing in the home they are surrendering, they should be looking for a place to move to rather quickly since the MFRS will normally be granted by the trustee and the repossession will be scheduled with the Sheriff's office unless an Answer is filed or a Hearing scheduled.

Application to Incur New Debt

A Chapter 13 normally lasts from three to five years. During that period of time anything could happen. For instance, if a debtor wants to purchase a new car, home or even a television that they will be making monthly payments on, the Chapter 13 Plan may need revised to allow enough extra money to pay this debt. In a situation like this, the debtor(s) will need to get permission from the court to make the purchase and their Chapter 13 plan payments may be adjusted if permission is granted.

However, I found that many Chapter 13 debtor(s) never think about asking the court for permission to change their Chapter 13 plan. Instead, they will purchase the item on their own and within a month or two realize they are having trouble making their Chapter 13 plan payment.

It might not be a bad idea to provide all the Chapter 13 debtor(s) with a booklet of information. Clearly point out that if they decide to create another debt while they are in the middle of their Chapter 13 plan to notify the attorney at once. If you tell them there may be the possibility their plan payment could be reduced (depending on the situation) they may be more cooperative in alerting the attorney before making the purchase. This will save everyone a lot of time and money.

Note: I am not suggesting in any way that you mislead the debtor(s) about the possibility their Chapter 13 plan payment could be reduced. As a virtual bankruptcy assistant you should *never* make statements like this, so make sure you use words like *could* and *possibly* instead of making direct statements when you are backed into a corner by debtor(s) to provide them with some type of response. In fact, there could be the possibility the debtor(s) Application to Incur New Debt could be denied. But if you present the issue to the debtor(s) in a manner that could be a possible benefit to them, they will cooperate more fully than if you say something like: *You cannot make any purchases until you check with the attorney first.* This statement sounds threatening and may cause the debtor(s) to not report anything affecting their case until it is too late or the case is dismissed for non-payment.

Motion to Convert

Several times I have encountered situations where a debtor starts out in a Chapter 13, but he or she loses their job and converts to a Chapter 7. When debtor(s) called the office and told me they were unable to make their Chapter 13 plan payment because they lost their job, the first thing I asked them is *when* they expect to start working again. If it appears they expect to be out of work for more than 90 days I inform the attorney and the attorney often directed me to draft a Motion to Convert.

The Motion to Convert can work the other way around also. In some situations a debtor may file a Chapter 7 bankruptcy but during the process they find a job and can afford to pay back all or a portion of their debts. Of course, the bankruptcy court as well as the creditors prefer to have a debtor pay back their debts and will gladly welcome a Motion to Convert From a Chapter 7 to a Chapter 13 in most cases.

Objection to Proof of Claim

The Objection to Proof of Claim is filed by the attorney representing the debtor prior to a 341 Meeting of Creditors. In some cases, it is filed after the hearing depending on the claim due date set by the bankruptcy court. The purpose of the Objection is to deny the claim or reduce the amount the creditor provides as being due and payable.

Summary of Pleadings

The pleadings I covered in this chapter only reflect the pleadings I personally used on a consistent basis. Your experience may be different because every pleading is unique to the case, just like every bankruptcy petition is unique and different. If the attorney you are working for wants you to start drafting their pleadings for them, the attorney will provide you with a template so you will have something to start with. The template will normally be in MS Word format and be emailed to you as an attachment. The template will contain the case heading style that is acceptable in the bankruptcy court your attorney practices in. You will fill in the names of the debtor(s), case number, judge's name, type of chapter this bankruptcy is for in the case heading area. Then you will proceed with the drafting of the pleading. Or, some attorneys still prefer to dictate their pleadings. Perhaps your attorney will provide you with a tape that you will transcribe and type into the pleading template he or she provides to you. Regardless of the procedure, make sure you customize your services to the needs of the attorney you are working for. Every attorney is unique and each one will have their own style and flair of doing things. Be sure and learn how to be adaptable, personable and eager to please. If you do, you will greatly succeed in this business.

Where Can I Find Pleading Samples?

If, after reading this information, you are curious about what pleadings look like and how they are used in bankruptcy, login to your PACER account, look up a case and review the case history. When you locate a pleading that has been filed in the case, you should be able to click on the link and see the actual pleadings that was filed. PACER will charge you 7¢ per page if you print out the pleading, but this is a small price to pay for training. If you buy a legal form from a company it will cost you $10 or more. Besides, pleadings used in consumer bankruptcy are often impossible to find.

Foreclosure Procedures

Foreclosures, repossessions and replevin actions are essentially the same thing. A foreclosure normally refers to a collector obtaining possession of *real* property. A repossession normally refers to a collector obtaining possession of *personal* property and a replevin normally refers to a collector obtaining possession of a *mobile home.*

The following are the procedures I performed in a replevin action at the creditor bankruptcy law firm I worked for back in 2001:

The Complaint is Filed

Before a creditor or mortgage company can begin the procedure of taking possession of a debtor(s) mobile home, they file a Complaint, Motion and Affidavit with the Common Pleas court in the county where the personal property is located. A copy of the debtor(s) signed contract and title were attached to the Complaint to verify the mortgage company had the right to repossess their home. The debtor(s) received a copy of these documents when they are filed, which is called *serving the Complaint.*

A Hearing Notice was also enclosed, allowing the debtor(s) five days to request a hearing to dispute the debt. Of course, most debtor(s) never requested a hearing because they knew they owed the money, but requesting a hearing could delay the repossession process because the court will schedule a hearing date in which the debtor(s) will appear and state their side of the story. The judge normally granted the Motion in favor of the creditor unless the debtor(s) could prove the debt or the amount owed was not accurate and the replevin action continued.

Because Complaints are served by the court by certified mail with personal service and the debtor(s) must be properly served before the process can continue. Some debtor(s) would purposely not accept certified mail thinking it would *buy them more time.* However, the opposite was always true. If good service cannot be obtained by certified mail, the Sheriff may be dispatched to serve the Complaint in person, which could be embarrassing for the debtor(s.) Ordinary mail service may also be performed by the creditor by filing a *Praecipe* with the Clerk of Court. If the post office did not return the piece of mail, the court considered this to be notice of proper service.

After proper service of the Complaint was completed, an Order was sent to the judge for his or her signature. Once the Order was signed by the judge, the mortgage company began the process of actually repossessing the mobile home.

Filing Bankruptcy After Service of Complaint

I found that most debtor(s) become very frightened when they were served a copy of the Complaint. Many of them would rush into the bankruptcy attorney's office and ask the attorney to file their bankruptcy petition immediately so they were not rendered homeless. When I worked on the debtor side of bankruptcy, I tried to keep the debtor(s) calm by reassuring them that just because they received a Compliant in the mail today, it does not necessarily mean they will be set out on the street tomorrow. Even after the Complaint is filed, the debtor(s) have five days to request a hearing and an Order still needs to be filed and signed by the judge. This should give the debtor(s) bankruptcy attorney enough time to properly prepare the bankruptcy petition and put a temporary stop to the replevin or foreclosure process while the debtor(s) have time to reorganize their debts.

However, some debtor(s) I encountered received a Complaint and waited weeks or even months before they scheduled an appointment to see the bankruptcy attorney. I don't know why people tend to do this, but if you work in the debtor arena for awhile you will see this pattern occur quite frequently. A situation like this makes your job as a virtual bankruptcy assistant working on the debtor side much harder because you must push everything aside and make it a top priority to gather the intake information and properly draft the bankruptcy petition for filing in a short period of time. I have worked many nights at the office until midnight drafting petitions for debtor(s) who waited until the day before their home was going to be sold at a Sheriff's sale just to save their home. If only the debtor(s) would have come in when they first received the Complaint life would have been so much easier. But we don't live in a perfect world, do we?

However, the filing of a bankruptcy petition will immediately put a stop to the replevin or foreclosure procedure. This is because the creditor may eventually be able to repossess the property but will not be entitled to a money judgment since the debtor(s) filed bankruptcy. This causes the creditor to refile additional paperwork with the court in order to proceed with the replevin or foreclosure action. This will help the debtor(s) to *buy some time,* especially if they are planning to surrender the home and get rid of the debt entirely. Of course, this is advice that only the attorney can provide to the debtor(s) but it is good information you need to know as a virtual bankruptcy assistant.

Overview of the Foreclosure Process

Repossessing a mobile home is different from foreclosing on real property (real property is anything attached to *God's green earth.*) That's because a mobile home is considered to be *personal* property. It is easy for a truck to hook up the mobile home, repossess the item and return it to the creditor, but that would be impossible to do for an actual home attached to a piece of land. Instead, real property must be sold and the title removed from the debtor(s) name.

Aside from filing a Complaint and all the other required documents, the foreclosure procedure for real property also involves posting a notice in the newspaper, allowing time for bids and finally setting up a time for the Sheriff's sale. If payments have not been met to satisfy the creditor, the Sheriff will deliver a notice giving the debtor(s) a period of time (normally 30 days) to vacate the property. At this point, the debtor(s) should have a place to move to or money to pay all the past due payments, late fees and extra added-on charges.

Although Sheriffs have been known to physically enter the home and set the furniture and all other contents outside on the lawn in order to repossess the home, I only witnessed this happen on two occasions. Debtor(s) normally have an adequate period of time and are notified by the court several times before this moment occurs. But there are some debtor(s) I encountered who refused to move after being given this *grace period.* In this type of situation, the Sheriff has no other choice but to comply with the court Order and remove them and their belongings off the property.

How Long Does the Foreclosure Process Take?

Because every mortgage company's collection procedures are different, it could take from two to nine months for the entire foreclosure process to be completed and the debtor(s) ordered to move from their home. While it is not suggested that anyone live *rent free* in their home until the last minute before the Sheriff sets them out on the street, if the debtor(s) are severely behind in their mortgage payments and cannot afford to keep the house, their attorney may advise them to use this short period of time to save their money for a down payment on a rental and to move as quickly as possible.

What if the Debtor(s) Want to Keep Their Home?

If the debtor(s) are severely behind in their mortgage payments and the replevin or foreclosure process has already begun, it was very doubtful the mortgage company would consider reaffirming on the debt if the debtor(s) filed a Chapter 7 bankruptcy. That is why the attorneys I worked with advised the debtor(s) to file a Chapter 13, which is a repayment plan. This way, debtor(s) may be able to keep their home and pay off the arrearages over a three to five year period. As long as the Chapter 13 plan is approved by the bankruptcy trustee, the mortgage company must accept the terms and allow the debtor(s) to remain in their home.

Also, there is a possible alternate solution called **Foreclosure Mediation.** This is normally done through a third party who negotiates for the bankruptcy attorney in reinstating the mortgage loan. A **Foreclosure Mediator** I interviewed said that he works with bankruptcy attorneys on a consistent basis. He normally can reinstate a loan by reducing the arrearages and lowering the interest rate. In most cases, the **Foreclosure Mediator** received a fee payment of 75% of the attorney fees. Most attorneys, he said, charged $1,000 for the service and he made $750 for a simple 15-minutes phone call.

However, learning this skill requires knowledge of the real estate and mortgage industry as well as effective sales-oriented skills. But for some people who are good at **Foreclosure Mediation,** they earn an excellent income.

Repossessions

Not all motor vehicles and household goods being repossessed involve the same type of documents required in the replevin or foreclosure action for a home. A repossession company can drive their tow truck out to the debtor(s) home, hook up the motor vehicle and repossess it without notice. When household goods are repossessed, normally a Sheriff or police officer will accompany the collector who has obtained permission from the court to repossess the item(s.) It is a very frightening situation for most debtor(s) to answer the doorbell and watch as their belongings are carried away. Then, after the repossession has taken place the creditor will normally file a judgment to obtain the amount of money still owed on the item(s) after they are sold.

For example: Mr. Doe's 2001 Chevrolet Celebrity is repossessed by the creditor. A total balance of $14,000 is still owed on the car. The creditor sells the car to a dealer for $8,000 and then seeks a money judgment against Mr. Doe for the remaining $6,000 still owed. Add another $1,000 to this total for the repossession charges, attorney fees and court fees and the debtor(s) have a debt of $7,000.

When Mr. Doe files bankruptcy this debt now becomes *unsecure* since the car is no longer in his possession. It is listed on Schedule F of the bankruptcy petition. If Mr. Doe files a Chapter 7, the entire $7,000 debt may be discharged by the trustee, or if Mr. Doe files a Chapter 13, he may only have to pay a portion of the $7,000 because the debt is treated as an unsecure, non-priority debt.

Chapter Summary

As I said before, you may or may not be involved in drafting pleadings or following through with cases acting in a paralegal capacity. But it is very helpful to familiarize yourself with different areas of bankruptcy so you can do a better job in the drafting of your bankruptcy petitions. Too often today, I find people who only know how to do one specific job. They never question what effect their job has on the industry as a whole. I believe it is very important to reach out and learn exactly how the work you do effects others as well as the operation of the entire organization. Knowing this information will ensure that you do a better job and the quality of your work will stand out from everyone else. These are skills that push you ahead in the world and you will ultimately become more successful than most people.

Chapter 8

Marketing and Growing Your Virtual Bankruptcy Assistant Service

Marketing and Growing Your Virtual Bankruptcy Assistant Service

Marketing is something that most people think begins after they have developed their product or service, purchased their beginning supplies and have reached a point where they need to make money. But this is not true! Marketing should begin the moment you give birth to your company.

I hear so many people say: *I am not a marketer.* But I wasn't either. Believe me folks, I was not born with the ability to build successful companies. I failed many times, but they were not failures; only mistakes that taught me great lessons. But regardless of what I tell people, they still call me a *marketing guru* and think I wave some magic wand and everything works the first time out.

This theory is only fantasy land folks. It doesn't work that way in the real world. When the majority of people decide to start their first business, they have heard over and over (1,000s of times on television infomercials) that they can order a start-up business kit and immediately make $60,000 a month or some astronomical figure. Therefore, the mind of the general public has been programmed to believe that anything that is <u>not</u> easy to do is not worth their time. But spend a few minutes talking to business owners in your own neighborhood. It won't take you long to find out that owning, operating and marketing a business is not always a *piece of cake.* The infomercials lie!

It is also important for you to not look at marketing as actually going out and getting customers for your business. Marketing is everything that makes up your day-to-day business. The way you answer emails, post your website on search engines, write a letter, talk on the phone or anything you do related to your business requires marketing skills. So if you want to own and operate your own business that you control, you need to learn how to love and enjoy marketing. Once you see how fun it can be your whole world will change.

As I stated before, marketing is not simply going door to door selling your service. Instead it is everything you do that works together to eventually sell your product or service. Below are the titles of three books I highly recommend that you purchase if you are starting your first business. These books are not about the notary business or bankruptcy business. In fact, they are not specific to any one type of business. Marketing is marketing regardless of which industry you are working in. But if you learn what works and doesn't work in marketing, you can apply that same skill to any business you own as well as many facets of your own personal life.

The books I highly recommend are:

- **Start Your Own Business: The Only Start-Up Book You'll Ever Need,** Author: Rieva Lesonsky, ISBN: 1932156658

- **What No One Ever Tells You About Starting Your Own Business: Real Life Start-Up Advice from 101 Successful Entrepreneurs,** Author: Jan Norman, ISBN: 0793185963

- **Small Time Operator,** Author: Bernard B. Kamoroff, ISBN: 0917510224

Also, go to any search engine and type in the words: *small business marketing.* Buy a few books or videos about the topic of marketing for small businesses. And this category can even be broken down even further. There are millions of small businesses, however your *type* of small business is a *home business.* Also, this category can be broken down even further. A virtual bankruptcy assistant is a home *service* business. So make sure the books and videos you purchase are specifically for marketing a home *service* business. Spend some time educating yourself with the basics. This crucial and important step will pay for itself a million times. You may not be making money with the information you are learning right now – but you'll make a lot of money in the future because you took the time to obtain this basic marketing education.

How I Built The Lawyer Assistant - the first online virtual bankruptcy assistant service

The Lawyer Assistant was the first company I ever started that I did not plan to start. That is because I originally started a business called *Bankruptcy Paralegal Services* (later changed to *Bankruptcy2Go.*) As I briefly discussed in the Introduction of this book, *Bankruptcy Paralegal Services* was a company dedicated to providing non-attorney bankruptcy petition preparation services to *John Q Public,* or people unable to afford an attorney. But I was forced out of business by the local bankruptcy court which led to the development of *The Lawyer Assistant* – a company that became one of the first companies on the internet to provide electronic forms processing services to bankruptcy attorneys nationwide.

Note: I would like to thank the bankruptcy trustees who filed complaints against me when I owned *Bankruptcy Paralegal Services.* Although I did not realize it at the time, if they had not filed any complaints I would have never changed my business from a consumer-related service to a business that served attorneys nationwide and provided a better income for my company.

My story begins back in March 2000 (just after the Y2K scare of 1999.) The bankruptcy attorney I was working for on a part-time basis decided to try an experiment. I would stop working in the office and instead process bankruptcy petitions from my home office. The attorney believed that taking the petition preparation work out of the office environment, the office would become less chaotic and result in more detailed bankruptcy petitions. He also believed that by paying me on a *per job* basis versus an hourly wage, he would save money.

During the experiment, I discovered that I could easily draft 15 petitions in a weekend compared to only 4 petitions if I worked in the office (due to constant interruptions). I also found that most clients were home in the evening and on weekends and I could quickly get answers regarding incomplete information on the Client Intake Forms without *playing telephone tag.* By making a simple 10-minute phone call to the client, the attorney determined that this reduced the phone calls to his office by 85% and his clients were more relaxed and cooperative talking to me versus the attorney. Happy clients make for easier and smoother bankruptcy filings and this effect spilled over into many more benefits for the office staff as well as the attorney.

My attorney and I continued the experiment for several more months and the results continued to improve. In fact, the attorney found he had more free time and was able to take a day off every week. He also noticed that his profits had increased by 50% in a short period of only 3 months. The experiment proved to be a great success!

This experiment also gave me a great idea. I decided to design a website and offer petition drafting services nationwide. But when I started researching on the internet I could not locate anyone drafting petitions for attorneys. All I found were *petition preparers* who prepared bankruptcy petitions for the general public. So I followed in this direction and the first company I started online was called *Bankruptcy Paralegal Services,* a name that was considered a violation of UPL but I didn't know it at the time.

Bankruptcy Paralegal Services is Born

In August of 2000, I started *Bankruptcy Paralegal Services.* There were very little overhead costs to start this company. I paid $10.99 for the domain name registration and a $7.99 monthly internet hosting fee though Bummer Hosting. I had most of all the office supplies I needed because the attorney had provided me with a desk, office chair and computer software. Using the Certificate of Deposit I purchased as collateral, I obtained a loan from the credit union to purchase a new computer for the business which I desperately needed.

Although I was earning the income from the bankruptcy attorney processing 15 to 20 bankruptcy petitions a week, I did not want to *put all my eggs in one basket.* How did I know that this attorney would continue to use my services forever? If I exclusively worked for him and lost his business, my company would also go out of business. Therefore, to create a cushion for myself in case this scenario ever played out, I began looking for ways to market my services and increase my customer base.

But where would I find customers who were interested in filing bankruptcy? I may have known how to prepare bankruptcy petitions, but *who* would I sell these services to and *how* would I find them? So while sitting at Fuddruckers restaurant eating a hamburger and fries one afternoon I picked up a copy of *The Other Paper.* This weekly publication was filled with classified ads directed toward consumers so I decided to run a classified ad and see what would happen. One ad that really paid off well for me appears at the right.

> **SAVE $100's** in attorney fees. File your own bankruptcy petition (minus court filing fees) with forms processing service fees of only $150. Visit our website today and download your **FREE** Client Intake Forms.

I kept the classified ad running continuously for several months while I found ways to advance my own bankruptcy education. One of the best ways I found to advance my knowledge was to work for bankruptcy attorneys. I simply signed up with a legal placement service in my area and started working temporary legal assignments in various areas of law.

In fact, I even accepted a temporary assignment from a creditor bankruptcy attorney so I could learn the *other side* of bankruptcy law. This experience proved to be extremely beneficial. Even though I did not enjoy working in creditor bankruptcy, I learned a lot about foreclosure and replevin procedures, as well as advanced areas of bankruptcy such as the appeals process and asset hearings where the trustee conducts bankruptcy estate sales. All of this advanced education enabled me to better assist debtor(s) and *Bankruptcy Paralegal Services* continued to grow at a steady rate.

Near the end of 2000, *Bankruptcy Paralegal Services* was producing a steady part-time income solely from the classified ads I was running in local newspapers. I also had begun running ads in other newspapers outside my state. Two of the services I used frequently were:

- **ACS, Inc** at http://www.advertisingresults.com/
- **Nationwide Newspapers** at http://www.nationwideadvertising.com/

Since I was still working fulltime outside my home office (and earning about $3,000 per month in income) I was in a position where I could take the business income and totally reinvest it into the growth of the company. The $3,000 per month fulltime income I was earning paid my rent, utilities and other monthly bills. So the small amount of business income was reinvested without any financial sacrifice. (This is where a husband would have come in handy. He could have worked and paid the bills while I built a company. But since I did not have a husband, I worked fulltime and drafted bankruptcy petitions in the evenings and on weekends.)

It sure made a difference to finally be able to invest all the income from the business back into marketing the business. It only took about five months before I was able to afford to quit my fulltime job and work at home fulltime. *Bankruptcy Paralegal Services* tripled its monthly income from $1,000 per month to $3,000 per month within only 90 days. However, even though $3,000 per month sounds like a lot of money, by the time I deducted the overhead expenses the business was still unable to pay me a steady salary. But it didn't matter at the time. I might not have been making any large profit, but I wasn't losing any money either.

My Prayer of Relief

In March of 2001 I went to my knees in prayer. I talked to God for several hours and explained my sincere desire to create a successful business. I promised God that if He would bless my business I would always give Him the credit as well as tithe 10% of my income to a Holy-Spirit filled ministry. I also told God that by taking me out of the *rat race* I felt He could better utilize my talents to enhance the lives of many people. I earnestly prayed this prayer to God every night asking Him for His help, guidance and mercy. It took a great leap of faith to go completely out on my own and trust Him to fulfill His part of the promise. I will never forget that moment in September 2001 because it was the moment my whole world changed. In fact, the whole world changed for everyone on the planet at that time also.

As you recall, on September 11, 2001 the Twin Towers in New York City were destroyed by terrorist attacks as well as the attack on the Pentagon in Washington

DC. These attacks created a ripple effect and within a few short weeks many Americans were out of work, factories closed and many large businesses filed for bankruptcy. From that point in time until the present, bankruptcy filings have grown to record-breaking figures. Although I was going through grief over the terrorist attacks like every other American, I realized that for the first time in my life I was in a position of being in the *right place at the right time.* I would be able to capture the market of debtor(s) seeking to file bankruptcy and provide them with virtual bankruptcy services if they wanted to file as a *pro se* debtor (without the aide of an attorney.)

Just when the business really began to take off, some of the *good ole' boys* in the local Columbus, Ohio legal community became jealous and outraged at my success. Instead of being smart and asking me to work for them (which would have been to their advantage), they filed complaints against me through the Columbus Bar Association and Ohio Bar. Next they filed complaints against me by delaying the discharge of three innocent debtor(s.) These complaints were not about the quality of my work but rather the information contained on my website. To make a long story short, I was charged with practicing law without a license on the internet.

Naturally, this came as a complete shock to me. I thought I had taken every precaution possible in an attempt not to violate the UPL (unauthorized practice of law) rules in my state. I had been a Board Member for the Paralegal Association of Central Ohio. I knew the UPL laws inside and out. I also had read and studied Section 110 of the Bankruptcy Code and could not understand how I violated any regulations. So I hired an attorney who specialized in internet law and asked him what I had done wrong. He was unable to provide me with an answer, so we made an appointment to meet with the U.S. Trustee and discuss the matter.

I printed out every page of my website and took it with me to the meeting at the bankruptcy court. I asked the trustees to point out on my website what I had done to constitute charges of UPL. Their reply was *Everything* and they handed back the printout from my website without even so much as looking at it. At this point I said, *My intention was never to violate any rules or laws. Just tell me what you want me to do and I will comply with your wishes.* The trustee's response was: *You cannot have anything on the website except for one page. The page cannot provide your name, address, phone number, email address of any other link of any kind. In fact, the only words you can have on your web site are "Bankruptcy Petition (not Paralegal) Services."* I immediately said, *Then how are people supposed to contact me?* The trustee answered in a robotic, monotone voice, *Oh well ... that's your problem.*

Right then I knew (beyond a shadow of a doubt) that these people had no concept of marketing on the internet. In fact, most of them didn't even know how to electronically file a document and had to attend training classes to learn how to use a mouse. It would not matter what I said or did at that point; they would still find fault against me because they couldn't understand what I was trying to explain to them. Therefore I had no choice but to admit defeat since I could not fight the federal government.

After leaving the trustee's office, I went home, renamed the business *Bankruptcy2Go,* secured a domain name, and transferred the business to another paralegal who lived in Georgia. I then wrote the trustee a letter telling him he had *won* and I was no longer in business. At this point, the business no longer was under my management and I received no income from it. Since the paralegal in Georgia was not limited by UPL regulations like I was in Ohio, the business was still able to continue growing. I eventually found a buyer for *Bankruptcy2Go* who lived in New Jersey, a state also with less-stringent UPL paralegal regulations than

Ohio. But when the Ohio trustees found out I had sold the business they brought the new owner into their litigation. While the Ohio trustee had no jurisdiction over paralegals in New Jersey, the new owner collapsed under the pressure and let *Bankruptcy2Go* die.

At this point I knew I had to develop something else to take the place of *Bankruptcy2Go*. I still loved working in the area of debtor bankruptcy law but no attorney within a 60 mile radius of Columbus, Ohio would hire me because of all the rumors generated by the bankruptcy court and the *good ole' boys* in power in Columbus, Ohio. I had to find a way to do the job I loved without violating any state or federal regulations.

How This Defeat Turned Into a Blessing

After transferring *Bankruptcy2Go* to the new owner, I began to doubt whether God was blessing my business or not. So I physically got down on my knees again and began crying out to God for help. I could not understand why God was causing everything to fall apart before my eyes after I prayed my first prayer. But God helped me to realize that He really was helping me. By tearing everything down that I created, God was able to rebuild my life. And rebuild it He did! But during that period of time, I felt like everything I had tried had not worked and I looked at my efforts as a total failure.

Within a few days after my prayer, a thought came to my mind (from God) to take the same service I provided to consumers and provide it to bankruptcy attorneys across the United States. The idea was flawless for several reasons:

1. I would still be doing something I dearly loved doing; preparing bankruptcy petitions for debtor(s.)

2. I would be free to work and never worry about breaking any unauthorized practice of law violations.

3. The attorney's name would be on the bankruptcy petition and my name would never appear. In fact, I could now prepare bankruptcy petitions for attorneys in the Columbus area and the local bankruptcy court would never know that I drafted them. Plus, they could not charge me with UPL since I was not violating any laws by working under the direction of a bankruptcy attorney.

4. Finally, I would make more money because working for attorneys provides a virtual bankruptcy assistant with a steady income stream. With *Bankruptcy Paralegal Services* and *Bankruptcy2Go*, once a bankruptcy petition was drafted and mailed to the debtor for filing with their local court, my services were never needed again. I had to spend a great deal of time and money advertising to generate new business. But working for attorneys would eliminate this step and stabilize my business income.

What an awesome God. I would never have come up with a plan that solved every single problem that quickly. But what can you expect from a powerful God who can speak things into existence? With this kind of power I am sure it is nothing to put a thought in my brain for me to act on. So, in May 2002 I developed *The Lawyer Assistant*.

The Birth of The Lawyer Assistant

Before starting this business I took the time and really did my homework. The first thing I did when I decided to start *The Lawyer Assistant* was to contact the Trustee's Office for the Northern and Southern District of Ohio. I wanted to find out if I would be violating any unauthorized practice of law regulations if I worked as a paralegal under the direction of attorneys outside my state. I immediately received approval to pursue this venture since there was no law stating a paralegal or virtual bankruptcy assistant could not work for an attorney who was located in another state other than where the paralegal or virtual bankruptcy assistant resided. Amazing! I finally received approval for an original idea from the same bankruptcy court who had brought UPL charges against me.

In addition I also made sure there was no law specifically requiring a virtual bankruptcy assistant to physically be located in the law office with the attorney he or she works for. It is a known fact that paralegals often take work outside the office gathering information for their attorneys. Paralegals and virtual bankruptcy assistants have never been limited to only working in the law office where their attorney was located. This would be impossible to do in many law firms, but I checked it out anyway and found my reasoning was correct. I now had no strings to bind me and knew deep down inside that I was headed for one of the most successful ventures of my life.

I couldn't wait to get started, but I wasn't about to make the same mistakes I made in the past. So I started by doing more research on the internet in an attempt to locate my competition. To my surprise, I could not locate any virtual bankruptcy assistants who offered nationwide petition preparation services to attorneys. I only found people preparing petitions for consumers like I did with *Bankruptcy Paralegal Services* and *Bankruptcy2Go.*

Against All Odds...

Most experienced marketers at this point would have advised me to avoid a situation where I would be developing a new service and offering it for the first time in the marketplace. Instead of paving the way with new products, marketers will normally advise a person to improve on products that already exist since they already are proven sellers. But I also remember reading an article in an old mail order publication that said *find a need and fill it.* So in my mind, a bankruptcy petition preparation service for attorneys was filling a need. My only problem was convincing the attorney he or she really had a need for my service and that my company could fill it. But since God had not let me down and seemed to be blessing everything I touched, I had the faith He would pave the way for me.

When I first started marketing *The Lawyer Assistant* in my local area, a number of attorneys would ask me, *Why should I pay you $150 to prepare my bankruptcy petition, when I can pay my employee $10 an hour to do it?* This was an excellent question and it deserved an excellent response. So I got busy developing a marketing strategy that proved how *The Lawyer Assistant* could save the attorney money. Some of the benefits I outlined for attorneys were:

- Eliminate all your Chapter 7 and Chapter 13 bankruptcy petition preparation for you and your office staff

- Eliminate 75% of client phone calls since the clients call our office for general questions that a virtual bankruptcy assistant is authorized to answer. All contact with your client's and/or documents faxed to us by your client is emailed to you for your files.

- Eliminate a majority of your client intake interview time since we conduct a telephone interview with your client to obtain any missing information or to verify figures in order to draft the bankruptcy petition. This crucial step ensures a more accurate and complete bankruptcy petition, which results in less paperwork and problems for you in the future.

- Be alerted to possible problems before the petition is filed. We provide attorneys who use our service with a summary sheet of all petitions we process. Important information, such as bringing your attention to unexempt equity, is just one example of how we alert our attorneys to problems that could develop which require their immediate attention.

- Your client files are maintained at our office and are released at any time upon your request. This helps to reduce storage space and you also have a *back-up* of client files if any computer crash should occur.

Thinking of this list of benefits was not an easy task. I had to examine every step of the bankruptcy process and present the services of *The Lawyer Assistant* in a positive and money-saving sales pitch to the attorney. However, this list proved to be an important key element in building *The Lawyer Assistant*. It was easy for attorneys to see how a fee of only $150 was a small amount to pay when the bankruptcy attorney was receiving $900 to $2,000 for each bankruptcy petition and their workload was greatly reduced.

With my marketing ideas in place, I now faced the task of getting the message out to all the bankruptcy attorneys. First I developed a brochure (see the actual one I used on Page 247 of this book.) I included a cover letter (see the actual one I used on Page 246 of this book) and mailed the brochure to every attorney within a 60-mile radius of Columbus, Ohio. Although this idea may work for you, unfortunately, it did not work for me because my reputation had been scarred in Columbus due to the complaints filed against me when I owned *Bankruptcy Paralegal Services*. But this didn't bother me. God reminded me that even Jesus Christ was not accepted in his own home town, so I couldn't expect any better treatment. In fact, when I was rejected by the bankruptcy attorneys in Columbus, Ohio it was a blessing in disguise since it forced me to market *The Lawyer Assistant* nationally on the internet and increase my income even more.

Understand How to Market to Attorneys

If you have never worked for an attorney before, you will probably be intimidated by them. But this is counter-productive thinking. As a virtual bankruptcy assistant all of your customers will be attorneys. If you are afraid to communicate with them you are not going to get anywhere in this business until you learn how. Below are a few suggestions to help you:

1. Join your local bar association as an *Associate* or *Supporting Member. Associate* or *Supporting Members* do not need to be attorneys. Once you join, start attending some of the open meetings and get used to attorneys and how to interact with them. It should only take a few meetings to ease your fears and build your confidence to make it easier to approach attorneys and talk to them.

2. Take the morning or afternoon off and visit your local courthouse. Because court hearings are normally open to the public, you can walk in, sit down in the courtroom and listen to the cases as they are presented. Watch and listen to how court proceedings are conducted and watch the attorneys presenting the case. Write down any words or legal phrases you do not understand and look them up in a legal dictionary. This excellent eduction will not cost you any money except maybe for a parking fee.

3. Work for an attorney. You do not need to be a paralegal to work for an attorney. Many attorneys hire people to answer the phone, file pleadings in court and do a variety of other jobs that a paralegal normally does not do. Look in your local paper for jobs available in law firms. Ask some of the members in the organizations you belong to for job references. Find out if your local bar association has a temporary service you can work through.

4. Work temporarily in law firms under temporary agencies. Two national agencies I know that supply legal staff to law firms are:

a. **Spherion Temporary Agency**
http://www.spherion.com/

b. **Special Counsel**
http://www.specialcounsel.com/home.asp

However, there are many more temporary agencies to choose from. Just visit http://www.google.com and type in the search words *legal temporary services.*

Why am I suggesting that you work for a law firm on a temporary basis? For many reasons. You will learn how law firms operate from the inside out. You will learn the *legal lingo* which is helpful when communicating with attorneys. You will learn not to be intimidated by attorneys and will feel comfortable in talking to them. You will learn to develop professional character traits and understand what is acceptable and not acceptable in the legal industry. You also will be able to impress attorneys with your hard work and dedication and these attorneys would be excellent for job references or to refer you to bankruptcy attorneys they know personally.

Of course any of these ideas will take time. This may be disappointing to some of you who wanted to purchase this book and immediately start making money. But remember the old saying: *Anything worthwhile takes time.* If you do not have the desire to take a few months and invest time into pre-training before you start your first virtual bankruptcy assistant business, you may be setting yourself for a longer wait until you are successful.

Attorneys Think Differently Than Most People

Attorneys are taught in law school to look at every side of an issue from all angles to determine the best form of defense in representing their client. This type of mental training often produces an attorney who will not act or think like you do. That is why it is extremely important, when you begin marketing your virtual bankruptcy assistant services to attorneys, to understand how they think to improve your communication with them. Regardless of whether you agree with their line of thinking, attorneys must be given a level of respect because they spent eight years in college and law school studying the law. I never had that level of persistence when it came to education - so I believe anyone that pursues an education for this length of time deserves respect and admiration. If you teach yourself to think like this, it will be a great start to improving your communication skills with the attorneys you work for.

Finding Attorneys on the Internet

One approach I used in locating bankruptcy attorneys on the internet was to visit every attorney search engine and directory I could find. I went to Google's search engine at http://www.google.com and typed in the search words *attorney directory, locate an attorney* and even *find a lawyer.*

In addition, I did numerous searches under the search words *bankruptcy attorney* and even just the word *bankruptcy.* I followed all the available relevant links and dug deep into the internet where most people do not have the patience to go. I even found bankruptcy attorneys on bar association websites but I had to go into each one individually and locate their particular web page (if one was available) to obtain their contact information. I spent several weeks working every day conducting marketing research and getting *The Lawyer Assistant* name recognized on the internet.

Next, I developed an Attorney Directory on my website. I developed a form for the attorney to fill out to submit their information. When I received the form, I added the attorney name and contact information to the directory. In return for filling out the form I personalized a set of the Client Intake Forms I developed and sent them a free set. The attorneys preferred my Client Intake Forms over the forms they were using, so they began using them. When they found the forms were so detailed and made their job easier, they began to trust that my virtual bankruptcy assistant services would make their jobs easier too.

As my popularity continued to grow through my internet contacts, the Attorney Directory became larger and larger. In fact, the Attorney Directory proved to be a blessing in disguise. I began to realize that this compilation of bankruptcy attorneys across the United States was also a solid customer base in which to build my business. So I compiled a list of the names and addresses of all the bankruptcy attorneys in the Attorney Directory and mailed them a cover letter, brochure and business card.

Within a couple of weeks (after sending out 200 brochures to bankruptcy attorneys) I was beginning to get phone calls on a daily basis from attorneys across the United States with questions about my service. Over 50% of the attorneys who called decided to give my service a try. It took about a month before I received any income (because I had to bill the attorney and wait on the payment), but the 30 day wait was well worth it. *The Lawyer Assistant* became a profitable company within four months of start-up.

The results from my mailing created a client base of 14 attorneys utilizing my bankruptcy petition drafting services. When those 14 attorneys discovered the benefits my service provided to their law firm, as well as increased profits, they passed along the news to their fellow attorneys. Within eight months after starting

The Lawyer Assistant I had a customer base of 56 attorneys and a workload of 125-150 petitions per week. Not only were attorneys benefiting financially from the service, I was making more money than I ever had in my life - only I did not have time to enjoy it.

How Did I Manage the Tremendous Workload?

With a heavy workload of 125-150 petitions per week and the fast level of business growth, I frantically looked for other virtual bankruptcy assistants to help me. Although I hired several friends and neighbors to call clients back to obtain answers to questions from the Client Intake Forms, it was becoming more difficult to keep up with the heavy workload. Unfortunately, at the time, no virtual bankruptcy assistants existed on the internet - only non-attorney petition preparers who did very sloppy work. I then resulted to making a plea for help to employed bankruptcy paralegals through the paralegal associations I belonged to. Again - no luck. Those paralegals were already so overloaded with work, they certainly did not want to come home and draft more bankruptcy petitions.

The paralegals I did manage to find that agreed to help me with the workload lacked the education in the preparation of a well-detailed petition. Many were treating the job like a data entry position instead of paying attention to the information they were entering. For instance, when the mortgage payment for real property is listed on Schedule A, that figure should immediately be transferred to Schedule J in order to maintain consistency within the document. Also, if a 401K payment was deducted from the income of a debtor on Schedule I, that 401K also needed to be reflected on Schedule B.

Additionally, I believed it was essential to make notes of potential problems and provide them to the attorney as a cover sheet. This page of notes was compiled during the drafting of the bankruptcy petition. It contained important information for the attorney, such as, calling his or her attention to unexempt property, or when Schedule I was less than the basic living expenses detailed on Schedule J. These notes helped the attorney pinpoint potential problems and get them resolved before the petition was filed - resulting in a huge reduction in time, paperwork (i.e., filing of Amendments to correct errors, etc.) and potential problems that would have resulted down the road.

Transition from Business Owner to Training Instructor

Being unable to find any legal staff that provided the level of detail in the bankruptcy petition preparation I decided to redirect my path and take my training methods to the masses. I sold *The Lawyer Assistant* to David Gonzalez, Esq. in Bronxville, New York and started on my educational quest. During my initial research I discovered that the present training programs for paralegals in debtor bankruptcy only concentrated on the law - not the actual preparation of the bankruptcy forms and schedules themselves. So I contacted the two largest organizations that provide training seminars to paralegals (Lorman Education and NBI-SEMS) and convinced them to let me do a few workshops to teach paralegals how to draft well-detailed bankruptcy petitions. Two were held in Columbus and one in Dayton, Ohio; however, the idea was still *too new* at the time and attendance was lower than expected. The workshops therefore were discontinued.

But although the workshops were *temporarily* discontinued, I continued in my quest. This time, instead of taking the education to the law-firm employees I introduced it to the notary signing agent field in September 2004. It was introduced by the publishing of my first bankruptcy book, How to Start a Bankruptcy Forms Processing Service, which was written to comply with the old law that was in effect at that time.

How Did the Term "Bankruptcy Forms Processor" Start?

Some of the material to write my book had previously been written and published under the title: "How to Start a Bankruptcy Paralegal Service." This information had been sold in a workbook format to attorneys nationwide who used the workbook to train their office staff. This was published during the time I owned *The Lawyer Assistant* and my attorney client base purchased copies.

Taking this material and rewriting it to fit the notary signing agents was a great task - but I believed that *somebody had to do it.* The only problem I faced was that I could not use the term *paralegal* in the title of my book to sell to the notary market. Why? Because most notary signing agents are not paralegals. While many paralegals are notary publics, few of them are aware of the mobile notary field working for mortgage companies.

Therefore, I asked my friend Gloria Joyce (who worked with immigration forms) what her job title was. Gloria said she was a immigration forms processor. So the phrase *bankruptcy forms processor* was originally coined from Gloria Joyce. The term *virtual bankruptcy assistant* was coined in 2006 in an effort to not confuse a *bankruptcy forms processor* with a *non-attorney preparer.* This seems to be a common problem for people who are marketing their services to bankruptcy attorneys. Some attorneys take a *dim view* to non-attorneys who prepare petitions for the general public. Using the title *virtual bankruptcy assistant* instead of *bankruptcy forms processor* may help in establishing more credibility for our service business and cause less confusion about the UPL issue.

Other Business Building Ideas

Before I begin this section I want you to know there are millions of ways to market. Some of the ideas I cover on the following pages may work for me but they may not work for you. That is why I cannot stress enough the importance of getting ideas from 100s of successful business owners who work in this field. One way I found of bridging this gap was to develop the weekly teleconferences which you can find more about on the 713Training.Com website. Each week we have a different special guest, or a unique topic of discussion, that provides attendees with exposure to a wide range of successful people. Each one explains the methods they used to achieve success and each one is unique as well as inspiring.

Armed with a wide variety of marketing ideas and techniques, you can use the creative area of your brain and develop your own. But first, let's cover some methods (as well as lessons I learned) when I was building *The Lawyer Assistant*. Just remember to always keep your eyes and ears open for even more ways to market your business and continuously strive to find new ways to locate your target market of bankruptcy attorneys.

Beware of Advertising in Legal Directories

Once your website is up and you begin marketing online, don't be surprised if one day you get a call from a salesperson asking you to advertise your forms processing services in their legal directory. I did. The first thing you need to find out is the target market of people the directory serves. For instance, FindLaw.Com is one of the top legal websites on the internet. It gets a lot of traffic and is used by large numbers of attorneys in the legal community but it is not the best marketing tool for virtual bankruptcy assistants.

If you go to the FindLaw.Com website you will see that its main purpose is helping consumers locate attorneys in their area. If a person has it in their mind to locate an attorney, it is very rare they will change their mind and hire a freelance virtual bankruptcy assistant - which is not your target market anyway.

Attorneys who visit legal directories often are looking for other avenues of marketing their law firm or networking with other attorneys. Again, attorneys using the directory for these purposes would very rarely be interested in hiring a freelance virtual bankruptcy assistant.

Therefore, I strongly suggest that you research all legal directories before entering into a contract to pay hundreds of dollars for a listing. If the legal directory is one that is targeted to attorneys who are seeking a virtual bankruptcy assistant, then you might have a fighting chance. But if the legal directory is designed to help consumers find attorneys in their area, you are wasting your money if you choose to advertise with them. In fact, you would be better off if you dropped 100,000 brochures from the top of the Sears Tower in Chicago and hoped that an attorney in the crowd would find it and hire you.

Developing a Company Brochure

In order to develop marketing skills you not only have to *think outside the box* but you must be able to think like your customer (or in my case, the attorneys I was target marketing), I can remember what it was like working at a law firm office. My attorney received 200 to 300 emails every day and he ended up deleting the ones that were not related to his cases. I could see this same thing happening to the emails I was sending out to market *The Lawyer Assistant,* so I had to develop another way of reaching the attorney.

One of the best ways to accomplish this was to mail a brochure and cover letter to the attorneys I was interested in working for. But before I provide you with the information that I used in my company brochure, you first need to develop a mailing list of well-qualified attorney candidates.

Well-qualified attorney candidates simply means a list of attorney names and addresses who you believe would be most interested in your service. I determined that I wanted to target very *small* law firms or attorneys who worked independently. The reason I ruled out marketing to large law firms was because they tend to practice in the Chapter 11 arena. Chapter 11 bankruptcies are filed by companies and they bring a larger income for the attorney. Bankruptcy attorneys who practice in the Chapter 7 and Chapter 13 arena are normally smaller law firms because the income an attorney receives working with the average *John Q Public* is substantially lower.

This fact is also an advantage for the freelance virtual bankruptcy assistant. Since smaller law firms need to closely monitor their overhead costs, most independent attorneys and small law firms will jump at the chance to save money and increase their profits by hiring a freelance virtual bankruptcy assistant. Your job as a marketer is to show them how your company can do this for them. Larger law firms, on the other hand, are not as concerned with overhead costs and will probably have an in-house staff drafting their bankruptcy petitions. In the future, larger law firms will probably use freelancers, but I found my virtual bankruptcy services were more accepted by the smaller law firms versus the larger ones.

How to Determine the Size of a Law Firm

I did searches on the internet and through online Yellow Pages to compile my mailing list of attorneys to send my brochure to. As I went through each one I could normally spot the small law firms by the name of their company. For example:

<u>Law Office of John Doe</u>

It is probably correct to assume that a law firm with the name of only one attorney is a sole proprietorship. Of course we don't know if John Doe has any employees or not, but any law firm with a name similar to this would be an excellent prospect for sending your brochure.

Doe and Smith, LLC (or LLP)

The *LLC* at the end of a law firm's name stands for *Limited Liability Corporation* and *LLP* stands for *Limited Liability Partnership.* Both are basically the same thing. There are major tax advantages, protection of personal assets and other benefits for a business that incorporates. When two attorneys decide to go into business together and split the costs 50/50 they will either form a partnership or incorporate into an LLC. Although we would not know if Doe and Smith, LLC had one or 100 employees, it is safe to assume attorneys with law firm names like these are probably small or medium-size.

However, if the law firm has several partner names before the LLC, they would probably be large law firms employing large numbers of attorneys and employees. For instance: *Smith, Doe, Sally and George LLC* will most likely be a large law firm. To make sure, visit their website and look for a link to the attorney profiles. If there are more than two attorneys at this law firm they may not make a good prospect for mailing your brochure to at this time. There are enough smaller firms to try first before taking on the big guys.

Smith & Associates or Smith Law Group

These two types of law firms are most likely sole-proprietorships. An attorney with the last name of Smith owns the law firm but he has one or more associates or a group of legal professionals working under him. These associates could be law students who are getting ready to pass their bar exam or other qualifying legal personnel. This type of law firm would probably be an excellent prospect for mailing your brochure to.

No Company Name

If you encounter a law firm with the same name as the attorney, you definitely know this is either an independent or small attorney firm. For instance: John Brown, Esq. is the name of the attorney who owns the company. The abbreviation *Esq.* after the attorney's name means *Esquire*, which is another name for an attorney. If the attorney has the title of *Emeritus* after his or her name, this means they are retired or semi-retired. They may still draw an income from the law firm, but they only provide legal services on a limited basis.

Note: The sample names of law firms previously referred to are fictional names and are not intended to refer to any existing law firm.

Developing the Cover Letter

Now that you have done some online research via the attorney directories or in the Yellow Pages, make a mailing list in MS Word (or whatever word processing software you use.) Most of the time you can copy and paste the name and address information from the online directory into MS Word, so make sure you have your word processing program open as you are researching the internet. The proper address format would be something like this:

Mr. John Doe, Esq.
Attorney at Law
123 Main Street, Suite A-5
Newark, Ohio 43055

Never send a brochure to *To Whom it May Concern* or simply the name of a law firm. You want the attorney to feel that you personally sought out his or her law firm and are interested in working directly for them. Never make your business look cheap and send out a general letter that looks like it was mass produced. Take the extra 10 seconds to address your letter to a specific attorney at the law firm. If that attorney is not interested, he or she may pass your brochure on to another attorney but if you don't address it to a specific attorney no attorney will probably ever see it.

You will also find that brochures and business cards are not destroyed as quickly as cover letters when they are sent to attorneys. Attorneys recognize the importance of having resourceful information at their finger tips. If they don't have a need for your services when your letter, brochure and business card arrive, there is more likelihood they will retain your business card for future reference. Make sure your business card contains contact information that will not change in case the attorney does not contact you immediately. You may not want to print your email address on your business cards if you expect it to change within the next year. Instead, always print your website address because that should not change and you can keep your website updated with your latest email address.

Once you have accumulated the mailing list it is time to develop the cover letter you will use. As I previously mentioned, each letter should be personalized for each attorney you are mailing to. If an attorney suspects you are just mailing out a standard form letter and didn't take the time to address them personally, they may think you would not provide personalized service to them through your business. So make sure you keep your business looking good at all times.

On Page 246 is an example of the cover letter I used when I was marketing *The Lawyer Assistant* to attorneys nationwide. Please don't copy my letter word-for-word. I prepared several different cover letters that were personalized for the attorney I was mailing my brochure to and my example is just one of the many different ones I developed.

The Lawyer Assistant
Victoria Ring, Certified Paralegal
1601 West Fifth Ave, Suite 123
Columbus OH 43212-2303
Office: 614-875-4496 - Fax: (614) 355-0184
http://www.lawyerassistant.com

April 29, 2006

Mr. John Doe, Esq.
Attorney at Law
123 Main Street, Suite 111
Groveport, Ohio 43125

Re: **Bankruptcy Paralegal Services**

Dear Mr. Doe:

I found your law firm on FindLaw.Com and noticed that you specialize in the area of debtor bankruptcy law. *The Lawyer Assistant* is an online company that provides bankruptcy attorneys nationwide with virtual bankruptcy assistant services. I have enclosed a company brochure for your review.

The Lawyer Assistant also provides attorneys with client intake interview services as well as drafting of Motions, Answers and other bankruptcy pleadings for one low price. In fact, we will personalize our services to fit your law firm's practice. Just tell us what you need and we will provide you with a price quote.

For a limited time, *The Lawyer Assistant* is offering you a **FREE 30-DAY TRIAL** to prove how reliable and valuable our service is. Simply have your next client fill out the Client Intake Forms (available free on our website at www.lawyerassistant.com.) Fax the forms to us and we will prepare the Chapter 7 or Chapter 13 petition for you. If you are not satisfied with our work in any way, you are not required to pay the invoice.

Thank you for your time and consideration of our services. If you have any questions or need additional information, do not hesitate to call the office and ask to speak to Victoria Ring.

Sincerely,

Victoria Ring, President
Certified Paralegal and Notary

Now For the Brochure .....

Beginning below and continuing on Pages __ through __ I have provided you with the brochure I developed for marketing *The Lawyer Assistant*. Of course, you will need to personalize it to fit your particular company. I purchased tri-fold brochure paper at my local Staples Office Supply store for $12.00 (100 brochures), then printed and folded them myself to save money.

Save hundreds of dollars per bankruptcy petition just like these attorneys did:

"Since you have been drafting the bankruptcy petitions for my clients, my 341 meetings have been much smoother due to the high level of detail you provide. Thank you for the excellent services."

"I was not aware of the value of your service until I took advantage of your 30-day free trial offer. You are not the typical document preparer. Instead you handle everything for me and every petition is ready to file with the court. Thank you."

How Our Petition Preparation Process Works:

Step 1:
You start by downloading a FREE set of Client Intake Forms from our website. Print the forms and have the client fill them out. They are designed to be consumer-friendly. Review them with your client for completeness and fax or mail to *The Lawyer Assistant*.
No payment is required.

SAMPLE BROCHURE PAGE 1

Step 2:
We draft the complete bankruptcy petition (normally within 24 hours) and compile a list of additional questions and/or summary analysis to alert you to any potential problems (if applicable.) Fax or email us with instructions on how to proceed and the petition is finalized.

Step 3:
If your client is currently receiving a wage garnishment, two letters will also be drafted for the creditor and payroll department of the employer to stop the garnishment immediately. The letters will be personalized with your law firm information, ready for your signature. There is no additional charge for this service. It is included in the $150.00 package price.

Step 4:
When the petition is complete, your law firm information and Attorney Compensation Statement will be drafted and personalized with your bar number. Then the entire petition is converted to PDF format and emailed to you for printing. The PDF file is also suitable for electronic filing, which we will also do for you if electronic filing is available at your local bankruptcy court.

After your review, if any page or pages within the petition needs to be changed, just let us know. We will immediately revise the affected pages and send them to you in PDF format at no additional charge within a few hours.

SAMPLE BROCHURE PAGE 2

Try Our Service FREE for 30 Days!!

The only way we can prove the tremendous cost savings to you as a bankruptcy attorney is to offer you our services free for 30 days. This way you can test us out before you decide to use our services on a regular basis.

Simply have your clients complete the Client Intake Forms, which are available free from our website. When the client has filled them out, fax them to us and we will immediately begin preparing your client's Chapter 7 or Chapter 13 bankruptcy petition.

After our work is completed and you are satisfied with the quality, we will send you an invoice for $150.00. You then have 30 additional days to pay the invoice and then you only are required to pay the invoice if you are satisfied with our work and find that our service saved you money.

Get Your Free Client Intake Forms!!

On the internet, go to http://www.lawyerassistant.com/intake_forms/
Print out the forms and give them to your client to fill out. Fax to us and we will handle the rest, often within 24 hours.

The Lawyer Assistant has drafted thousands of petitions for other attorneys and law firms across the United States.
We hope you join our family of
satisfied and repeat clients.

SAMPLE BROCHURE PAGE 3

Visit our website and you'll find a lot of free and low-cost services specifically designed for the debtor bankruptcy attorney. These include:

- Free Debtor and Creditor pleading templates in MS Word format for your immediate use.
- Free Client Intake Forms specifically designed to obtain most of the required information to prepare a detailed bankruptcy petition.
- Training CD, *How to Prepare a Bankruptcy Petition.* This CD contains a 2-1/2-hour on-screen video. It has already helped train a variety of attorneys, paralegals and virtual bankruptcy assistants unfamiliar with preparing bankruptcy petitions.
- Nationwide Attorney Directory so you can network with other bankruptcy attorneys in your area.
- Our exclusive *Easy Bankruptcy Office* income and expense software with contact manager.

SAMPLE BROCHURE PAGE 4

Putting it All Together

Fold the cover letter into three folds like a standard business letter. Place a brochure and your business card in the envelope and mail to all the attorneys on the mailing list you created in MS Word. There is no need to put anything else in the envelope because a letter, brochure and business card are the perfect weight to go through the mail at the standard first-class letter postage rate.

How Many Brochures Should You Mail Out?

You should mail out as many brochures as your budget will allow. However, when you are first creating your mailing list do not allow mailing costs to be the main thought on your mind. Instead, concentrate solely on finding the attorneys you feel will be the best prospects to use your virtual bankruptcy assistant service. Even if you end up with 1,000 names on your mailing list you don't have to mail brochures to all of them at once. Just mail them out in the quantity you can afford in postage each week and eventually you will mail to the entire list. You may want to go ahead and stuff the envelopes so they are ready to mail. Then each week purchase the amount of stamps you can afford and mail out that many brochures.

What Happens Next?

If you mailed out a good brochure with a professional cover letter, attorneys may start calling you within a few days to obtain more information. The largest majority of the attorneys will visit your website first - so make sure you have one already in place that provides good information and projects a professional image before you start mailing brochures. If the attorney likes your website he or she will probably call you on the phone if they need your services. If not, they may keep your business card and pass the information on to another bankruptcy attorney they know who may need your services. But if you don't hear back from an attorney you mailed your brochure to within 30 days, my suggestion would be to call their office (if the attorney is local) and schedule an appointment to sit down and talk with them about your virtual bankruptcy assistant service.

At that meeting you may want to take a portfolio with you containing:

1. A blank copy of the Client Intake Forms to show the attorney the high level of detail you obtain before drafting the bankruptcy petition.

2. A copy of a sample bankruptcy petition that you compiled during your training. Make sure the names, social security numbers and other financial data is bogus and is not confidential information you obtained on a real person. Attorneys are very careful about releasing their work to someone they do not know for confidentiality purposes. If you present them with a sample of your work and it contains confidential client information, they will not be impressed.

3. A sample of the type of Attorney Summary Page you provide to the attorneys you work with that details specific areas of the bankruptcy petition that requires their attention. Attorneys love this attention to detail and will appreciate the time you save them by providing this much needed information.

As stated before, the way an attorney's mind works has always been interesting to me. They are trained to look at all sides of an issue in order to make a rational and fair decision. Therefore, when you have a discussion with an attorney they normally will always be one step ahead of you. Make sure you are honest, quick to admit your mistakes and fix them as quickly as possible. Treat attorneys with the respect they deserve and everyone should get along fine.

Other Ideas for Marketing

There are as many ways to market as there are stars in the sky. Every once in awhile I will receive an email from someone who has read one of my books or articles and they will say something like: *Can you tell me how to market my business?* People like this must think I have the time to write a 200-page email attempting to answer their question. Little do they realize that even a 200-page email would never scratch the surface in providing the millions of different marketing methods available around them on a daily basis.

The best way to learn how to market your services is to learn to think like your customer. If you find out exactly what they want, you can adjust your marketing techniques or even your company operations to fill this need. The only way to learn how your customer thinks is to listen to them with an open mind and put yourself in their place. And don't be afraid of failure if you try something and it doesn't work. This happens to every marketer many times over. In fact, the only way we can truly learn how to successfully market to our customers is to make mistakes, fix them and fine tune our marketing technique until something works.

When I started *The Lawyer Assistant* I must have tried 100 or more different marketing methods. I worked hard every day and tried everything I could think of that might work. A few months later my business jumped from preparing 20 petitions a month to an average of 50. My friends would ask me: *What did you do to increase your business so quickly?* I replied: *I don't know. I just kept trying something new every day and finally something worked.*

Although big companies who have the budget to afford a marketing department are able to pinpoint the effects of different methods they use in marketing, when you are a one-person operation, marketing on the internet, it is impossible to do this. For me, it didn't really matter what specific method worked in growing my business. I was just happy the business was growing. Besides, after *the ball got rolling,* the attorney clients I drafted petitions for told other attorneys about my service and I no longer had to advertise. Instead, *The Lawyer Assistant* grew rapidly from word-of-mouth advertising.

How Word-of-Mouth Advertising Helped Jo Anne Sessom Start Her Virtual Bankruptcy Assistant Service

On November 22, 2005, we were very grateful to have Jo Anne Sessom of JW Bankruptcy Forms Processing as our special guest at the weekly teleconference. Jo Anne explained to the attendees that her business began by word-of-mouth advertising. She was sitting at the beauty shop getting her hair done when she was talking about her new business venture with the hair stylist. It just so happened that the hair stylist was going through a divorce at the time and hired an attorney to represent her. She told her attorney about Jo Anne's service and the attorney called Jo Anne to find out more information. Within less than 90 days after starting her business, Jo Anne had three (3) attorney clients.

Jo Anne advised everyone who is starting any type of service business to ALWAYS talk about your business to everyone you meet. This does not mean that you should bore people to death and force them to endure a long, boring sales speech. It means that you should mention to people what type of business you have started. If they are interested, they will ask you more questions. If they are not interested, they will change the subject. This gives you the cue you need about whether to pursue talking about the subject or not. But regardless of whether the person is interested or not in your new business venture, they will still remember what you do. And who knows? That person may tell someone else, who will tell someone else, who happens to know an attorney who needs your services. Although this scenario may sound far-fetched to beginners, it happens more often than you may realize.

We really enjoyed having Jo Anne Sessom provide us with her experiences in marketing her business as well as the learning curve she experienced when attempting to learn how to draft Chapter 7 bankruptcy petitions. I invite you to listen to the entire teleconference recording, which is available free at www.713training.com/teleconference/ Also, if you would like to contact Jo Anne she has given permission to release her contact information. Visit www.713training.com/directory/colorado/sessom.html

Marketing Through Magazine Advertising

I didn't do a lot of printed magazine advertising for *The Lawyer Assistant* because the cost was relatively high. However, there were three magazines that I received a good response rate with when I ran a classified ad:

- **Law Office Computing**
  http://www.lawofficecomputing.com/

- **The Paralegal Reporter**
  http://www.paralegals.org/

- **Legal Assistant Today**
  http://www.legalassistanttoday.com/

I also urge you to subscribe to these magazines so you can keep up-to-date on the legal and paralegal world. While not every article in these publications will be specifically about bankruptcy, bankruptcy law can be involved in a wide variety of other types of law. You will always pick up something to help you in these magazines, so make sure you at least request a sample copy if you cannot afford to subscribe at the present time.

Marketing on the Internet

Trying to make a direct sale for your services to an attorney by email is not the way to market your services. Not only does it make you look cheap and inexperienced in business but you can also be accused of spam and be reported. If one attorney is offended by your marketing email, he or she can contact your ISP (Internet Service Provider) and complain about your company. The ISP will then contact you and in some circumstances people have actually lost their email accounts.

To make sure you maintain a professional image and are never reported for sending out spam mail — turn your marketing message into a press release or an article. You can read samples of press releases online by going to any search engine and typing in *press release.* This will help you to get a *feel* for the information in a press release so you can customize yours to fit the product or service you are selling.

A press release (or an article) is written to *inform* the reader, not sell them something. At the bottom of the press release or article you can place a one or two-sentence blurb for people to visit your website to find out more information. But this is the only type of acceptable advertising in a news-related article.

Note: On Page 257 is a sample of one press release I used when I marketed *The Lawyer Assistant*.

Once you have a press release or article written that ties in with your service and informs the reader about a newsworthy item, you can post it on the internet for millions to read. One good thing about press releases is that they can remain online for many years. A few places I posted articles and press releases online were:

- **Free Press Release.Com**
  http://www.free-press-release.com/submit/

FOR IMMEDIATE RELEASE!

How a Debtor Bankruptcy Attorney Can Increase Profits for Their Law Firm

Electronic filing and the internet have opened the doors for attorneys working in the area of debtor bankruptcy law to minimize their overhead and increase their law firm's profits substantially.

Instead of hiring an office staff and paying employees for the time they are non-productive, a bankruptcy attorney can hire a freelance virtual bankruptcy assistant and pay them only for the work they complete. The freelance virtual bankruptcy assistant can be located in any U.S. state because all case information can be accessed online or by creating a virtual network that enables both the virtual bankruptcy assistant and attorney access to cases stored on their computers.

Victoria Ring of *The Lawyer Assistant* said: *I draft bankruptcy petitions, Chapter 13 plans and other pleadings for bankruptcy attorneys in twenty-three different states. Many of these attorneys have no office staff or if they do, it is normally a part-time receptionist who answers the phone, makes copies and schedules appointments. All the forms processing work is performed by* The Lawyer Assistant *and attorneys have reported income increases of 400% or more using our services.*

To find out how your law firm may be able to boost profits and increase the efficiency of the bankruptcy petition preparation process, visit our website at www.lawyerassistant.com

SAMPLE PRESS RELEASE

- **PR Web**
  http://www.prweb.com/

- **Idea Marketers**
  http://www.ideamarketers.com/library/category.cfm?acatid=51

If any of these links become obsolete, you can go to any search engine, type in the search words *submit legal article* and start going through the list. Be sure to read any guidelines for submitting your material or it may not get posted. While this type of marketing takes a great deal of time, you will not have to spend one penny in advertising and articles normally stay online for many years. Articles and press releases are one of the best ways to market your services, but it is a time consuming task.

Subscribe to Bankruptcy Ezines

If you are not very good at writing press releases and articles, the next best thing is to market through ezines (electronic newsletters.) Again, you will not be using the direct sales approach. Instead, you will communicate with other bankruptcy professionals and find out what their needs are so you can effectively sell your services to them. Some ezines I subscribed to were:

- **Bankruptcy Roundtable**
  http://groups.yahoo.com/group/bankruptcy_roundtable_USA/

- **Chapter 7 Bankruptcy**
  http://finance.groups.yahoo.com/group/BeltranAssoc-Chapter_7_Bankruptcy/

- **Turnarounds and Workouts Newswire**
  http://www.bankrupt.com/mail_lists/discussion.twn.html

- **Bankruptcy and Creditor's Rights Newsletter**
  http://www.hklaw.com/Publications/Subscribe.asp

- **Legal Assistant Today Bulletin**
  http://www.legalassistanttoday.com/bulletin/

- **Bankruptcy Newsletter from the Law Office of John Rogers**
  http://johnrogerslaw.lawoffice.com/CM/Custom/Bankruptcy.asp

If any of these links become obsolete, you can locate additional discussion groups by going to any search engine and typing in the search words *bankruptcy discussion group* or *bankruptcy paralegal discussion groups.*

How Do the Changes in the New Bankruptcy Law Effect Marketing for the Virtual Bankruptcy Assistants?

Since the new bankruptcy law went into effect on October 17, 2005 the bankruptcy attorneys as well as the court system faced a major transitional phase. If you recall, the federal government waited until the last minute to implement the final changes in the new bankruptcy law so the attorneys did not have time to prepare for the transition. It took them some time to clean-up from the tremendous rush of filings where people waited until the last minute to file bankruptcy on October 17. Next, it took some time to update their office procedures to conform to the new law. Therefore, during this period of time some virtual bankruptcy assistants did not receive an overwhelming response from their marketing efforts like I did back in 2001. But do not be dismayed. At the time of this writing, bankruptcy attorneys are working hard to get through this transitional period so try to understand their position and find ways you can still assist them during this period of time.

In January 2006, I spoke with a paralegal who worked for a major creditor bankruptcy law firm in Atlanta, Georgia. He told me that every wall in his office was lined with stacks of bankruptcy filings that were caused as a result of people waiting until the last minute to file bankruptcy under the old law. This is important to know as a virtual bankruptcy assistant because it helps you to understand what may currently be going on in the field of bankruptcy. Also remember that filings made under the old law continued to be handled under the old law. It took several months before the new bankruptcy law was even fully used within the court system after the law was passed.

Start a Local Legal Clinic

One paralegal I interviewed had an excellent idea. She ran help wanted ads in college newspapers that were targeted to law students who were getting ready to take the bar exam. One ad she frequently used that worked well for her was:

> **NEW** attorneys needed for possible legal clinic start-up in the area of consumer bankruptcy. Please call 000-0000

She received over 100 telephone calls from attorneys who were getting ready to either take the bar exam or had recently passed it. Out of the 100 attorneys who originally called, three were interested in her idea so she set up an appointment for an initial business meeting with all the parties.

The result of the meeting was the development of a legal clinic that was located inside a high-traffic mall. Consumers came into the clinic, the paralegal conducted the initial client intake interview and drafted the bankruptcy petition. The attorneys also met with the clients, had them sign a Retainer Agreement and collected the monies for the bankruptcy representation. The legal clinic turned out to be very successful and the paralegal as well as the attorneys earned more money compared to working in a law firm.

Summary of Marketing

As I stated before, there are as many ways to market a product or service as there are stars in the sky. I have provided you with the resources and methods I personally used to start building *The Lawyer Assistant*. But (as I said before) what worked for me may not necessarily work for you. Even if I drove to your house and wrote all your advertising materials for you, you are still a unique individual and you have your own unique personality. Your business is an extension of who you are and it will always be different from the others. Just make sure you build it with a solid foundation so it will not collapse during a storm.

Marketing can be compared to asking 25 cooks how to prepare a meal and getting 25 different answers. As you build your business and come into contact with other business owners you will hear a lot of different ideas and methods they used to build their companies. Don't think you have to do the same thing. Just like a good cook, you can collect bits and pieces of the recipes from a variety of sources and form you own unique way of cooking that works for you and within your budget.

Below is a list of marketing moves that business owners often miss. If you follow these marketing secrets you will gain a competitive edge in attracting new clients and increase referrals.

- Appeal to your clients' self-interest. Clients will hire you only if they know how they will benefit. Clients always ask: *What's in it for me?* Make sure all your marketing materials (including your web site) answers this question over and over again.

- Make sure client's know how your services are different from your competition. Client's do not hire you because your service is like everyone else. They hire you because you are different. These positive differences is what gives you a competitive edge. Make sure you emphasize to client's exactly how your service is different from the others. You might even *tastefully* compare your services with Company A and Company B and then proceed to show how your service will save the client money or provide them with a better product.

Note: Many new business owners are often worried about competition. One way to virtually eliminate any competition is to offer unique, high-quality services your competition cannot provide. Strive to place your business in a class *all its own* and you may never be in a position where competition is a worry or concern.

- Continually strive to achieve the highest possible level of trust. Everyone, including you and me are skeptical to part with our money. You can increase the creditability of your business by doing the following:

a. Talk to client's in plain English. Don't try to impress them with your high-level of intelligence. Remember that client's are not interested in you, they are interested in hiring you to do a service for them.

b. Allow client's to discuss their problems. Listen to your client's. Let them talk and explain their situation to you. As they are talking, you can think of ways you are going to present the perfect solution to their problem — your services.

c. Collect testimonials and make them available for potential clients. Testimonials should also appear on your web site and they should all be verifiable.

In other words, you must ask your client for permission to mention their law firm if you plan to use their testimonial. I have not known of any attorney to refuse this offer. By adding the law firm's name to the testimonial, it provides the potential client with verifiable evidence the testimonial is real.

Also, evaluate your own thought-process of selection when you decide to hire a professional. What do you look for? How do you determine if the professional is trustworthy? Your own self-evaluation will help you to understand how your client's will perceive your business.

- When you begin an explanation, always go back to square one. When you simply assume the client understands the basic facts, you will almost always be wrong. The explanation you provide to potential client's may be the same explanation you have repeated many times before, but it will be the first time the client has heard it. Therefore, always start at the beginning, lay the foundation for your explanation and speak in plain English.

- Do not use advertising to deliver your marketing message. Instead, use advertising to arouse interest in your services and increase the desire to request more information from you. This will save you a lot of money and it helps to build a customer client base of target-marketed prospects.

- Invite clients to call you with questions. Normally when people call my office with questions about my services they will immediately place an order. Often the potential client is only interested to know if you are a real business and to find out if you really know what you are doing. An attorney will never trust a offsite virtual bankruptcy assistant with sensitive client information unless they trust them. Therefore, expect to receive phone calls from attorneys interested in your service and be prepared to show them the confidence you have in your own abilities to do a highly professional job for them.

- Place the needs of your clients above money. Although you need to generate an income for your business in order for it to grow and survive, you should never place *making money* at the top of your priority list. If you provide your clients with good quality, dependable service, the money will come on its own without much effort.

- Use supportive and bonding-type words. Cold, impersonal words will turn clients off. Instead, attack clients by using bonding-type words like *welcome, share, invite* and *good.* Here are a few do's and do not's to help you begin formulating some good ideas:

Do Not Use:	You may call our office during normal business hours.
Use This Instead:	Please feel free to call our office if we can help you in any way.
Do Not Use:	Please have a seat, I will be with you in a minute.
Use This Instead:	Thank you for stopping by. It is good to see you. Please give me a minute and I will be right with you. May I get you some coffee while you're waiting?
Do Not Use:	I'm sorry but I cannot find your order right now.
Use This Instead:	Let me take your phone number and I will call you back with the information.
Do Not Use:	We can provide you with the service but it is going to cost you several hundred dollars.
Use This Instead:	Yes! We can provide that service with a 100% money-back guarantee for only $349.00.

- Never turn down work. Many new business owners make the big mistake of turning down offers of work from clients that may be outside their normal services. Get in the habit of never turning down extra work. Even if you are incapable of doing the job yourself, it is smarter to hire a freelance contractor to complete the job for you. This way, your business will earn a profit without you actually doing the work yourself.

- Charge a reasonable fee for your service. Never make the mistake of pricing your service too low with the intention of getting more work. Take it from someone who knows. Your skill as a virtual bankruptcy assistant is unique and in great demand (whether you realize it or not at this time.) You are already saving the attorney a great deal of money. If you discount your services too low, your product will look cheap and you will attract the *wrong kind* of attorney.

Suggested fees for drafting bankruptcy petitions:

Pricing Guidelines if you are NOT EXPERIENCED:
Chapter 7 - $250.00

Pricing Guidelines if you ARE EXPERIENCED:
Chapter 7 – $350.00 (50 debts or less)
Chapter 7 - $450.00 (51 debts or more)

These pricing guidelines are NOT written in stone. They should only be used as a guideline for pricing your bankruptcy forms processing services. Most attorneys charge from $1,500 to $2,000 to clients for Chapter 7 representation. Your fee should be based on approximately 15% of the attorney fee if you have little or no experience and 25% or more after you have experience. Therefore, when an attorney contacts you to obtain more information about your virtual bankruptcy assistant services, he or she will probably ask you for a price to draft their petitions. Never answer this question directly. Instead, throw the negotiation back into the attorney's lap by saying: *I base my fee on several factors as I work with each attorney to determine a fair and reasonable price. What do you charge your clients for a Chapter 7?* Then, wait on an answer. Once the attorney provides you with the amount he or she charges their client, you can quickly do a calculation in your head of 15% to 25% of their fee. If the attorney feels the price is too high, you can tell the attorney: *My fee will be reduced as your volume increases, however, before you decide whether to use my services or not, allow me to do the first one for you with no payment upfront. If you are not satisfied with my work, you do not pay the invoice.*

WARNING: Do NOT price your Chapter 7 bankruptcy petition services less than $200. This technique will NOT bring more business. Instead, it will cheapen your business, harm your ability to grow and hurt the industry.

- Make sure you get paid. Unlike working for an employer, when you own a business everything you do is free labor until the clients check clears the bank. Learn how to talk openly, honestly and proudly about your prices. Be prepared to explain how your services are a measure of your knowledge, skill and expertise. When a client asks why another virtual bankruptcy assistant charges less than you do, you could respond by saying: *I wonder what the assistant is leaving out?*

- Finally, always place the Lord Jesus Christ at the forefront of your business. Of course this suggestion does not work for the unsaved. But if you know Jesus Christ as your Lord and Savior, I encourage you to pray and talk with Him on a daily basis about your plans and goals. Ask God to direct your paths and help your business to prosper. Also remember to tithe 10% of your business profit (income minus expenses) in the manner that God directs you; then pray for God's blessing. Your tithing does not need to necessarily be given to a church or ministry. (Many of the Christian churches are corrupt in this day and age anyway.) Instead, you can use the money to feed poor families in your area or buy toys for children in the cancer hospital or any other worthwhile purpose that truly helps people in need. You might also want to include a Chick Tract which is an excellent witnessing tool. You can order a supply at www.chick.com. You will always find that when you give from your heart God will richly bless you.

May God bless you and bring you to the knowledge of His perfect will in your life. Some people get angry when I include God in my books, but I don't care. I fully believe that God answered my prayer and gave me the knowledge to develop and train others who will become very successful in this field. I just hope that you are one of those successful people.

Chapter 9

Resource Links for
Virtual Bankruptcy Assistants

Resource Links for Virtual Bankruptcy Assistants

The web site references that appear in this chapter have not paid to be listed. Instead, these are the web sites that I personally used in building *The Lawyer Assistant.* But keep in mind that web sites move and merge with larger web sites. Therefore, if any of the links in this chapter become outdated, go to any search engine and type in the company name to locate their new web site location.

Setting Up Your Business

- http://www.dnwiz.com/
  Available domain names for ideas in naming your business.

- http://www.google.com
  Search engine

- http://www.bummerhosting.comg
  Recommended Web Hosting

- Geoff Gratz, Email: ggratz@columbus.rr.com
  Recommended Computer Technician

- http://www.dell.com/outlet/
  Save Money on Computers

- http://www.maxemail.com
  Recommended Efax Service

- http://www.quillcorp.com
  Quill Corporation

- http://www.vikingop.com
  Viking Office Supplies

- http://www.reliable.coms
  Reliable Office Supplies

- http://www.staples.com
  Staples Office Supplies

- http://www.officemax.com
  Office Max Office Supplies

- http://www.chick.com
  Chick Tracks

General Bankruptcy Information

- http://www.13network.com/
  The attorney is the only one that can sign up to access the Chapter 13 Network online. Have your attorney contact the Chapter 13 trustee and request a user name and password to access the service.

- http://www.pacer.psc.uscourts.gov/
  As a virtual bankruptcy assistant, you can sign up for your own PACER account.

- http://www.uscourts.gov/rules/bk-localrules.html
  Local rules of court for all the U.S. bankruptcy courts.

- http://www.bankruptcyaction.com/bankruptcyexemptions.htm
  Find out if state or federal exemptions are used for bankruptcy filings in your area.

- http://www.atla.org/Networking/Tier3/ListServers.aspx
  Legal related web list server.

- http://www.usdoj.gov/ust/eo/ust_org/office_map.htm
  Locate U.S. Bankruptcy Trustees in all 50 states

- http://www.legalresearchbydave.homestead.com/
  Free legal research website.

- http://www.lexisnexis.com/
  The main website used by the legal community for research.

- http://www.carquotes.com/blackbook.asp
  Find market values for motor vehicles in the Black Book.

- http://www.kbb.com/
  Find market values for motor vehicles in Kelly Blue Book.

- http://www.boats.com/nada/nada.jsp
  Find market values for boats.

- http://www.nadaguides.com
  Find market values for motor vehicles at NADA.

- http://www.duhaime.org/diction.htm
  Online legal dictionary.

- http://legal.hopcott.net/
  Excellent resource for legal-related books and materials.

- http://www.legalcity.net/
  Submit articles and press releases to targeted areas of the legal community or read materials submitted by others to increase your own knowledge.

- http://www.knowlespublishing.com/
  An excellent source for legal related books and CDs.

- http://www.lawidea.com/
  A resource directory of over 17,000 links to legal related websites.

- http://www.mybankruptcyassistant.com/
  A bankruptcy petition preparation service for attorneys. Obtain some great ideas and excellent resources.

- http://www.weitzlux.com/statebaraccociations_449.html
  Locate your local state bar association. Paralegals normally can become members of the bar, but they will be classified as *associate* members. It is a good idea to join the bar association in your area and add this to your resume and any other list of credits.

- http://www.freelancers.com/newlisting.asp
  A great place to announce your freelance forms processing services.

- http://www.ibill.com/about/
  If you do not have a merchant account for your business where you can accept Visa, Mastercard, Discover and American Express credit cards, you may want to check out the professional services of Ibill instead of Paypal.

- http://www.titlesearch.com/
  If you ever need a title search performed on a piece of real estate, this is an excellent online resource.

- http://www.irs.gov/file/content/0,,id=105693,00.html
  I used this website to locate the mailing address of IRS offices. This is necessary to know when clients owe back taxes. Although debtor(s) may currently reside in one location, they may have moved. Find out the city and state they lived in when the tax debt was made and you can easily locate the correct IRS office to notify when the bankruptcy petition is filed.

- http://www.bankruptcy-courts.net/
  General information on Chapter 7, 13 and 11 bankruptcy procedures.

- http://www.bankruptcyaction.com/
  Complete U.S. bankruptcy information including business bankruptcy predictor, bankruptcy exemptions for all states, lawyer locator covering lawyers in all states, do-it-yourself bankruptcy, bankruptcy statistics, bankruptcy news and more.

- http://www4.law.cornell.edu/uscode/11/
  The complete bankruptcy code online. Use the search feature and quickly locate and cite references for your attorney.

- http://www.bankrupt.com/conferences/
  Directory of upcoming bankruptcy seminars, meetings and conferences.

- http://www.nbi-sems.com/
  The Institute for Paralegal Education

- http://www.bankruptcydata.com/Courts/Courts.htm
  Links to all the bankruptcy courts in the United States. Locate addresses, telephone numbers, read bankruptcy headlines and much more. Creditor's lists, plan summaries and reports can be viewed on a *pay per view* basis.

Means Test Information

- http://www.usdoj.gov/ust
  Means Income Tables

- http://www.collectlaw.com/lawsandarticles.htm
  NARCA Legislative Alert - Senate Bill 256 - Summary

- http://abiworld.net/newsletter/financialadvisors/vol2num3/summary.html
  Summary of the BAPCPA of 2005

- http://www.nacba.org/ubb/chicagofaqc73.asp
  Chapter 7 Means Test Questions and Answers

- http://www.usdoj.gov/ust/bapcpa/bci_data/median_income_table.htm
  Median Income by State

- http://www.usdoj.gov/ust/bapcpa/meanstesting.htm
  Means Testing Information (provided by the US Trustee Program)

- http://www.irs.gov/businesses/small/article/0,,id=104696,00.html
  National Standard for Housing and Utility Expenses

- http://www.usdoj.gov/ust/bapcpa/bci_data/national_expense_standards.htm
  National Standards for Living Expenses

- http://www.irs.gov/businesses/small/article/0,,id=104623,00.html
  National Standards for Transportation Expenses

Credit Counseling Requirement

- http://www.usdoj.gov/ust/eo/bapcpa/ccde/cc_approved.htm
  Approved Credit Counseling Agencies

- http://www.cccsatl.org/index.asp?pg=titlepg_BK_options
  Online Credit Counseling

- http://www.cfefa.org/
  Debt Counseling Agency

Paralegal Education

- http://www.ashworthcollege.com/
  This college offers an excellent on-line paralegal education. You can earn your Paralegal Certificate and/or Associate's Degree in the comfort of your home. Although there are hundreds of online colleges like Ashworth, this is where I personally obtained my degree.

- http://calparalegal.com/
  Constitutional Educational Research Foundation

- http://www.theparalegalschool.com/
  The Washington Online Learning Institute

Places to Find Attorneys on the Internet

- http://www.bestlawyers.com/
- http://www.lawyertree.com/
- http://www.attorneyfind.com/
- http://lawyers.findlaw.com/
- http://www.martindale.com/
- http://www.lawyers.com/
- http://www.legalengine.com/findalawyer.htm

- http://www.bankruptcylawyers.com/
- http://www.abcworld.org/condir.html
- http://law.chapter7.com/
  A legal directory specifically for locating Chapter 7 bankruptcy attorneys.
- http://www.nacba.org/
  National Association of Bankruptcy Attorneys
- http://www.nabt.com/
  National Association of Bankruptcy Trustees

Marketing and Web Design Links

- http://www.webthemes.com/do-it.html
  Market your website to search engines and link pages.

- http://groups.yahoo.com/group/LegalLinkExchange/
  Make sure you announce your legal service on this board.

- http://selfpromotion.com/
  This is one of the best websites I know of that provides you with excellent information on properly marketing your website on the internet.

- http://www.virtualpromote.com/promoteb.html
  Another fantastic website filled with marketing information and links to help your business to grow.

- http://www.boxedart.com/
  A great place to find templates and graphics for your web pages.

- http://www.basictemplates.com/
  Another great place to find webpage templates that will help you to present a professional online presence for your company.

Press Release Submission

- http://www.free-press-release.com/submit/
  Free Press Release.Com

- http://www.prweb.com/
  PR Web

- http://www.ideamarketers.com/library/category.cfm?acatid=51
  Idea Marketers

National Advertising

- http://www.advertisingresults.com/
  ACS, Inc.

- http://www.nationwideadvertising.com/
  Nationwide Newspapers

Legal Employment

- http://www.spherion.com/
  Spherion Temporary Agency

- http://www.specialcounsel.com/home.asp
  Special Counsel

- http://www.legalstaff.com
  Legal Staff

Legal Software

- http://www.abacuslaw.com/
  Case management software program.

- http://www.timeslips.com/
  Another case management software program.

- http://www.timematters.com/
  Time billing software program

- http://www.hotdocs.com/
  A popular software program that allows your master template pleadings and forms to be used over and over again to maintain consistency and prevent repetitive typing

Bankruptcy Software

- http://www.bestcase.com/
  In my opinion, this is the best bankruptcy petition preparation software on the market.

- http://www.lawfirmsoftware.com/
  A! Law Firm Software

- http://www.bankruptcysoftware.com/
  Bankruptcy 2005

- http://nationallawforms.com/bankruptcy/software-bankruptcy.htm
  Bankruptcy Case

- http://www.lawdisks.com/bcydisk.htm
  Bankruptcy Disk

- http://www.syscommedia.net/bankruptcy_plus_software.asp
  Bankruptcy Plus

- http://www.legal-pro.com/
  Bankruptcy Pro

- http://www.ezfiling.com/
  EZ Filing

Legal Associations

- http://www.aafpe.org/
  American Association for Paralegal Education

- http://www.abanet.org/home.html
  The American Bar Association

- http://www.abiworld.org/
  American Bankruptcy Institute

- http://www.alanet.org/home.html
  Association of Legal Administrators

- http://www.clla.org/
  Commercial Law League of North America

- http://www.paralegalmanagement.org/ipma/
  International Paralegal Association

- http://www.nala.org/
  National Association of Legal Assistants

- http://www.paralegals.org/
  National Federation of Paralegal Associations

- http://www.paralegalgateway.com/
  Paralegal Gateway

Publications and Chat Boards

- http://www.bankruptcybooks.com/
  A wide range of hard-to-find bankruptcy books.

- http://bankruptcymaster.com/
  Bankruptcy Master is the most comprehensive and reliable resource for the legal, collection and credit professionals practicing bankruptcy law.

- http://www.legalassistanttoday.com/bulletin/
  All virtual bankruptcy assistants should subscribe to this excellent online newsletter.

- http://chat-cards.com/wwwboard/bankruptcy/messages.html
  Bankruptcy forum chat board.

- http://chapter7.com/forum/list.php?f=1
  The Bankruptcy Forum

- http://lawofficecomputing.com
  Law Office Computing Magazine

- http://groups.yahoo.com/group/bankruptcy_roundtable_USA/
  Bankruptcy Roundtable

- http://finance.groups.yahoo.com/group/BeltranAssoc-Chapter_7_Bankruptcy/
  Chapter 7 Bankruptcy

- http://www.bankrupt.com/mail_lists/discussion.twn.html
  Turnarounds and Workouts Newswire

- http://www.hklaw.com/Publications/Subscribe.asp
  Bankruptcy and Creditor's Rights Newsletter

- http://johnrogerslaw.lawoffice.com/CM/Custom/Bankruptcy.asp
  Bankruptcy Newsletter from the Law Office of John Rogers

- http://www.bankruptcymedia.com/bkfinder/pastissues.html
  Free Bankruptcy Ezine to Subscribe To and Read Previous Issues

- http://www.irs.gov/businesses/small/article/0,,id=104598,00.html
  Bankruptcy Article

- http://www.usdoj.gov/ust/eo/bapcpa/meanstesting.htm
  Article from US Department of Justice

- http://www.fbamich.org/index.cfm?location=154&ParentID=156
  Another Bankruptcy Article

Web Resources Available from 713Training.Com

- http://www.713training.com/teleconference/index.html
  Weekly teleconferences

- https://www.713training.com/administrator/signup.php
  Join the Bankruptcy Teleconference Club

- http://www.713training.com/directory/index.html
  The Nationwide Bankruptcy Forms Processor Directory

- http://www.713training.com/directory/whyorder.html
  Add your services to the nationwide directory

- http://www.713training.com/trainingvideos/index.html
  Training Video: How to Draft a Bankruptcy Petition

- Free Video Training Sample
  http://www.50statenotary.com/bankruptcybook/samplevideo.html

- http://www.713training.com/marketingvideo/index.html
  Marketing Video: How to Market Your Virtual Bankruptcy Assistant Service

- http://www.713training.com/workbook/index.html
  The Virtual Bankruptcy Assistant Training Workbook

- http://www.713training.com/seminars/index.html
  Power Marketing Seminars

- http://www.713training.com/freetraining/index.html
  Free Getting-Started Ebook

- https://www.713training.com/intake_forms/index.html
  Client Intake Forms

Chapter 10

Legal Dictionary for Virtual Bankruptcy Assistants

Legal Dictionary for Virtual Bankruptcy Assisants

The following information was compiled by Rick Raddatz of Radco Publishing. Rick sorted through a wide variety of legal dictionaries and hand picked the legal terms that relate to virtual bankruptcy assistants. I am sure you will gain a great benefit from this exclusive dictionary and will refer to it often.

341 Meeting
In a bankruptcy proceeding, a meeting of creditors at which the debtor is questioned under oath by creditors, a trustee, an examiner, or the U.S. Trustee about his or her financial affairs.

-A-

Administrative Office of the United States Courts (AO)
The federal agency responsible for collecting court statistics, administering the federal courts' budget, and performing many other administrative and programmatic functions, under the direction and supervision of the Judicial Conference of the United States.

Admissible
A term used to describe evidence that may be considered by a jury or judge in civil and criminal cases.

Adversary proceeding
A lawsuit arising in or related to a bankruptcy case that begins by filing a complaint with the court, that is, a *trial* that takes place within the context of a bankruptcy case.

Affidavit
A written or printed statement made under oath.

Affirmed
In the practice of the court of appeals, it means that the court of appeals has concluded that the lower court decision is correct and will stand as rendered by the lower court.

Alternate Juror
A juror selected in the same manner as a regular juror who hears all the evidence but does not help decide the case unless called on to replace a regular juror.

Alternative Dispute Resolution (ADR)
A procedure for settling a dispute outside the courtroom. Most forms of ADR are not binding on the parties, and involve referral of the case to a neutral party such as an arbitrator or mediator.

Answer
The formal written statement by a defendant in a civil case that responds to a complaint, articulating the grounds for defense.

Appeal
A request made after a trial by a party that has lost on one or more issues that a higher court review the decision to determine if it was correct. To make such a request is *to appeal* or to *take an appeal.* One who appeals is called the *appellant;* the other party is the *appellee.*

Appellant
The party who appeals a district court's decision, usually seeking reversal of that decision.

Appellate
About appeals; an appellate court has the power to review the judgment of a lower court (trial court) or tribunal. For example, the U.S. circuit courts of appeals review the decisions of the U.S. district courts.

Appellee
The party who opposes an appellant's appeal, and who seeks to persuade the appeals court to affirm the district court's decision.

Assets
Property of all kinds, including real and personal, tangible and intangible.

Assume
An agreement to continue performing duties under a contract or lease.

Automatic Stay
An injunction that automatically stops lawsuits, foreclosure, garnishments, and most collection activity against the debtor the moment a bankruptcy petition is filed.

-B-

Bankruptcy
A legal procedure for dealing with debt problems of individuals and businesses; specifically, a case filed under one of the Chapters of Title 11 of the United States Code (the Bankruptcy Code).

Bankruptcy Administrator
An officer of the Judiciary serving in the judicial districts of Alabama and North Carolina who, like the United States trustee, is responsible for supervising the

administration of bankruptcy cases, estates, and trustees; monitoring plans and disclosure statements; monitoring creditors' committees; monitoring fee applications; and performing other statutory duties.

Bankruptcy Code
The informal name for Title 11 of the United States Code (11 U.S.C. Sections 101-1330), the federal bankruptcy law.

Bankruptcy Court
The bankruptcy judges in regular active service in each district; a unit of the district court.

Bankruptcy Estate
All interests of the debtor in property at the time of the bankruptcy filing. The estate technically becomes the temporary legal owner of all of the debtor's property.

Bankruptcy Judge
A judicial officer of the United States district court who is the court official with decision-making power over federal bankruptcy cases.

Bankruptcy Petition
A formal request for the protection of the federal bankruptcy laws. (There is an official set of Forms and Schedules for bankruptcy petitions.)

Bankruptcy Trustee
A private individual or corporation appointed in all Chapter 7 and Chapter 13 cases to represent the interests of the bankruptcy estate and the debtor's creditors.

Brief

A written statement submitted in a trial or appellate proceeding that explains one side's legal and factual arguments.

Burden of Proof

The duty to prove disputed facts. In civil cases, a plaintiff generally has the burden of proving his or her case. In criminal cases, the government has the burden of proving the defendant's guilt.

Business Bankruptcy

A bankruptcy case in which the debtor is a business or an individual involved in business and the debts are for business purposes.

-C-

Case File

A complete collection of every document filed in court in a case.

Case Law

The law as established in previous court decisions. A synonym for legal precedent. Akin to common law, which springs from tradition and judicial decisions.

Caseload

The number of cases handled by a judge or a court.

Cause of Action

A legal claim.

Chambers

The offices of a judge and his or her staff.

Chapter 7

The chapter of the Bankruptcy Code providing for *liquidation,* that is, the sale of a debtor's nonexempt property and the distribution of the proceeds to creditors. In order to be eligible for Chapter 7, the debtor must satisfy a *Means Test.* The court will evaluate the debtor's income and expenses to determine if the debtor may proceed under Chapter 7.

Chapter 7 Trustee

A person appointed in a Chapter 7 case to represent the interests of the bankruptcy estate and the creditors. The trustee's responsibilities include reviewing the debtor's petition and schedules, liquidating the property of the estate, and making distributions to creditors. The trustee may also bring actions against creditors or the debtor to recover property of the bankruptcy estate.

Chapter 9

The chapter of the Bankruptcy Code providing for reorganization of municipalities (which includes cities and towns, as well as villages, counties, taxing districts, municipal utilities, and school districts).

Chapter 11

A reorganization bankruptcy, usually involving a corporation or partnership. A Chapter 11 debtor usually proposes a plan of reorganization to keep its business alive and pay creditors over time. People in business or individuals can also seek relief in Chapter 11.

Chapter 12

The chapter of the Bankruptcy Code providing for adjustment of debts of a *family farmer,* as that term is defined in the Bankruptcy Code.

Chapter 13

The chapter of the Bankruptcy Code providing for adjustment of debts of an individual with regular income, often referred to as a *wage-earner* plan. Chapter 13 allows a debtor to keep property and use his or her disposable income to pay debts over time, usually three to five years.

Chapter 13 Trustee

A person appointed to administer a Chapter 13 case. A Chapter 13 trustee's responsibilities are similar to those of a Chapter 7 trustee; however, a Chapter 13 trustee has the additional responsibilities of overseeing the debtor's plan, receiving payments from debtors, and disbursing plan payments to creditors.

Chapter 15

The chapter of the Bankruptcy Code dealing with cases of cross-border insolvency.

Chief Judge

The judge who has primary responsibility for the administration of a court; chief judges are determined by seniority.

Claim

A creditor's assertion of a right to payment from a debtor or the debtor's property.

Class Action

A lawsuit in which one or more members of a large group, or class, of individuals or other entities sue on behalf of the entire class. The district court must find that the claims of the class members contain questions of law or fact in common before the lawsuit can proceed as a class action.

Clerk of Court

The court officer who oversees administrative functions, especially managing the flow of cases through the court. The clerk's office is often called a *court's central nervous system.*

Collateral

Property that is promised as security for the satisfaction of a debt.

Common Law

The legal system that originated in England and is now in use in the United States that relies on the articulation of legal principles in a historical succession of judicial decisions. Common law principles can be changed by legislation.

Complaint

A written statement that begins a civil lawsuit, in which the plaintiff details the claims against the defendant.

Confirmation

Approval of a plan of reorganization by a bankruptcy judge.

Consumer Bankruptcy

A bankruptcy case filed to reduce or eliminate debts that are primarily consumer debts.

Consumer Debts

Debts incurred for personal, as opposed to business, needs.

Contingent Claim

A claim that may be owed by the debtor under certain circumstances, e.g., where the debtor is a cosigner on another person's loan and that person fails to pay.

Contract

An agreement between two or more persons that creates an obligation to do or not to do a particular thing.

Counsel

Legal advice; a term also used to refer to the lawyers in a case.

Court

Government entity authorized to resolve legal disputes. Judges sometimes use *court* to refer to themselves in the third person, as in *the court has read the briefs.*

Court Reporter

A person who makes a word-for-word record of what is said in court, generally by using a stenographic machine, shorthand or audio recording, and then produces a transcript of the proceedings upon request.

Creditor

A person to whom or business to which the debtor owes money or that claims to be owed money by the debtor.

Credit Counseling

Generally refers to two events in individual bankruptcy cases:

1. the *individual or group briefing* from a nonprofit budget and credit counseling agency that individual debtors must attend prior to filing under any chapter of the Bankruptcy Code; and

2. the *instructional course in personal financial management* in chapters 7 and 13 that an individual debtor must complete before a discharge is entered.

There are exceptions to both requirements for certain categories of debtors, exigent circumstances, or if the U.S. trustee or bankruptcy administrator have determined that there are insufficient approved credit counseling agencies available to provide the necessary counseling.

-D-

Damages
Money that a defendant pays a plaintiff in a civil case if the plaintiff has won. Damages may be compensatory (for loss or injury) or punitive (to punish and deter future misconduct).

Debtor
A person who has filed a petition for relief under the Bankruptcy Code. defendant An individual (or business) against whom a lawsuit is filed.

Debtor's Plan
A debtor's detailed description of how the debtor proposes to pay creditors' claims over a fixed period of time.

Declaratory Judgment
A judge's statement about someone's rights. For example, a plaintiff may seek a declaratory judgment that a particular statute, as written, violates some constitutional right.

De Facto
Latin, meaning *in fact* or *actually.* Something that exists in fact but not as a matter of law.

Default Judgment

A judgment awarding a plaintiff the relief sought in the complaint because the defendant has failed to appear in court or otherwise respond to the complaint.

Defendant

In a civil case, the person or organization against whom the plaintiff brings suit; in a criminal case, the person accused of the crime.

De Jure

Latin, meaning *in law.* Something that exists by operation of law.

De Novo

Latin, meaning *anew.* A trial *de novo* is a completely new trial. Appellate review de novo implies no deference to the trial judge's ruling.

Deposition

An oral statement made before an officer authorized by law to administer oaths. Such statements are often taken to examine potential witnesses, to obtain discovery, or to be used later in trial.

Discharge

A release of a debtor from personal liability for certain dischargeable debts. Notable exceptions to dischargeability are taxes and student loans. A discharge releases a debtor from personal liability for certain debts known as dischargeable debts and prevents the creditors owed those debts from taking any action against the debtor or the debtor's property to collect the debts. The discharge also prohibits creditors from communicating with the debtor regarding the debt, including through telephone calls, letters, and personal contact.

Dischargeable Debt

A debt for which the Bankruptcy Code allows the debtor's personal liability to be eliminated.

Disclosure Statement

A written document prepared by the chapter 11 debtor or other plan proponent that is designed to provide *adequate information* to creditors to enable them to evaluate the chapter 11 plan of reorganization.

Discovery

Procedures used to obtain disclosure of evidence before trial.

Dismissal with Prejudice

Court action that prevents an identical lawsuit from being filed later.

Dismissal without Prejudice

Court action that allows the later filing.

Disposable Income

Income not reasonably necessary for the maintenance or support of the debtor or dependents. If the debtor operates a business, disposable income is defined as those amounts over and above what is necessary for the payment of ordinary operating expenses.

Docket

A log containing the complete history of each case in the form of brief chronological entries summarizing the court proceedings.

Due Process

In criminal law, the constitutional guarantee that a defendant will receive a fair and impartial trial. In civil law, the legal rights of someone who confronts an adverse action threatening liberty or property.

-E-

En Banc

French, meaning *on the bench.* All judges of an appellate court sitting together to hear a case, as opposed to the routine disposition by panels of three judges. In the Ninth Circuit, an en banc panel consists of the chief judge and 14 other, randomly selected, judges.

Equitable

Pertaining to civil suits in *equity* rather than in *law.* In English legal history, the courts of *law* could order the payment of damages and could afford no other remedy. See damages. A separate court of *equity* could order someone to do something or to cease to do something. See, e.g., injunction. In American jurisprudence, the federal courts have both legal and equitable power, but the distinction is still an important one. For example, a trial by jury is normally available in *law* cases but not in *equity* cases.

Equity

The value of a debtor's interest in property that remains after liens and other creditors' interests are considered. (Example: If a house valued at $60,000 is subject to a $30,000 mortgage, there is $30,000 of equity.)

Evidence

Information presented in testimony or in documents that is used to persuade the fact finder (judge or jury) to decide the case in favor of one side or the other.

Exculpatory Evidence

Evidence indicating that a defendant did not commit the crime.

Executory Contracts

Contracts or leases under which both parties to the agreement have duties remaining to be performed. If a contract or lease is executory, a debtor may assume it (keep the contract) or reject it (terminate the contract).

Exempt Assets

Property that a debtor is allowed to retain, free from the claims of creditors who do not have liens on the property.

Exemptions, Exempt Property

Certain property owned by an individual debtor that the Bankruptcy Code or applicable state law permits the debtor to keep from unsecured creditors.

For example, in some states the debtor may be able to exempt all or a portion of the equity in the debtor's primary residence (homestead exemption), or some or all *tools of the trade* used by the debtor to make a living (i.e., auto tools for an auto mechanic or dental tools for a dentist). The availability and amount of property the debtor may exempt depends on the state the debtor lives in.

Ex Parte

A proceeding brought before a court by one party only, without notice to or challenge by the other side.

-F-

Face Sheet Filing

A bankruptcy case filed either without schedules or with incomplete schedules listing few creditors and debts. (Face sheet filings are often made for the purpose of delaying an eviction or foreclosure.)

Family Farmer
An individual, individual and spouse, corporation, or partnership engaged in a farming operation that meets certain debt limits and other statutory criteria for filing a petition under Chapter 12.

Federal Public Defender
An attorney employed by the federal courts on a fulltime basis to provide legal defense to defendants who are unable to afford counsel. The judiciary administers the federal defender program pursuant to the Criminal Justice Act.

Federal Question Jurisdiction
Jurisdiction given to federal courts in cases involving the interpretation and application of the U.S. Constitution, acts of Congress, and treaties.

Felony
A serious crime, usually punishable by at least one year in prison.

File
To place a paper in the official custody of the clerk of court to enter into the files or records of a case.

Fraudulent Transfer
A transfer of a debtor's property made with intent to defraud or for which the debtor receives less than the transferred property's value.

Fresh Start
The characterization of a debtor's status after bankruptcy, i.e., free of most debts. (Giving debtors a fresh start is one purpose of the Bankruptcy Code.)

-G-

Grand Jury

A body of 16-23 citizens who listen to evidence of criminal allegations, which is presented by the prosecutors, and determine whether there is probable cause to believe an individual committed an offense.

-H-

Hearsay

Evidence presented by a witness who did not see or hear the incident in question but heard about it from someone else. With some exceptions, hearsay generally is not admissible as evidence at trial.

Home Confinement

A special condition the court imposes that requires an individual to remain at home except for certain approved activities such as work and medical appointments. Home confinement may include the use of electronic monitoring equipment with a transmitter attached to the wrist or the ankle to help ensure that the person stays at home as required.

-I-

Impeachment

The process of calling a witness's testimony into doubt. For example, if the attorney can show that the witness may have fabricated portions of his testimony, the witness is said to be *impeached;* The constitutional process whereby the House of Representatives may *impeach* (accuse of misconduct) high officers of the federal government, who are then tried by the Senate.

In Camera

Latin, meaning in a judge's chambers. Often means outside the presence of a jury and the public. In private.

Inculpatory Evidence

Evidence indicating that a defendant did commit the crime.

In Forma Pauperis

In the manner of a pauper. Permission given by the court to a person to file a case without payment of the required court fees because the person cannot pay them.

Information

A formal accusation by a government attorney that the defendant committed a misdemeanor.

Injunction

A court order preventing one or more named parties from taking some action. A preliminary injunction often is issued to allow fact-finding, so a judge can determine whether a permanent injunction is justified.

Insider (of corporate debtor)

A director, officer, or person in control of the debtor; a partnership in which the debtor is a general partner; a general partner of the debtor; or a relative of a general partner, director, officer, or person in control of the debtor.

Insider (of individual debtor)

Any relative of the debtor or of a general partner of the debtor; partnership in which the debtor is a general partner; general partner of the debtor; or corporation of which the debtor is a director, officer, or person in control.

Interrogatories
A form of discovery consisting of written questions to be answered in writing and under oath.

Issue

1. The disputed point between parties in a lawsuit;
2. To send out officially, as in a court issuing an order.

-J-

Joint Administration
A court-approved mechanism under which two or more cases can be administered together. (Assuming no conflicts of interest, these separate businesses or individuals can pool their resources, hire the same professionals, etc.)

Joint petition
One bankruptcy petition filed by a husband and wife together.

Judge
An official of the judicial branch with authority to decide lawsuits brought before courts. Used generically, the term judge may also refer to all judicial officers, including Supreme Court justices.

Judgeship
The position of judge. By statute, Congress authorizes the number of judgeships for each district and appellate court.

Judgment
The official decision of a court finally resolving the dispute between the parties to the lawsuit.

Judicial Conference of the United States
The policy-making entity for the federal court system. A 27-judge body whose presiding officer is the Chief Justice of the United States.

Jurisdiction
The legal authority of a court to hear and decide a certain type of case. It also is used as a synonym for venue, meaning the geographic area over which the court has territorial jurisdiction to decide cases.

Jurisprudence
The study of law and the structure of the legal system.

Jury
The group of persons selected to hear the evidence in a trial and render a verdict on matters of fact.

Jury Instructions
A judge's directions to the jury before it begins deliberations regarding the factual questions it must answer and the legal rules that it must apply.

-L-

Lawsuit
A legal action started by a plaintiff against a defendant based on a complaint that the defendant failed to perform a legal duty which resulted in harm to the plaintiff.

Lien
A charge on specific property that is designed to secure payment of a debt or performance of an obligation. A debtor may still be responsible for a lien after a discharge.

Litigation

A case, controversy, or lawsuit. Participants (plaintiffs and defendants) in lawsuits are called litigants.

Liquidation

A sale of a debtor's property with the proceeds to be used for the benefit of creditors.

Liquidated Claim

A creditor's claim for a fixed amount of money.

-M-

Magistrate Judge

A judicial officer of a district court who conducts initial proceedings in criminal cases, decides criminal misdemeanor cases, conducts many pretrial civil and criminal matters on behalf of district judges, and decides civil cases with the consent of the parties.

Means Test

Section 707(b)(2) of the Bankruptcy Code applies a *Means Test* to determine whether an individual debtor's Chapter 7 filing is presumed to be an abuse of the Bankruptcy Code requiring dismissal or conversion of the case (generally to Chapter 13).

Abuse is presumed if the debtor's aggregate current monthly income (see definition above) over 5 years, net of certain statutorily allowed expenses is more than (i) $10,000, or (ii) 25% of the debtor's nonpriority unsecured debt, as long as that amount is at least $6,000.

The debtor may rebut a presumption of abuse only by a showing of special circumstances that justify additional expenses or adjustments of current monthly income.

Misdemeanor
An offense punishable by one year of imprisonment or less.

Mistrial
An invalid trial, caused by fundamental error. When a mistrial is declared, the trial must start again with the selection of a new jury.

Moot
Not subject to a court ruling because the controversy has not actually arisen, or has ended.

Motion
A request by a litigant to a judge for a decision on an issue relating to the case.

Motion To Lift The Automatic Stay
A request by a creditor to allow the creditor to take action against the debtor or the debtor's property that would otherwise be prohibited by the automatic stay.

Motion In Limine
A pretrial motion requesting the court to prohibit the other side from presenting, or even referring to, evidence on matters said to be so highly prejudicial that no steps taken by the judge can prevent the jury from being unduly influenced.

-N-

No-Asset Case
A Chapter 7 case in which there are no assets available to satisfy any portion of the creditors' unsecured claims.

Nolo Contendere

No contest. A plea of nolo contendere has the same effect as a plea of guilty, as far as the criminal sentence is concerned, but may not be considered as an admission of guilt for any other purpose.

Nondischargeable Debt

A debt that cannot be eliminated in bankruptcy. Examples include a home mortgage, debts for alimony or child support, certain taxes, debts for most government funded or guaranteed educational loans or benefit overpayments, debts arising from death or personal injury caused by driving while intoxicated or under the influence of drugs, and debts for restitution or a criminal fine included in a sentence on the debtor's conviction of a crime.

Some debts, such as debts for money or property obtained by false pretenses and debts for fraud or defalcation while acting in a fiduciary capacity may be declared nondischargeable only if a creditor timely files and prevails in a nondischargeability action.

Nonexempt Assets

Property of a debtor that can be liquidated to satisfy claims of creditors.

-O-

Objection to Dischargeability

A trustee's or creditor's objection to the debtor being released from personal liability for certain dischargeable debts. Common reasons include allegations that the debt to be discharged was incurred by false pretenses or that debt arose because of the debtor's fraud while acting as a fiduciary.

Objection To Exemptions

A trustee's or creditor's objection to the debtor's attempt to claim certain property as exempt from liquidation by the trustee to creditors.

Opinion

A judge's written explanation of the decision of the court. Because a case may be heard by three or more judges in the court of appeals, the opinion in appellate decisions can take several forms.

1. If all the judges completely agree on the result, one judge will write the opinion for all. If all the judges do not agree, the formal decision will be based upon the view of the majority, and one member of the majority will write the opinion.

2. The judges who did not agree with the majority may write separately in dissenting or concurring opinions to present their views.

3. A dissenting opinion disagrees with the majority opinion because of the reasoning and/or the principles of law the majority used to decide the case.

4. A concurring opinion agrees with the decision of the majority opinion, but offers further comment or clarification or even an entirely different reason for reaching the same result.

5. Only the majority opinion can serve as binding precedent in future cases.

Oral Argument

An opportunity for lawyers to summarize their position before the court and also to answer the judges' questions.

-P-

Panel

1. In appellate cases, a group of judges (usually three) assigned to decide the case;
2. In the jury selection process, the group of potential jurors;
3. The list of attorneys who are both available and qualified to serve as court appointed counsel for criminal defendants who cannot afford their own counsel.

Party In Interest

A party who has standing to be heard by the court in a matter to be decided in the bankruptcy case. The debtor, the U.S. trustee or bankruptcy administrator, the case trustee and creditors are parties in interest for most matters.

Petition Preparer

A business not authorized to practice law that prepares bankruptcy petitions.

Per Curiam

Latin, meaning *for the court.* In appellate courts, often refers to an unsigned opinion.

Peremptory Challenge:

A district court may grant each side in a civil or criminal trial the right to exclude a certain number of prospective jurors without cause or giving a reason.

Petit Jury (or Trial Jury)

A group of citizens who hear the evidence presented by both sides at trial and determine the facts in dispute. Federal criminal juries consist of 12 persons. Federal civil juries consist of at least six persons.

Petition

The document that initiates the filing of a bankruptcy proceeding, setting forth basic information regarding the debtor, including name, address, chapter under which the case is filed, and estimated amount of assets and liabilities.

Petty Offense

A federal misdemeanor punishable by six months or less in prison.

Plaintiff

A person or business that files a formal complaint with the court.

Plan

A debtor's detailed description of how the debtor proposes to pay creditors' claims over a fixed period of time.

Plea

In a criminal case, the defendant's statement pleading *guilty* or *not guilty* in answer to the charges.

Pleadings

Written statements filed with the court which describe a party's legal or factual assertions about the case.

Postpetition Transfer

A transfer of the debtor's property made after the commencement of the case.

Prebankruptcy Planning

The arrangement (or rearrangement) of a debtor's property to allow the debtor to take maximum advantage of exemptions. (Prebankruptcy planning typically includes converting nonexempt assets into exempt assets.)

Precedent

A court decision in an earlier case with facts and legal issues similar to a dispute currently before a court. Judges will generally *follow precedent* meaning that they use the principles established in earlier cases to decide new cases that have similar facts and raise similar legal issues.

A judge will disregard precedent if a party can show that the earlier case was wrongly decided, or that it differed in some significant way from the current case.

Preferential Debt Payment

A debt payment made to a creditor in the 90-day period before a debtor files bankruptcy (or within one year if the creditor was an insider) that gives the creditor more than the creditor would receive in the debtor's Chapter 7 case.

Presentence Report

A report prepared by a court's probation officer, after a person has been convicted of an offense, summarizing for the court the background information needed to determine the appropriate sentence.

Pretrial Conference

A meeting of the judge and lawyers to plan the trial, to discuss which matters should be presented to the jury, to review proposed evidence and witnesses, and to set a trial schedule. Typically, the judge and the parties also discuss the possibility of settlement of the case.

Pretrial Services

A function of the federal courts that takes place at the very start of the criminal justice process after a person has been arrested and charged with a federal crime and before he or she goes to trial.

Pretrial services officers focus on investigating the backgrounds of these persons to help the court determine whether to release or detain them while they await trial.

The decision is based on whether these individuals are likely to flee or pose a threat to the community. If the court orders release, a pretrial services officer supervises the person in the community until he or she returns to court.

Priority
The Bankruptcy Code's statutory ranking of unsecured claims that determines the order in which unsecured claims will be paid if there is not enough money to pay all unsecured claims in full.

Priority Claim
An unsecured claim that is entitled to be paid ahead of other unsecured claims that are not entitled to priority status. Priority refers to the order in which these unsecured claims are to be paid.

Probation
Sentencing option in the federal courts. With probation, instead of sending an individual to prison, the court releases the person to the community and orders him or her to complete a period of supervision monitored by a U.S. probation officer and to abide by certain conditions.

Probation Officer
Officers of the probation office of a court. Probation officer duties include conducting presentence investigations, preparing presentence reports on convicted defendants, and supervising released defendants.

Procedure

The rules for conducting a lawsuit; there are rules of civil procedure, criminal procedure, evidence, bankruptcy, and appellate procedure.

Proof of Claim

A written statement describing the reason a debtor owes a creditor money, which typically sets forth the amount of money owed. (There is an official form for this purpose.)

Pro Per

A slang expression sometimes used to refer to a pro se litigant. It is a corruption of the Latin phrase *in propria persona.*

Property of The Estate

All legal or equitable interests of the debtor in property as of the commencement of the case.

Pro Se

Representing oneself. Serving as one's own lawyer.

Prosecute

To charge someone with a crime. A prosecutor tries a criminal case on behalf of the government.

Pro Tem

Temporary.

-R-

Reaffirmation Agreement

An agreement by a debtor to continue paying a dischargeable debt after the bankruptcy, usually for the purpose of keeping collateral or mortgaged property that would otherwise be subject to repossession.

Record

A written account of the proceedings in a case, including all pleadings, evidence, and exhibits submitted in the course of the case.

Redemption

A procedure in a Chapter 7 case whereby a debtor removes a secured creditor's lien on collateral by paying the creditor the value of the property. The debtor may then retain the property.

Remand

Send back.

Reverse

The act of a court setting aside the decision of a lower court. A reversal is often accompanied by a remand to the lower court for further proceedings.

-S-

Sanction

A penalty or other type of enforcement used to bring about compliance with the law or with rules and regulations.

Schedules

Lists submitted by the debtor along with the petition (or shortly thereafter) showing the debtor's assets, liabilities, and other financial information. (There are official forms a debtor must use.)

Secured Creditor

A secured creditor is an individual or business that holds a claim against the debtor that is secured by a lien on property of the estate. The property subject to the lien is the secured creditor's collateral.

Secured Debt

Debt backed by a mortgage, pledge of collateral, or other lien; debt for which the creditor has the right to pursue specific pledged property upon default. Examples include home mortgages, auto loans and tax liens.

Senior Judge

A federal judge who, after attaining the requisite age and length of judicial experience, takes senior status, thus creating a vacancy among a court's active judges. A senior judge retains the judicial office and may cut back his or her workload by as much as 75%, but many opt to keep a larger caseload.

Sentence

The punishment ordered by a court for a defendant convicted of a crime.

Service of Process

The delivery of writs or summonses to the appropriate party.

Settlement

Parties to a lawsuit resolve their dispute without having a trial. Settlements often involve the payment of compensation by one party in at least partial satisfaction of the other party's claims, but usually do not include the admission of fault.

Sequester

To separate. Sometimes juries are sequestered from outside influences during their deliberations.

Small Business Case

A special type of Chapter 11 case in which there is no creditors' committee (or the creditors' committee is deemed inactive by the court) and in which the debtor is subject to more oversight by the U.S. trustee than other Chapter 11 debtors. The Bankruptcy Code contains certain provisions designed to reduce the time a small business debtor is in bankruptcy.

Statement of Financial Affairs

A series of questions the debtor must answer in writing concerning sources of income, transfers of property, lawsuits by creditors, etc. (There is an official form a debtor must use.)

Statement of Intention

A declaration made by a Chapter 7 debtor concerning plans for dealing with consumer debts that are secured by property of the estate.

Standard of Proof

Degree of proof required. In criminal cases, prosecutors must prove a defendant's guilt *beyond a reasonable doubt.* The majority of civil lawsuits require proof *by a preponderance of the evidence* (50% plus), but in some the standard is higher and requires *clear and convincing* proof.

Statute

A law passed by a legislature.

Statute of Limitations

The time within which a lawsuit must be filed or a criminal prosecution begun. The deadline can vary, depending on the type of civil case or the crime charged.

Sua Sponte

Latin, meaning *of its own will.* Often refers to a court taking an action in a case without being asked to do so by either side.

Subordination

The act or process by which a person's rights or claims are ranked below those of others.

Subpoena

A command, issued under a court's authority, to a witness to appear and give testimony.

Subpoena Duces Tecum

A command to a witness to appear and produce documents.

Substance Abuse Treatment

A special condition the court imposes that requires an individual to undergo testing and treatment for abuse of illegal drugs, prescription drugs, or alcohol. Treatment may include inpatient or outpatient counseling and detoxification.

Substantial Abuse

The characterization of a bankruptcy case filed by an individual whose debts are primarily consumer debts where the court finds that the granting of relief would be an abuse of Chapter 7 because, for example, the debtor can pay its debts.

Substantive Consolidation

Putting the assets and liabilities of two or more related debtors into a single pool to pay creditors. (Courts are reluctant to allow substantive consolidation since the action must not only justify the benefit that one set of creditors receives, but also the harm that other creditors suffer as a result.)

Summary Judgment

A decision made on the basis of statements and evidence presented for the record without a trial. It is used when it is not necessary to resolve any factual disputes in the case. Summary judgment is granted when on the undisputed facts in the record one party is entitled to judgment as a matter of law.

Supervised Release

Term of supervision served after a person is released from prison. The court imposes supervised release during sentencing in addition to the sentence of imprisonment. Unlike parole, supervised release does not replace a portion of the sentence of imprisonment but is in addition to the time spent in prison. U.S. probation officers supervise persons on supervised release.

-T-

Temporary Restraining Order

Akin to a preliminary injunction, it is a judge's short-term order forbidding certain actions until a full hearing can be conducted. Often referred to as a *TRO.*

Testimony

Evidence presented orally by witnesses during trials or before grand juries.

Transfer

Any mode or means by which a debtor disposes of or parts with his/her property.

Transcript
A written, word-for-word record of what was said, either in a proceeding such as a trial, or during some other formal conversation, such as a hearing or oral deposition.

Trustee
The representative of the bankruptcy estate who exercises statutory powers, principally for the benefit of the unsecured creditors, under the general supervision of the court and the direct supervision of the U.S. trustee or bankruptcy administrator.

1. The trustee is a private individual or corporation appointed in all Chapter 7, Chapter 12, and Chapter 13 cases and some Chapter 11 cases.

2. The trustee's responsibilities include reviewing the debtor's petition and schedules and bringing actions against creditors or the debtor to recover property of the bankruptcy estate.

3. In Chapter 7, the trustee liquidates property of the estate, and makes distributions to creditors.

4. Trustees in Chapter 12 and 13 have similar duties to a Chapter 7 trustee and the additional responsibilities of overseeing the debtor's plan, receiving payments from debtors, and disbursing plan payments to creditors.

-U-

United States Trustee
An officer of the Justice Department responsible for supervising the administration of bankruptcy cases, estates, and trustees; monitoring plans and disclosure

statements; monitoring creditors' committees; monitoring fee applications; and performing other statutory duties.

Undersecured Claim

A debt secured by property that is worth less than the amount of the debt. unlawful detainer action A lawsuit brought by a landlord against a tenant to evict the tenant from rental property usually for nonpayment of rent.

Undue Hardship

The most widely used test for evaluating undue hardship in the dischargeability of a student loan includes three conditions:

1. The debtor cannot maintain based on current income and expenses a minimal standard of living if forced to repay the loans;

2. There are indications that the state of affairs is likely to persist for a significant portion of the repayment period; and

3. the debtor made good faith efforts to repay the loans.

U.S. Attorney

A lawyer appointed by the President in each judicial district to prosecute and defend cases for the federal government.

The U.S. Attorney employs a staff of Assistant U.S. Attorneys who appear as the government's attorneys in individual cases.

U.S. Trustee

An officer of the U.S. Department of Justice responsible for supervising the administration of bankruptcy cases, estates, and trustees; monitoring plans and disclosure statements; monitoring creditors' committees; monitoring fee applications; and performing other statutory duties.

Undersecured Claim
A debt secured by property that is worth less than the full amount of the debt.

Unliquidated Claim
A claim for which a specific value has not been determined.

Unscheduled Debt
A debt that should have been listed by the debtor in the schedules filed with the court but was not. (Depending on the circumstances, an unscheduled debt may or may not be discharged.)

Unsecured Claim
A claim or debt for which a creditor holds no special assurance of payment, such as a mortgage or lien; a debt for which credit was extended based solely upon the creditor's assessment of the debtor's future ability to pay.

Uphold
The appellate court agrees with the lower court decision and allows it to stand. See affirmed.

-V-

Venue
The geographic area in which a court has jurisdiction. A change of venue is a change or transfer of a case from one judicial district to another.

Verdict
The decision of a trial jury or a judge that determines the guilt or innocence of a criminal defendant, or that determines the final outcome of a civil case.

Virtual Bankruptcy Assistant
An independent contractor who works for bankruptcy attorneys via the internet.

Voir Dire
Jury selection process of questioning prospective jurors, to ascertain their qualifications and determine any basis for challenge.

Voluntary Transfer
A transfer of a debtor's property with the debtor's consent.

-W-

Wage Garnishment
A non-bankruptcy legal proceeding whereby a plaintiff or creditor seeks to subject to his or her claim the future wages of a debtor. In other words, the creditor seeks to have part of the debtor's future wages paid to the creditor for a debt owed to the creditor.

Warrant
Court authorization, most often for law enforcement officers, to conduct a search or make an arrest.

Witness
A person called upon by either side in a lawsuit to give testimony before the court or jury.

Writ

A written court order directing a person to take, or refrain from taking, a certain act.

Writ of Certiorari

An order issued by the U.S. Supreme Court directing the lower court to transmit records for a case which it will hear on appeal.

Graphico Publishing
http://www.graphicopublishing.com

Printed in the United States
49469LVS00006B/17-56

9 780976 159179